Rowan Manahan has been providing career advice since the tender age of 22 (initially for colleagues and friends, and then on a full-time, professional basis) and is the founder of *Fortify Services*, providing consultancy and outplacement services to the public and private sectors and a career management service for individuals.

Consulting with employers on the hiring line and working with job-seekers on a daily basis, Rowan has developed a strategic methodology and toolset for job-hunting in the 21st century. He makes his living providing simple, workable solutions to frustrated job-hunters, and the techniques that he advocates have proven successful for clients operating at all levels of the organisation chart. He has been variously described as: *The Career Doctor, The Insultant* and *A Reverse-Engineering Guru*, but prefers the simple, understated moniker that he developed for himself while at university – *Manahan-The-Magnificent.*

Rowan lives in Dublin with his wife, Marie, and his two daughters, Lynn and Jane. He loves good minds, great music, smelly cheese and chop-sockey videos. He is in the enviable situation of bouncing out of bed every Monday morning with a smile on his face and sees no valid reason why everyone else can't too.

WHERE'S MY OASIS?

*The essential handbook
for everyone wanting
that perfect job*

ROWAN MANAHAN

LONDON

1 3 5 7 9 10 8 6 4 2

First published in the United Kingdom in 2004 by
Vermilion, an imprint of Ebury Press
Random House UK Ltd
Random House
20 Vauxhall Bridge Road
London SW1V 2SA

Random House Australia (Pty) Limited
20 Alfred Street, Milsons Point, Sydney
New South Wales 2061, Australia

Random House New Zealand Limited
18 Poland Road, Glenfield
Auckland 10, New Zealand

Random House (Pty) Limited
Endulini, 5A Jubilee Road, Parktown 2193, South Africa

Random House UK Limited Reg. No. 9540009
www.randomhouse.co.uk
Papers used by Vermilion are natural, recyclable products
made from wood grown in sustainable forests.

A CIP catalogue record for this book is available from the British Library.

ISBN: 0091899982

Printed and bound in Great Britain by Mackays of Chatham plc, Chatham, Kent

Names and identifying characteristics of people in this work
have been changed to protect the privacy of the individuals.

Female and male pronouns are alternated chapter by chapter throughout the
book to avoid clumsy 'he/she', 'his/her' alternatives.

This book is dedicated to Marie

For the idea

For the girls

For finding me my oasis

For everything that matters to me...

ACKNOWLEDGEMENTS

To Pat Kenny, Marian Richardson, Pat Costello and the team for all of their support over the years.

Likewise to Richard Curran and David Murphy in the *Independent*.

To Ivan without whom...

To Amanda, Julia and the coven in Vermilion.

To Mum and Foley for all the trips to the library.

Grateful thanks to *Shifu* Han Kim Sen for all of his guidance and, in particular, for allowing me to include the section on breathing.

To Mark Cumisky for all of the toothsome discussions.

Quotes from Tom Peters are used with kind permission – thank you Tom (www.tompeters.com).

And last but very much not least, for all of the Jaffa Cakes and late night rants, to the Mooses: Dr Verbeeg, Nobby, Eurmal, VK, Muff, Bad Bob, Muurfman, Kohai and TBWNW.

> 'Knowing is not enough;
>   we must apply.
> Willing is not enough;
>   we must do.'
>
> **JOHANN WOLFGANG VON GOETHE**

CONTENTS

PART 4: FACE-TO-FACE 2 — 207
(FROM THE HANDSHAKE ONWARDS)

PART 6: I THINK I WANT TO DO SOMETHING DIFFERENT WITH MY LIFE   337

APPENDICES 401

A WORD FROM THE AUTHOR

> *Reader, if you seek his monument, look around you.*
>
> **CHRISTOPHER WREN'S EPITAPH (Wren is interred in his masterpiece, St Paul's, in London)**

Who am I, what am I and why am I qualified to write this book?

I do not work for a placement agency.
I am not an academic or a journalist.
I am not a Human Resources manager, although I work with them every day.
I am a **career management** professional.
I am an **outplacement** consultant.
I am a highly experienced **interviewer**.

I spent 10 years working for multinationals before setting up my own company, *Fortify Services*, providing consultancy and outplacement services to the corporate and public sectors. (Outplacement is a service offered to people who have been made redundant by their employer. In a nutshell, it means that if you are downsized, you will have someone who knows you well and who knows all of the tricks and traps of the job-hunting process helping you to get back into employment.)

We also provide a specialist hiring service to employers, offering an objective, tailored, best-practice approach to hiring and retaining the most talented people in the market. So, in writing this book, I wear two hats – I am both poacher and gamekeeper. I have seen every mistake a candidate can make from the interviewer's side of the table and I have counselled thousands of people through the rollercoaster ride of the modern job-hunt.

COMMON SENSE?

Job-hunting is common sense – most of the mistakes that people make in the process are obvious and readily avoidable if you just sit and think about it for a while. The problem is that people are reluctant to share their experiences in this arena, sometimes because of embarrassment, often because they don't want to give away their competitive advantage. Thus, job-hunting sense isn't common at all – very few people seem to know how to approach this most important of career skills.

With my poacher hat on, I will guide you through the process, sharing the accumulated knowledge, mistakes and successes of thousands of job-hunters who have gone before you. With my gamekeeper hat on, I can provide you with further insight and let you know what the person on the other side of the table is thinking, why he is asking the questions he is asking and how he comes to a decision at every stage of the hiring process.

There have been numerous books written on this subject, so why another one? Three reasons:

1 The jobs market always changes but the pace of that change has dramatically accelerated in recent years. As a result, a book on interview techniques that was current, useful and groovy five years ago may only address half of what you need to know today.

2 I have not yet seen an holistic book that takes you through each step of managing your career and the job-hunting process in a cohesive way. Many of my clients read books on this subject and the most common feedbacks I get from them are: the authors are frequently unqualified to write on this topic; their perspective may be too

limited; the book doesn't go far enough; or the advice offered is no longer relevant/effective. But most importantly, up to now you had to buy anything from two to five books to get the full picture. Books by different authors, with different backgrounds or perspectives. There tended to be a lot of cross-over between titles, resulting in conflicting advice – leaving the reader wondering, 'To whom should I listen?' My intention in writing *Where's My Oasis? (WMO?)* is that it will become your three-ring reference binder, a handbook that you can continually refer to as you progress in your career.

3 All too many of the books on job-hunting offer solutions with a par-roted approach. I have lost count of the number of times I have heard clichéd answers, delivered in a sing-song voice by naïve, well-meaning candidates. Nothing turns an interviewer off faster than spotting one of these pre-prepared answers which that interviewer has, in all likelihood, heard a hundred times before... This book will arm you with the insights you need and will help you prepare to go out and do battle across the table, but it will *not* spoon-feed you with a facile approach. Landing a worthwhile job is a big deal these days; it's not going to happen for you unless you are prepared to put in the effort required.

USING THIS BOOK

There is probably more information here than you really, immediately, need. Some of it may no longer be relevant to your circumstances or some of it may only pertain to senior roles that are some years away for you at present. Feel free to skip and bounce. The Index and Contents will quickly enable you to dip into any specific areas you wish to address and there is no particular advantage to reading the book starting at page one. I have endeavoured to cross-reference the material throughout, so if you are 'dipping in', you will be able to quickly find points or details referred to.

FAQs: there are Frequently Asked Questions dotted here and there through the book. These are the most common areas of concern that clients have raised with me over the years. Some of them are answered in a single paragraph, some require a whole chapter. There's a complete list of these in the Appendices (see page 408).

Learning Curves: I will be using a series of Case Studies based on clients I have worked with, the first of which is Chapter 1 of Part 1. Throughout the book, all names (and, in some cases, industries) have been changed to protect client confidentiality, but the people you will be reading about are real. They have all gone through this process – some successfully, some less so – and each of them has something to teach you.

FEEDBACK

In closing, let me impress upon you how much your input matters. I have conducted countless recruitment Interviews over the years and, on the other side of the table, I have coached thousands of clients through the process. What you are reading here is my collation of *their* words, *their* experiences and *their* accumulated wisdom.

If you find *WMO?* useful, please let me know. Send me your experiences, your triumphs and disasters, your whinges and moans, your feedback on what aspects of the book were useful and what just didn't work for you. As I sit here writing this, I am acutely conscious that many aspects of *WMO?* will be out of date in a ridiculously short timeframe. We *will* be bringing out updates and revised editions, so do your bit – share!

Thanking you

Rowan
rowan@wheresmyoasis.com

PROLOGUE: A PERFECT DAY

When you start to doubt yourself, the real world will eat you alive.

HENRY ROLLINS

You get out of bed, well-rested but nicely keyed-up. You slept well because you are looking forward to giving a good account of yourself today. Your interview clothes are laid out at the end of the bed, perfectly co-ordinated and immaculately pressed. You have a leisurely breakfast (you have taken the day off) and complete your grooming. You give the company a call to confirm that you will be attending the interview this afternoon and that you are looking forward to meeting Mr Brown and Ms Green there. (You know who both of these people are, where they were educated, the qualifications they have gained, what their areas of responsibility are and what difficulties are facing their aspects of the business. Furthermore, you have discovered a sporting interest of Ms Green, have read two articles that she has written for a technical journal in the past year and are aware from the grapevine that Mr Brown likes to probe on one particular key area when he interviews.)

You read the major headlines for the day and do a quick online search of any breaking news in the sector and in the company that you're interviewing with this afternoon. Finding one item of interest pertaining to a competitor, you note it for use later.

You spend the rest of the morning reading over your condensed notes for the interview and performing a final rehearsal of your presentation – you include the competitive item of interest on your final slide. You print out three fresh copies of your *Curriculum Vitae*, hard copies of your presentation and your list of questions for the interviewers.

You drive to the company HQ and have a light lunch in a nearby hotel, which you spotted when you visited the area a week ago. At the top of your notepad you make a final note of the Nuggets (see page 196) you want to deliver and head off, timing your arrival to seven minutes before your interview is due to begin. You leave your coat and briefcase in the car, just carrying a good-quality leather notepad holder and your laptop computer (battery fully charged).

You introduce yourself at reception and use their bathroom, all the while breathing slowly and calmly to ground yourself. You are brought up to the interview room by an administrator who chats with you on the way. You shake hands with Mr Brown and Ms Green and take your seat. A technician plugs your laptop into an LCD projector and ensures that all is working properly. You thank him as he leaves.

They give you an overview of the meeting – they want to have a 'preliminary chat' for about half an hour, then see your presentation and then talk for another 30 to 40 minutes. They commence with some background questions and ask you about several areas that you have highlighted on your CV. You see them exchange a glance and a smile as you make a particularly strong point about a success you had recently and how you understand that there will be a similar issue arising shortly in their company. You can see from their watches (you don't look at your own) that they have already run behind schedule. Then they invite you to make your presentation.

You mention that things seem to be running a little long and ask if they want you to compress your presentation time. They say no, so you deliver for 14 minutes (the brief said 15) and they are visibly impressed by the depth of your thinking and your confidence. You clarify a couple of points when their body language shifts early in the pitch, skim another less important one to gain back that time and catch them unawares with the announcement from the competitor company from this morning (which gets a laugh and a rueful smile).

You hand over hard copies of the presentation (crisply laser-printed on nice scrunchy paper) and re-take your seat for Q&A, comfortably dealing with their questions – there was only one area of inquiry that you had not anticipated and it is a minor matter anyway. Checking against your Nugget list on your notepad (which they can't see as you wrote it in very faint pencil) you recall that you still have two important areas you want to make them aware of. As the questioning goes on, you introduce both of them without difficulty.

The interview winds up and they ask you if you have any questions. You check your list and tick off the points that have already been covered in the discussion, which leaves a couple of strong questions for clarification – as you had intended. They seem in no hurry to wrap up and stay chatting on about the state of the market with you. Mr Brown confirms your contact details as you take your leave and says they will be in touch in the next 24 hours. You have been under the spotlight for just over two-and-a-half hours.

The same administrator sees you out of the building and you are courteous and attentive to her, chatting as you leave. The next morning, you get a call inviting you to meet the Managing Director for a discussion later in the week.

Why is it never that simple…?

INTRODUCTION (WHAT'S ALL THIS ABOUT AN OASIS? I JUST WANT A DECENT JOB!)

> *Reality is what refuses to go away when I stop believing in it.*
>
> **PHILIP K. DICK**

There is no denying that the business of finding, getting and holding on to a job has become increasingly difficult. The post-war covenant of the 'job-for-life' has been irrevocably broken in the private sector, and the papers are full of articles stating that no one can afford to live on a Public Service salary these days. So where does that leave you? Well, a good starting point is to accept the realities of the marketplace, generate an understanding of how that marketplace goes about hiring and build your approach on those foundations. Simple as that. Sorry. (You were expecting maybe some rocket science?)

UGLY FACT NO. I

JOB SECURITY IS A THING OF THE PAST. REALLY.

Irrespective of your performance, of how well your department or division is doing; irrespective of the strides taken by your organisation on a local, national, continental or global level, your job can evaporate overnight. Psychiatrists tell us that one of the most fundamental coping mechanisms that human beings use is denial – in fact, most of us go through life denying the one certainty, death. In my experience, too many people apply this kind of thinking to their careers as well.

If your expectations are realistic and your approach to the job-hunt is just a little bit more professional than the next person's, your chances will dramatically improve. If you take it up a notch and maintain a focus on your *career*, instead of merely job-hunting, you will be head and shoulders above the average. Learn to combine a long-term focus on your career with meticulous preparation and presentation for every aspect of the job-hunting process and you will be head, shoulders and *torso* above the competition. Ask anybody you know who has to conduct selection interviews as part of their job and they will tell you that professional, courteous, well-researched and prepared candidates are very rare animals. Interviewers have a tendency to lunge across the table and grab such people with both hands (see page 38, The Bogeyman).

DON'T JOB-HUNT – CAREER-HUNT

You would never take a journey in your car without a clear destination in mind – you would just end up panicking when you arrived at the first junction and didn't know which way to turn. And yet many people take *exactly* that approach to their working lives. They drift into something that they can do, or that they have some modicum of talent for, whether or not it gives them any real sense of satisfaction; and they follow the path of least resistance in that job, drifting along with the current, hoping for a promotion.

In the past, you could at least rely on the organisation to not dump you unless there was a very good reason – as long as you were not downright incompetent and the company was not haemorrhaging money, you were reasonably safe. Today, there is no such security. This makes it all the more imperative that you pursue a career that you:

(a) **are good at,** and it would be a good idea if you were *very* good at some aspects of it – *way* better than average; and

(b) **enjoy** more often than not – if you are miserable more than half of the time in your work, it is not good for your mental or physical wellbeing (see page 372, Stress). It is also likely that someone will notice that unhappiness. Happy workers are productive workers, and organisations in today's cut-throat marketplace are desperately in need of productivity from their workforces. They will therefore want to hold on to the most productive and best-motivated staff if times get tougher and they have to trim the workforce…

CAREERING ALONG?

You can define the word 'career' in two ways – as a noun or as a verb.

NOUN: A job or occupation undertaken for a significant period of a person's life, usually with opportunities for progress. Somebody's progress in a chosen profession or during that person's working life. (Well, that doesn't sound too bad. *Significant period… progress…*' It might even be a bit of fun and pay a few bills along the way.)

VERB: Move swiftly and in an uncontrolled way in a specified (or unspecified) direction. Rush forward while lurching or swaying. (One phrase you never want to hear over the PA on a train, plane or bus is, 'Folks, I'm sorry to have to tell you this, but we are careering out of control…'.)

A CONSIDERED APPROACH…

My recommended approach to managing your career is very straightforward (still no rocket science – sorry), highly structured and can be encapsulated in these three maxims:

- **Get shortlisted.**
- **Chance favours the prepared mind.**
- **At the end of the day – remember it's only a job.**

GET SHORTLISTED

If you are not a player, you can't compete. Get your fundamentals – the nuts and bolts of job-hunting – correct from the outset. You don't have to think particularly strategically to do this, but there *are* pitfalls for the unwary. *WMO?* will provide you with useful insights for every stage of the process and will help you to significantly tighten up your approach.

CHANCE FAVOURS THE PREPARED MIND

That was Louis Pasteur's answer to a question on his approach to science and discovery. Thomas Jefferson was a bit more wry: 'It's funny – the harder I work, the luckier I seem to get.' If your current approach has not been consistently working, starting to think this way will make all the difference. You may have been getting to interview and even second interview, but just not getting the final call-back. A skimming or tactical approach to the process of landing and keeping a job will only take you so far...

Managing your career on an ongoing basis and undertaking job-hunts as required are both enormously demanding activities. In many cases, the effort involved in finding, researching and securing a job is more challenging and time-consuming than performance of the job itself. Only you can decide how much effort to put into staying on top of your career or any job-hunt and how much exertion that job is worth to you. But I have always felt that it is better to be a little over-prepared and not need it than to be under-prepared and suddenly find yourself tongue-tied in the midst of a vital interview. So the Chance Favours the Prepared Mind maxim (which I liken unto that moment in *The Wizard of Oz* when Dorothy says, 'Toto, I have a feeling we're not in Kansas any more') brings you through a more strategic approach to career management and playing in the bigger leagues.

REMEMBER IT'S ONLY A JOB

Maintaining a sense of perspective in your career is central to any balanced approach to life. Unless you are working in the medical field or in an intrinsically dangerous environment, it is very unlikely that an error on your part is going to result in anybody's death. So try and bring a 'nobody-is-going-to-die-here' perspective to bear on the process as you go through it.

Every day, people are told that they are going to meet their maker. Despite the great strides we have taken in medicine, doctors still have to deliver that awful piece of news all the time. And I am willing to bet hard cash that *no one* who has just been told they have six months to live has ever said, 'Gee, I wish I'd spent more time at the office.'

Whether you love or hate your job, whether you live to work or work to live, remember at the end of the day, it is **ONLY A JOB!** This is particularly important to bear in mind as you choose the career moves you make, but it is also a valuable perspective to maintain as you job-hunt. That process can become all-consuming, to the detriment of your relationships with your family and friends. It is critical that you learn to prioritise and manage your time, and build in enough leeway for domestic tasks, the hunt, your family, your friends and yourself (see page 18, Managing Time Effectively).

MAKING AN INVESTMENT

The professional, targeted approach that I am recommending necessitates a considerable investment of time, effort and energy (and perhaps a little cash along the way). What is your return on that investment? Well thus far, your outlay consists of the few pounds that you have spent on this book and now you are going to invest some, a lot or a whole lot of time. Against what? For an entry-level job that pays you £15,000, you will earn £150,000, £225,000 or £300,000 over 10, 15 and 20 years respectively. (I am not for a moment suggesting that you will be working for the same company in 10, 15 or 20 years, but you will be working at something.) Those numbers assume no pay rises and no promotions;

allow a measly 3 per cent raise every year (but still no promotions), and your return on investment looks like this:

BASE SALARY	10 YEAR EARNINGS	15 YEAR EARNINGS	20 YEAR EARNINGS	25 YEAR EARNINGS
£15,000	£172,000	£279,000	£403,000	£547,000
£20,000	£229,000	£372,000	£537,000	£729,000
£30,000	£344,000	£558,000	£806,000	£1,094,000
£40,000	£459,000	£744,000	£1,075,000	£1,458,000
£50,000	£573,000	£930,000	£1,344,000	£1,823,000
£75,000	£807,000	£1,307,000	£1,886,000	£2,557,000
£100,000	£1,146,000	£1,860,000	£2,687,000	£3,646,000

If you are mathematically inclined and want to get a more accurate picture for yourself, the multipliers (including just a 3 per cent raise every year) are:

5 Years:	Base Salary x 5.31
10 Years:	Base Salary x 11.46
15 Years:	Base Salary x 18.60
20 Years:	Base Salary x 26.87
25 Years:	Base Salary x 36.46

Managing your career is a pain in the neck. You simply should not have to work this hard just to stay afloat – but you do. You do because of the lack of certainty that seems to be the norm in the marketplace now and you do because your competition is getting smarter and slicker with their approach to job-hunting. You can play the denial game, you can play the bargaining/fantasy game ('Oh, it's not really that bad out there, and I'm doing a good job – they'd be fools to let me go'). It's your livelihood, so feel free.

If, however, you do accept the realities of the marketplace you can either choose to regard the effort involved in managing your career as a pain in the neck or you can regard it as an investment. If you have an opportunity coming up and you will have your chance at interview – what's the five-year return on your investment? £80,000? £133,000? £200,000?

I contend that an ongoing effort to keep your career on track, with a few bursts of heavy activity when you are considering a move, doesn't sound so bad when you put it in the light of that kind of return for the effort involved.

WARMING UP

LEARNING CURVE 1 – STAGNATION

Alan, mid-30s, married, nursing qualification and marketing degree
Alan's career was stagnating. He had joined a multinational company as a Sales Representative and had progressed into the Marketing Department, but he could not advance any further without gaining significant people-management experience; in his role as a Brand Manager, this was not available to him.

Alan's initial consultation with us consisted of a close examination of the progress of his career to date and some preliminary discussion of his aspirations and the sort of stumbling blocks he had encountered in the recent past. We then started to provide him with management's perspective on his situation. Put simply, promoting him represented an unnecessary risk for his company and, if his own company wouldn't give him a break, it was highly unlikely that a competitor company would either. A classic 'Catch-22' situation.

We went back to Alan's medium- and long-term ambitions and began to identify the gaps in his training, knowledge, experience and current approach against those ambitions. We also scrutinised his company – their hiring patterns, recent promotions and approach to succession planning. More importantly, we examined the company's strategic plan, seeking to identify when promotion opportunities were likely to arise. The final step in this planning phase was to timeframe Alan's personal development and career-advancement programme. We agreed an end-date and laid out the key milestones and the steps that he would have to take along the way.

Alan's self-directed efforts began with a great deal of reading. His degree course had not focused in on the core skills of managing people and it was imperative that he should become fully conversant with the best theories in this subject area. He then gradually started demonstrating his new-found knowledge in team settings and in discussions with his Manager. He sketched out his intentions, hopes and objectives in advance of these meetings with us and debriefed after each interaction. He learned a great deal about his personal style from this reading and test-piloting approach and became capable of predicting outcomes in his dealings with colleagues and management.

We then worked closely with Alan to produce an agenda for his next annual review meeting with his boss – Alan had clear objectives delineated for this meeting and had laid down sufficient groundwork in advance that his Manager spontaneously raised some of the items that were on that agenda. For the first time, Alan outlined his short- and medium-term career plans and elicited support from his boss for these aspirations. Together, they identified several immediately useful training initiatives and agreed to meet on a monthly basis to review his progress.

These monthly meetings proved invaluable for Alan, as he gained immediate feedback from his boss and was in a position to advance his ideas and contributions for the company. The Manager began copying him in on correspondence relating to the salesforce and undertook to provide him with a secondment opportunity into Sales Management as soon as possible. Alan continued his reading and formal training through this period, until this opportunity arose – he effectively 'job-swapped' with a Regional Sales Manager in a nearby affiliate for a six-month period.

Meanwhile, Alan updated his CV with us, intending to go out to the market and get some practice in interview settings. He took several practice interviews, with no intention of accepting the jobs. He declined one offer and was being considered for several more when a full-time Sales Management position finally arose within his company in his own territory. He submitted his (pre-prepared) plan for the sales team to launch a new product and was invited to interview. He fleshed out his ideas in the interview and secured the job.

LEARNING POINTS:

- If you don't **actively manage** your career, it will stagnate and can leave you in a dreadfully vulnerable position. This is known as **Career Management Deficiency** and it is a very common and dangerous disease.

- It takes **courage** to specify what you want from your career, because that kind of goal-setting opens you up to the prospect of failure. However, without a long-term plan, you are merely following the path of least resistance and hoping for the best – you would never undertake a long journey by road without a clear destination in mind, plus a map if the locale was unfamiliar. Why on earth would you do less for your career? (See page 363, Ten Year Plan.)

  > 'The greatest danger for most of us lies not in setting our aim too high and falling short; but in setting it too low and achieving our mark.'
  >
  > **MICHELANGELO**

- Kick-starting or revitalising your career like Alan did requires you to be completely **honest** with yourself – if you don't push yourself, you will aim too low, and if you are deluding yourself, you can aim way beyond your true level of capability (see page 80, 360°).

- A considered, **steady build** is a very effective approach – it does not require you to re-invent yourself overnight, nor does it expect management (or a potential employer in a new organisation) to take an enormous risk by promoting or hiring you.

Chapter 2

A ROAD MAP THROUGH THE DESERT

So much to do, so little done.

CECIL RHODES'S EPITAPH

Regardless of your immediate circumstances, there are a number of defined stages to the process of landing a job. Let's start from the perspective that really counts – how an employer views the process:

1 Decides that a position needs to be created or filled.

2 Lets it be known that the position exists – seeks internal applicants, puts it out on the grapevine, talks to placement agencies or advertises (typically in that order).

3 Screens potential applicants – usually in writing first and then face-to-face.

4 Determines the best candidate – interviews, psychometric profiling, platform tests and more interviews. This part of the process has become far more searching than it used to be, with even junior level positions being screened much more thoroughly.

5 Makes an offer (reference and background checks are usually conducted at this juncture).

6 Makes the hire (more often than not with a safety-net, such as a probation period).

7 And they all lived happily ever after (or at least until the next downsizing, rightsizing, merger, acquisition, profit call or whatever...).

From *your* standpoint then, the process can be broken down as follows:

1 The primary decision stage – what sort of jobs am I going to apply for? This is the critical question that you must answer. Get this wrong and you will truly understand the meanings of the words 'stress' (see page 372) and 'misery'…

2 The primary research stage – exactly what organisation do I really want to work for? The cultural fit and the boss fit. A badly thought-out move can turn your working life into a living hell.

3 The written stage – CVs, cover letters, application forms. Setting yourself apart from all the other candidates in the large pile of paper.

4 The secondary research stage – getting ready for the interview. The big stuff which (a) enables you to impress them with your professionalism and thoroughness and (b) gives you a real insight into the workings and style of the organisation, further answering the questions that arose at Stage 2.

5 The face-to-face stage(s) – making your pitch to them.

6 The second decision stage – do I really want to work for/with these people? Now that I have met them, do I (metaphorically) want to introduce them to my mother? Will I be happy here? Do I believe the seduction spiel I have just heard?

7 And they all lived happily ever after…?

MOMENTS OF TRUTH

SWEDISH MANAGEMENT GURU RICHARD NORMANN DEFINED THE 'MOMENTS OF TRUTH' CONCEPT IN 1984 AND JAN CARLZON WROTE THE BOOK IN 1987. IN SHORT, IT RELATES TO THE IMPRESSION OF QUALITY THAT A PERSON GETS WHEN THEY FIRST COME INTO CONTACT WITH AN ORGANISATION – HOW THE PHONE IS ANSWERED, IF THE RECEPTION AREA IS CLEAN, IS EVERYTHING HANDLED COURTEOUSLY AND PROFESSIONALLY?

There are moments of truth on both sides of the job-hunt, but for now let's focus our attention on the viewpoint of the hiring organisation. The defining moments for them are:

1 When they answer your phone call (see page 124, The Power of the Phone).
2 When they read your written representation of yourself (see page 50, Thinking Like Them...).
3 When they see you for the first time (see page 182, Looking the Part).
4 When you open your mouth for the first time (see page 209, Introducing Yourself Well).
5 When you actually take up the job – do you match up to what they thought you were like?

It is imperative that you shine in these moments and that you take the time and trouble to learn what is impressive about you and how to present all of that to them to your best advantage. The structure of this book closely mirrors the order of these moments of truth. If you have an immediate or particular difficulty or concern, you may want to skip ahead to that section...

THE GRAPH OF CONTROL

Who holds the cards in this process? That varies according to what stage you are at.

Most people have a perception that they are effectively impotent in the job-hunting process. Not so. You have 100 per cent control over: (1) whether you apply at all; (2) the quality of your written representation of yourself; (3) the breadth and depth of your research/preparation for the interview; and (4) the outward appearance that you present on the day. You have virtually total control over your punctuality for the interview (acts of God notwithstanding) and it is only at this juncture that the pendulum starts to swing over to the employer's side.

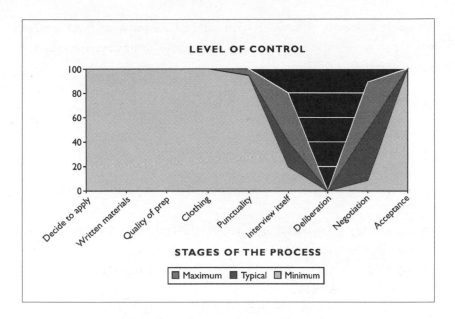

A badly prepared candidate might have as little as 10–20 per cent control in the interview room, while a very well-prepared player can be up to 80 per cent in charge. You have no control whatsoever over their deliberation process once you have left the room – you don't know what guidelines they have been issued ('No one under thirty' 'Let's get more females than males if possible – our gender balance isn't right at the moment' 'The last Chinese/Irish/Hispanic/black/left-handed/red-haired guy didn't work out – avoid them this time if you can'). More importantly, you don't know what calibre of candidates you are up against. You may be perfectly competent and have a solid track record of success, but you ended up in competition with a Messianic figure in the final interview…

If they do make you an offer and you enter into a period of negotiation over remuneration, terms and conditions, you once again have a degree of control: 50/50 if the position was hotly contested, 10/90 if the salary is set in stone and you are the supplicant, and 90/10 if you are the Messiah figure and they desperately need you. Finally, you have *total* control over whether you say 'Yes' or 'No' at the end of the day.

So don't despair – you actually *do* have a lot of control in this process, and *WMO?* will equip you with the tools and techniques to lever that control to your maximum benefit.

Chapter 3

MANAGING TIME EFFECTIVELY

One of the most common stressors (see page 372, Stress) in the career management process is that there never seem to be enough hours in the day. If you aren't operating some kind of diary system, you will find job-hunting or career transition very difficult indeed. For a start, you should sit down with the family calendar and look at the big annual items:

- Christmas
- Birthdays/anniversaries
- Your annual holidays/weekends away/short trips
- Bank holiday weekends
- National holidays

These are 'gone' before the year even begins and therefore you should block them out of your calendar and transfer them into your diary early in the year. Likewise, important family events – school plays, sports events and prize-giving – are all important dates in a child's calendar and should be treated with the appropriate respect and planned for well in advance.

Our lives are so busy now, most of us can't really account for the time that we spend and don't realise how much we devote to different tasks. If you plan your time out one week ahead, you are working to a simple constraint of 7 x 24 = 168 hours. As a simple exercise, try filling in the way in which you used time in the past week, in the box below:

ITEM	HOURS	%
Sleep		
My job (or job-hunt)		
Commuting		
Education/training		
Partner/immediate family		
Friends/phone calls		
Vegging out – TV, reading		
Entertainment		
Shopping		
Laundry		
Meals		
Cooking		
Other domestic		
Time for me		
TOTAL	168	100.0

It is worth developing the habit of keeping track of this as it will allow you to plan much more effectively for when you are under pressure coming up to an interview (or a deadline at work). Sit down on a Sunday night or Monday morning with the Weekly Planner (see page 413, Appendix 6) and account for, and plan, your time under the headings below. Colour the different categories, so that you can see at a glance what is 'eating' your time.

BLUE **Domestic**	This includes sleep, shopping, laundry, looking after kids, cleaning, cooking and day-to-day meals.
BLACK **Work**	Commuting, training, course-work, working at home, taking calls, reading or studying for work.
RED **Vital**	The job-hunt: thinking, dreaming, researching, writing, rehearsing, lunches, meetings; *anything* related to managing your career or finding your next job.
GREEN **Soul Food**	Time for you, time for your partner, big-fun time for your kids or nieces and nephews. Taking a long bath, having a facial or a massage, a long walk, reading a great book, going to the cinema, a special meal. Because the job-hunt can be so demanding, we sometimes don't think to do these things. Or if we do, we feel guilty about doing them. Plan for them (12–20 hours a week of green time) and use this time as a reward for all of your efforts. Learn to turn the mobile off in this time. More importantly, learn to turn *your head* off in this time.

This kind of planning feels a little trite and foolish at first – it's like being back in primary school! But it is *essential* that you take this structured, meticulous approach to the process of managing your career. Air traffic controllers are only allowed to spend three to four hours on the scope before taking a mandatory break, because there is so much at stake if they make an error. How long can you productively work for? Ten hours a day? Twelve? Fifteen?

We are all capable of a Herculean effort of this sort every now and then, but if it became the norm in your job, you would be at risk of burn-out very quickly. Sleep deprivation is against the Geneva Convention for a very good reason: a person deprived of sleep for 72 hours will begin to experience aural and visual hallucinations and quickly deteriorate into a psychotic or catatonic state. (Maybe someone should explain that to new-born babies.) If your job-hunt is consuming your every waking moment and is coming between you and a good night's sleep, you have lost the oh-so-important balance. You are not job-hunting effectively, you are probably snapping irritably at those closest to you and you are *definitely* not giving off the right vibrations to a potential employer.

Most men (and a minority of women) go through this if they have an enforced period of unemployment. What is happening is the primitive hunter inside you is feeling unsettled. 'Why won't they let me hunt?' roars the cave-man. This primitive cave-man is of little or no value to you in a modern job-hunt (see page 372, Stress). You need to give him something to occupy himself – a sport or a hobby – or he will drive you *crazy* with his incessant whining. In the 21st century, more and more of us are becoming Knowledge Workers. Your Knowledge Worker brain is the part that is useful to you as you manage your career. Cultivate it, feed it (with hobbies, sleep and plenty of green time) and listen to it.

It is relatively easy to assess your limitations and intellectually recognise that you can only operate effectively for a certain number of hours per day. Emotionally accepting these limitations is much harder, particularly if you are out of work and the pressure (real or imagined) is mounting. This is when the cave-man starts bellowing in your head. It takes a while, but you must learn to ignore him. You cannot ever entirely control your circumstances, but you can learn to control your reactions to them. Channel the need to hunt into productive activities – research, networking, polishing your CV, interview practice – and if your inner cave-man is telling you that this is not enough, do some physical exercise to burn off the excess energy and then tell him to shut up!

You need to get your inner Knowledge Worker back in charge of your time and bring the job-hunt (and the cave-man) to heel. A typical weekly map for someone in a 9–5 job (or in full-time education) might look like this – the working week:

TIME	MONDAY	TUESDAY	WEDNESDAY	THURSDAY	FRIDAY	SATURDAY	SUNDAY
6.00							
7.00							
8.00							
9.00							
10.00							
11.00							
12.00							
13.00							
14.00							
15.00							
16.00							
17.00							
18.00							
19.00							
20.00							
21.00							
22.00							
23.00							
00.00							

▓ Work

Then add in your normal daily activities – the domestic routine:

TIME	MONDAY	TUESDAY	WEDNESDAY	THURSDAY	FRIDAY	SATURDAY	SUNDAY
6.00							
7.00							
8.00							
9.00							
10.00							
11.00							
12.00							
13.00							
14.00							
15.00							
16.00							
17.00							
18.00							
19.00							
20.00							
21.00							
22.00							
23.00							
00.00							

▒ Domestic
▓ Work

Now add in your 'vital' time – in this instance 18 hours of job-hunting activities:

- Desk-based research during lunchtime on Monday.
- Meeting with a person who has some knowledge of your desired sector on Tuesday evening.
- A visit to the library on Wednesday to gen up on the trade magazines.
- Discussion with your mentor on Thursday evening, and so on…

TIME	MONDAY	TUESDAY	WEDNESDAY	THURSDAY	FRIDAY	SATURDAY	SUNDAY
6.00							
7.00							
8.00							
9.00							
10.00							
11.00							
12.00							
13.00							
14.00							
15.00							
16.00							
17.00							
18.00							
19.00							
20.00							
21.00							
22.00							
23.00							
00.00							

Domestic   Vital
Work

Finally, add in your balancing time – 'soul food' – to fill out the sheet. In this example, we've allowed 22 hours of soul food:

- A short, quiet lunch on Tuesday.
- Two hours to yourself on Wednesday night (pub/gym/long walk/a film or video).
- A long lunch with a friend (picnic in the park?) on Thursday.
- Dinner with your partner on Friday.
- A swim with the kids on Saturday lunchtime, and so on…

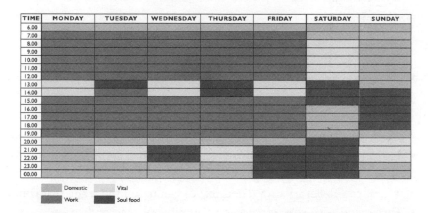

Domestic   Vital
Work   Soul food

Some people seem to have a knack for time management, but make no mistake, it *is* a learnt skill. Get on top of it, get used to managing the time available to you and learn how to build in 'me' time as you go. If you are being pulled in too many directions and you feel like you are always running to stand still, life is not going to be a barrel of laughs for you. Job-hunting is a stressful business at the best of times (see page 372, Stress); and if you find that you can't wind down and restore your equilibrium, your chances for success will be severely diminished.

Chapter 4

ROUTES OF ENTRY INTO THE JOB MARKET

A master of comedy, his genius in the art of humour brought gladness to the world he loved.

STAN LAUREL'S EPITAPH

The people I meet who have grown disillusioned with the whole process of job-hunting are typically the ones who haven't had the time, inclination or knowledge to give the task the level of thought that it deserves. And that thinking starts with, 'How am I going to find this new job? The job that will make me happy and keep me happy? The job that will pay all my bills and leave me with a few pounds to spare? The job that has good career prospects? The Holy Grail of jobs?'

People who have become disenchanted with their careers, or with the process of trying to move out of an unfulfilling job, typically don't have ready answers for those questions. What is your route of entry into your new job/career going to be? How will you get your foot in the door? If you have been reading stories about the thousands of job-cuts and redundancies that are going on out there every day and simultaneously noticing a dwindling number of advertisements for new jobs in the newspapers, you could be forgiven for thinking that there are few or no jobs to apply for. Wrong.

THE JOBS ARE OUT THERE – YOU JUST HAVE TO FIND THEM

Look at the unemployment figures on your Government's website (search for "notified redundancies"). Even if those numbers have been increasing, it will be at a very slow rate – much slower than all the alarming tales of factory closures and staff cuts following mergers would make you think. If it bleeds, it leads – bad news makes for higher circulation and ratings. You will never see a story on the evening news that starts, 'Ninety per cent of the 500 people who lost their jobs in Widgets Incorporated in the spring have successfully regained employment, many of them in comparable or better positions.' That's not a particularly fascinating story, it's nigh-on impossible to research and it's not nearly as dramatic as the 'FIVE HUNDRED people lost their jobs following a factory closure by Widgets Incorporated' story that they led with back in the spring.

So don't despair, there are lots of jobs out there and they are being filled every day. People retire, resign, die, take career breaks, go on long-term sick leave, decide to work part-time, get promoted, get transferred, get fired or disappear off the face of the planet every day. Your sector or area of expertise may be quiet right now, it may even be in decline, but as long as it's not completely dead, there are people starting work in that sector every Monday morning. The jobs are there – you just have to get serious about looking for them. The major routes of entry in the jobs market are:

- Responding to **advertised** positions
- Registering with placement **agencies**
- **Cold calling** on an organisation you would like to work for – face-to-face, by phone, by letter or e-mail
- **Networking** – hearing about opportunities on the grapevine
- Job-hunting **groups**, both formal (typically government-sponsored) or informal
- Being **headhunted**
- The **internet** (see the next chapter).

WHAT ABOUT ADVERTISED POSITIONS? IS THAT A GOOD WAY TO FIND A JOB?

Certainly – as long as your target organisation's preferred *modus operandi* in recruitment drives is to advertise and as long as you pay due attention to the difficulty of trying to distinguish yourself from the herd of CVs that inevitably respond to a big job advertisement.

You should be devouring the recruitment sections of all of the major newspapers, the relevant local papers, trade magazines and journals (most, if not all, available at your local library). You should have your target organisations' websites bookmarked and visit their career pages weekly. You should phone their Human Resources (HR) departments and find out which placement agencies they like to use, or which newspapers/journals they typically advertise in.

If there is an organisation that you want to work for in your vicinity, you should be ready to apply to them on the spot. Your reading and research should be complete, your CV 95 per cent written. You should know, from the grapevine, that an advertisement is going to be placed in the paper this week and be ready, not reacting.

DON'T PLACEMENT AGENCIES HAVE ALL OF THE BEST JOBS?

Placement agencies do have some excellent positions for certain sectors, but many people make the mistake of regarding them as a 'friend in camp' as they pursue their job-hunt. It is important that you don't lose sight of their real agenda – placement agencies (and headhunters) make their money by selecting the best candidates for the vacancy in their client's organisation and putting those candidates forward with the *minimum* of effort and time spent. Every phone call they make, every e-mail and letter they send, is money out of their pockets in the long run. So, if you are in any way unsure as to what it is you want to do next, or how to approach the market, don't expect to get any help from this quarter. Some guidelines for dealing with placement agencies:

- Position yourself crisply, leaving no doubt in the agency's mind that you know what you have to offer, know what you want to do next and are committed and focused on this career path. If you haven't yet firmly decided on your career path, keep away from agencies until you have.
- Make them work for their money – extract the maximum information from them that you can, every time you have contact with them.
- That being said, expect to have to work hard at the relationship – if you call them, don't expect them to call back. It can be a pleasant surprise if they do, but most won't.
- Deal with the players. Find out who the directors or owners of the agency (or local branch of the bigger agencies) are and deal directly with them – they will care more about the business and provide better service than younger, less experienced members of staff might.
- Many employers are using multiple agencies to find the best candidates. Register with a number of them and don't be afraid to play them off against one another – you may be able to glean a few extra morsels of information from playing this game.

WHAT ABOUT DIRECTLY CONTACTING AN ORGANISATION THAT I WANT TO WORK FOR? DOES THAT WORK?

Otherwise known as cold calling – it very, very occasionally yields results (about 5–8 per cent of the time in the private sector). You can't mess around with an untargeted approach if you are going to pursue this route – if you truly want to work for a specific organisation, you are going to have to *woo* them.

Find out *everything* about them (see page 162, Research, and page 168, Networking) and then send in your carefully crafted, immaculately tailored *Curriculum Vitae* and letter. DO NOT send your carefully crafted, immaculately tailored CV and letter to the Human Resources department unless you want to work in Human Resources. HR are the sentries of an organisation. They stand on the drawbridge and ask, 'What's the password?'

Send your missive to the King or Queen. Send it to the person who has the power and vision to give you the job you want. And don't give up. People with power and vision respect guts, tenacity and a thick skin. If the General Manager of Microsoft sends you a Dear John letter (also known ruefully by most job-hunters as a PFO letter), write to the Vice President for the Region. If he PFOs you, write to Bill Gates, gently carping about the lack of imagination being displayed by his Regional and Local Managers. If Bill sends you a PFO, write to Steve Jobs in Apple, enclosing copies of your correspondence with Microsoft and copy Bill in on your letter to Steve. They will remember you. Keep going until you get the response you want. You have nothing to lose – never surrender.

I HEARD THAT NETWORKING IS VERY IMPORTANT FOR JOB-HUNTING, BUT IT SEEMS SO CRASS...

The other cry against networking that I hear all the time is, 'Nepotism.' Allow me to let you in on a little secret here – employers HATE hiring. It is difficult, time-consuming and expensive, and it rarely results in the perfect appointment. In these highly competitive times, it would be foolish for any employer to spend a lot of unnecessary cash on a recruitment drive if a few phone calls could short-circuit that process. If an employer lets it be known on his network that he is looking for a certain type of person to fulfil a certain type of role, so much the better if the person that is ultimately hired is in some way a known quantity to that employer.

So get out there and start networking. If you find the whole idea skin-crawling, then restrict your forays into this arena to research and perhaps getting a tip-off if a position is going to arise in a target organisation. There is nothing worse than opening the newspaper and seeing someone's grinning mugshot in a company announcement of a newly filled job that you would have loved to go for... except it wasn't advertised. Hate networking? Get over it and get out there (see page 168, Networking).

HOW DO JOB-HUNTING GROUPS WORK?

A job-hunting group can range from a coffee morning once in a while in a friend's house to a government-sponsored suite of offices with expert advisers, a comprehensive library and a range of 'friendly' organisations already in place. Informal groups tend to restrict their efforts to people of a certain educational standard or of a certain profession, while the formal groups typically have a much broader remit.

No matter what your circumstances, these can be an excellent avenue to explore. Start looking at advertisements in your local press and go and talk to your local unemployment or social welfare office. Whether you are returning to the workplace having raised your family or you have a PhD in laser physics, you will get some interesting ideas and approaches from talking with people who think about the subject of job-hunting all the time.

HEADHUNTING – WAITING FOR THEM TO COME TO YOU

There you are, sitting at your desk one fine day and the phone rings. The receptionist tells you it's a personal call from a name you don't recognise and the caller introduces herself by saying, 'My name is XXXX, I work with Blah-blah Executive Search & Selection and I was given your name as a possible candidate for CEO of the Universe. Is this a good time for you, can you speak freely now?'

Wow, flattering or what? As you would expect, these calls don't happen very often, nor do they get made to people below a certain salary threshold; but, boy, is it nice when they happen! But how do you *make* them happen? Getting on to a headhunter's radar scope is not easy; the top-end players in this arena receive *massive* numbers of unsolicited CVs every day, most of which they ignore. You need to take a very sophisticated, lengthy and probably expensive approach in order to put yourself on the map in this way and this, not surprisingly, begins and ends with networking (see page 168).

If you are going to approach these people, your CV needs to be really top-notch (even more so than if you were sending it to a placement agency). It needs to reek of professionalism and point to a rapidly progressing career with an unfailing level of contribution and accomplishment throughout. Then they just might call you back. Always preface any contact you make with a headhunter by phoning first. Do a bit of research to find out who handles your sector and do some background on her. If you are in her bracket and have the right sort of credentials, you won't get the brush-off; if you are in any way a stretch of her imagination, you are going to have to do some very careful positioning to get your foot through her door.

MIX AND MATCH

As you would expect from the hanging sentences in all of the sections above, an all-your-eggs-in-one-basket approach is not likely to do the trick any more. You will need to apply elements from all of the routes in order to start getting results. In order of priority, I would place the major routes as follows:

1 Networking – first, last and always.
2 Researching and using the internet – also throughout the process.
3 Placement agencies and advertised positions a joint third.
4 Cold calling – *never* do this until you have acquired every morsel of information you can and have 'warmed up' the call (if at all possible) with your network.
5 Job-hunting groups.
6 Sitting by the phone waiting for a headhunter to call you.

This is what I mean when I talk about investment. Keeping tabs on all of this requires a very organised approach and even then takes a *colossal* amount of time. If you are just firing off a stock CV every now and then in response to ads in the papers and desultorily calling one or two placement agencies every six months, you are operating at the bottom of the food chain. Full-on career management requires professionalism, *total* commitment and large reserves of enthusiasm and energy every step of the way.

UGLY FACT NO. 2

FINDING A JOB IS A FULL-TIME JOB IN ITSELF.

Whoever coined that phrase was right on the money. In starting out on your job-hunt, think VERY carefully about your routes of entry. If you think you are too busy to pursue the hunt fully and effectively, your first purchase should be a good book or course on the subject of time management (see page 18, Managing Time Effectively). You need to be blocking out big chunks of time for your job-hunt and all of the research and preparation that it will entail. Why? Because someone else out there **IS** and he will be hired ahead of you if you don't. Full stop. End of argument (see page 38, The Bogeyman).

Chapter 5

THE INTERNET

Here a mound suffices for one for whom the world was not enough.

ALEXANDER THE GREAT'S EPITAPH

The internet has expanded more rapidly than any mass-media tool in history. From the first printing presses in the 15th century to books becoming a common household item took hundreds of years. It took radio 38 years to reach 50 million listeners. Television grew much more quickly – just 13 years to reach 50 million viewers. Once the internet moved from being purely the province of military and academic users, it took just 5 years to reach over 100 million users.

For many job-hunters, the internet has transformed the way in which they approach the market and any job moves they intend to make. For most employers, the internet has likewise transformed the preliminary stages of the recruitment process. But no more than that. The internet is *not* a short-cut to a new job, nor is it a magic pill which will in some way prop up a shoddy approach to job-hunting on your part.

It is, however, a marvellous resource for finding jobs that you might otherwise never hear about. And it is a very important development in the way in which job-hunters can research potential sectors or employers in advance of applying. This is (of course!) a double-edged sword – now that information is so freely available, employers have far higher expectations of candidates in the early stages of screening and selection. So, if you have Luddite tendencies, you are going to have to work much harder than your competition to glean information about the market and the organisations that you want to work for. Far better to make the investment in time, effort and money and

> **'Nobody gives you power – you just take it.'**
> **ROSEANNE BARR**

embrace the best that technology has to offer the modern job-hunter. In the vast majority of jobs, you will need to have these skills anyway, so start acquiring them as soon as possible and don't sit there with your hand out, waiting for someone to give them to you.

RESEARCH

Let me first refer you to Part 3: Chapter 6 on this subject. Information has never been more readily available. The internet is groaning with low-hanging fruit about the sectors you are interested in, the organisations that you would like to work for and the people that you will be working with. Go and find it! Far too many job-hunters show up for a networking discussion with someone 'in the know' having done no groundwork. This is a huge missed opportunity. It would be like having a discussion about mathematics with Albert Einstein without bothering to learn your three-times tables. Yes, you can walk away from the discussion with a clear understanding of the basics but, with a bit of groundwork, you could have walked away with an understanding of the workings of the universe!

Another advantage of internet research is that it helps you to maintain confidentiality regarding your job-hunt. As soon as you start having conversations with people about the state of the market and the politics surrounding a particular post, you are showing your hand and risking your confidentiality.

ONLINE JOB ADVERTISEMENTS

These appear in a number of different locations, but the key ones are:

- Job boards
- Online recruitment companies
- Online newspaper recruitment advertising
- The 'Careers with Us' section that you will find on most corporate websites.

Life was so much simpler when all you had to do was buy your national and local papers on the day they had the appointments pages. One complaint I constantly hear about the internet as a route of entry is that there are so many jobsites covering such a broad range of industries and locations that it can be very difficult for beleaguered job-hunters to narrow down their options and find a local job in their particular sector. Employers further confuse this morass by advertising their vacancies on multiple sites.

I would suggest that you dip your toe in the water first and get comfortable using three or four of the more reputable sites. Then you can start searching for sites that cover local jobs or job-specific national sites, refining your results down to those in your desired geography.

ONLINE JOB-SEEKING – THE FUNDAMENTALS

The mechanics of the process may be slightly different, but the same conventions apply whether you are licking stamps and envelopes or hitting the 'send' button on your computer. You need to:

1 Have the appropriate qualifications/training.
2 Have the requisite level of experience.
3 Be a 'minimal risk' hire.

4 Be seen to be focused on the prospective employer's needs, not yours.

5 Distinguish yourself from the competition by representing the above well in writing.

Your application may be read by a human being or it may be interrogated by a piece of software that has been programmed to look for certain phrases. Of course, this is increasingly happening when you send in a hard copy by post so, once again, there's little or no difference between the old and the new methods of applying.

DOWNSIDES

One important distinction between the two methods is that many job-sites invite you to submit an online CV which sits there for all to see. And that 'all' can include your present employer. The better sites will offer degrees of confidentiality and you should tailor your online CV accordingly.

Another problem with having your CV sitting there passively while employers browse through is that you have to try to appeal to the broadest range of employers possible in order to generate any leads. Tricky once more – we have shown, time and again, that targeted and tailored documents have a much higher strike rate than CVs which smack of one-size-fits-all.

The biggest problem *I* see when I work with employers using this route is that there are simply far too many CVs languishing up on the web and the time-and-effort cost of shuffling through them is now greater than it would be if we put a blind advertisement in a major newspaper and had the usual deluge of CVs arrive in response. It would appear that we are coming full circle and that the providers of these sort of online services are frantically having to play catch-up with employers' needs in order to retain any perceived value.

Nevertheless, large numbers of people do get hired *via* this route every day, and if this is particularly true for your sector it's time to pre-pare a couple of different text-only versions of your CV and cover letter and get to work. If you play the online route well, what you lose in control, you will make up for in the breadth of your reach.

My final *caveat*: given that the total number of jobs filled is increasingly dependent on *some level of personal contact*, make absolutely sure that the organisations you want to work for have used and continue to use the web as a key method of finding talent. Call HR. Talk to current or past employees. Use the network early and often and hone your approach accordingly. This is true for all of your possible routes of entry, but none more so than the online approach.

Chapter 6

THE HORRORS AHEAD

> *Advice is seldom welcome, and those who need it the most like it the least.*
>
> **LORD CHESTERFIELD**

It is only fair to point out a few of the less pleasant elements you can expect to have to deal with in managing your career and in your next job-hunt. If you find this chapter disturbing or depressing, I make no apologies – this is my unvarnished stance on the state of play in the marketplace and it has been my experience that attempting to compete without this sort of insight, or with some kind of naïve worldview, is a recipe for failure.

THE STRESS OF THE ENFORCED JOB-HUNT

Data from the United States show that the upshot of all the mergers, hostile take-overs, corporate re-engineering programmes and globalisation initiatives of recent years, combined with the diminution of employee rights legislation, is that you can expect to have to change job up to seven times in your life. Have to. I'm not talking about the moves that you make voluntarily to better organisations with better prospects and better pay and conditions, I'm talking about seven *enforced* job changes.

Seven times ploughing through the appointments section of your newspaper with a red crayon in your hand. Seven times rattling every bush in your network to find out when a job is coming up in a company you could just about tolerate working for. Seven times explaining to your spouse/partner that it has happened… again. Seven times talking to your Bank Manager about deferring mortgage or other payments while you secure new employment…

Take the example of junior doctors. They come out of university and step into a veritable maelstrom of interviews (and most of them are *lousy* at it, by the way). In the hospital setting, they change rotation every six months for three to five years and then annually after that until they gain a permanent position. They know that all of this is coming and yet how many of them think about managing their careers and their job-hunts in a structured way? *Veeeery* few. *'Interview skills? (shudder) But I'm a doctor.'*

So fair reader, irrespective of your occupation, education level and degree of brilliance at your chosen calling, acknowledge and respect the fact that you need to get good at this thing we call Career Management. If you are reasonably proficient, you will be offered the job at one out of every four interviews. Rounding up, that means if you face the worst-case scenario of seven enforced changes, you're going to have to get to, and sit through, around thirty interviews in your career (plus, of course, any that you take as a result of voluntary changes). **Get good at this!**

Career Management is not an innate talent – you have to learn how. Nor is it a frivolous luxury – it has become a necessity. Nor is it a one-off investment of time, effort or money. The skills and tactics described in this book should become part of your daily routine. You brush your teeth every day so they don't look, feel and smell unattractive and so that they don't fall out of your head. Do you think that your career could benefit from a more-than-occasional polish and flossing?

THE BOGEYMAN

The Bogeyman is not the person who is going to read your CV and decide your life's fate in a matter of seconds. Nor is he the person who interviews you, probing relentlessly into your past weaknesses and failures. No, the Bogeyman is the person who is better prepared than you to compete for the job that you so desperately want (or need).

The Bogeyman is the person who has wanted this job (not just any old job, but *this* job) since he was 19 years of age. He has been networking, training, educating himself, reading and researching every day since his 19th birthday. He doesn't have friends – he has contacts. He doesn't have a family, just a circle of influence. He doesn't have a social life, just more entries in his little black book. His CV would make you weep. His writing style is so tight, you wonder why he isn't making a living as an advertising copywriter or a Pulitzer Prize-winning journalist.

And why does he do all this? Just so he can beat you (and every other contender – there's nothing personal here) hands-down for his dream job. He has what my mother used to refer to as 'naughty thoughts' about his dream job. Do you?

BOGEYMEN – THE GRASSHOPPER ANALOGY

Why does a fit, strong, aggressive young man who has no martial arts training ('*Young Grasshopper*') lose when he faces an old Master? What has the Master learnt as a result of all of his training? He can't turn back time, or make himself sprightlier, and yet he has rendered it virtually impossible for the young man to win. The old Master knows all about balance, breathing, attitude, distance, timing, targeting, blocking and the efficient generation of force. There are other factors, but those eight are the keys to determining victory in a hand-to-hand situation.

So, a truly skilled martial arts expert faced with a belligerent amateur would have the odds massively stacked in his favour. It would be as if both parties were holding eight dice (to represent the determinants): the Master would only lose if he rolled eight ones and the amateur could only win if he rolled eight sixes. Not impossible I grant you, but *highly* improbable.

There is another, less tangible, X-factor here. The Master *knows* that he is going to win. He *knows* what is going to happen when he punches his opponent in the solar plexus. He *knows* that his fist will be properly formed, he *knows* that his stance will be strong and that his waist will co-ordinate the punch to increase its power. He knows *exactly* where the solar plexus is and that he will not miss. He *knows* that his opponent will not be capable of withstanding the blow. There is no cockiness, no arrogance here, just the certainty born of hard training. His opponent, on the other hand, is throwing out a punch and merely hoping for the best. I know who I'm betting on.

Wouldn't it be lovely to walk into an interview with that degree of certitude? To know that there is *nothing* they can ask you that you haven't anticipated and prepared for. Bogeymen have that surety. Fortunately, Bogeymen are rare. I hope you never come up against one. More to the point – I hope that, as a result of reading this book and refining your approach to managing your career and any job-hunts you may need (or want) to undertake, you *become* the Bogeyman (see page xxiii, A Perfect Day).

SILVERBACKS

Silverbacks are the older, greyer (and supposedly wiser) people in your organisation who make life hard for you. You have just been appointed to a new job and you were hired by the Managing Director/CEO. The function you are fulfilling is quite new and the direction that the organisation needs to move in is something of a sea-change, too. All of a sudden, you find yourself stymied on every initiative by the Silverbacks – the layer of management that stands between you and the ultimate decision-maker.

'That's not how we do things around here, sonny/my dear.'

'We've been making a tidy profit around here for quite a long time you know.'

'Have you any idea how much that new-fangled idea will cost?'

'Now why would you want to go and re-invent the wheel like that? Sure, aren't we doing fine as we are?'

Managing upwards against this kind of inertia can be enormously frustrating. If you suspect that this is going to be a factor in a new job, you need to ensure that access to the decision-maker is built into your contract. Without this, madness, ulcers and death can ensue.

A significant percentage of the clients that I deal with are making major job moves *solely* because of Silverbacks. They have been backed into a corner, feel utterly impotent, derive zero satisfaction from their work and are constantly grinding their teeth in frustration. Silverback avoidance is an okay reason to move job (although if it is in an excellent organisation which you otherwise enjoy, you might want to consider alternatives just short of assassination); but the horror starts when, having left an organisation because of ponderous management, you encounter it again in your new job. Researching a new organisation (see page 162) is not just about impressing them at interview with all the cool stuff you have been able to dig up, it's also about ensuring your survival and happiness in the new environment.

FANATICS

The Fanatics that I am talking about are the guys and gals in the very good suits on the other side of the table. Some of them used to be Bogeymen. But now they have made it. And they hold your life in their hands.

I train senior management across the gamut of organisation types in a variety of skills, including the fine art of making seriously impactful presentations. The CEOs and CFOs of publicly quoted companies have to present to the financial community and shareholders anything from one to four times a year. The content of these presentations tends to be fairly repetitive (and dry) but the delivery has to be *razor* sharp, every time.

I have worked with one CEO who regularly sets aside 40–60 hours per quarter for intensive rehearsal of these presentations. He might double that level of effort for an AGM or EGM. He's not doing this because he is poor at presenting and he does not use this time for deciding what is going to go into, or come out of, the presentation; or what colours and graphics he is going to use. This *massive* amount of time is just for *rehearsal*.

(Laurence Olivier spent six weeks in rehearsal for his final appearance on stage as Richard III – a role he had been performing all of his adult life. Do you imagine he put in that level of effort because he had *forgotten his lines*?)

That CEO recognises the level of scrutiny that he will be facing from the analyst audience and so he agonises over every syllable that he includes or omits from his delivery. Once we're happy with the substance of his presentation, we listen to the alliterative quality of his language, ensure that it is not too sibilant, pay attention to the rhythm of his phrasing. *Then* we get into the pace, the pauses, the emphasis he places on a word ('*this* word or *that* word'), how he's going to bridge from one idea to the next without losing his audience or his credibility…

Now, just supposing you are going for an interview as Vice-President-in-Charge-of-Whatever in that CEO's company. Just how well-prepared do you think he expects you to be? I have interviewed prospective senior managers with this Fanatic and let me tell you, he fires slipshod, badly primed candidates out of the building using a CANNON!

The guy is a Fanatic. And proud of it. And guess what? He surrounds himself with like-minded people. So, maybe you aren't quite ready for the Vice President job just yet. Maybe you are going for a position three or four rungs down the organisational ladder from there. In that organisation, chances are a Junior Fanatic – a Fanatic-in-Training – is interviewing you. I hope you are well prepared for that interview, because that guy probably has a cannon hidden somewhere around his office too…

THE THREE PHASES

An average life in the Western world lasts 70-something years. Each of the phases of that life has different characteristics:

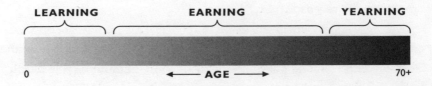

- The **Learning** phase typically stretches from the age of five to the early twenties and is characterised by freedom. Your thinking is unfettered, you are chock-full of dreams and aspirations and (happily) some-

> 'There are three ingredients to the good life: learning, earning and yearning.'
> **CHRISTOPHER MORLEY**

one else is footing the bills! Schooldays, for many of us, really were the happiest days of our lives. No one expected very much of you, other than passing a few exams along the way, and you could just swing along, having a great old time…

- The next phase is the **Earning** years; the period from leaving formal education to retirement. The overriding concern in this Earning phase is *security* (I spell that word as follows: **$ecurity** or **S CURITY**, as this phase tends to be all about generating sufficient income to pay the monthly bills). For many, this involves sublimating the dreams of youth as a life of routine takes over. Few in the Earning years question the choices they have made because, typically, this questioning process can be quite disconcerting. Routine generation of wealth becomes paramount and you get swept along with the current. This is fine if you made sound choices in your late teens and early 20s with regard to your career. But if you didn't… for routine, read 'RUT'.

- The **Yearning** phase is about looking back over a life not quite fulfilled and saying 'If only… if only…' With the wisdom of years comes regret for the road not taken, the too-conservative choices made. Studies conducted on the geriatric population and on terminally ill people consistently demonstrate that regrets arise as a result of decisions *not* taken. The wise old owls that I talk to all agree that it is better to look back and think, 'I wish I hadn't…' rather than wistfully saying, 'I wish I had…'

Mark your age on the chart opposite. How far along are you in the Earning years? How many job/career changes have you been through already? If you retired tomorrow, how would you look back over your working life? With indifference? Regret? Pride? Delight? Anger?

As you progress through this book and the process that it mirrors, you are, at the very least, going to have to contemplate some uncomfortable choices about yourself, your personal style and your level of happiness, and I make no apologies for this. Better to take the time and spend the effort at this early stage and improve the choices that you make for later, rather than to have those choices made for you at a time that may not suit you.

Chapter 7

TOOLS OF THE TRADE

> *If the only tool you have is a hammer, you tend to see every problem as a nail.* **ABRAHAM H. MASLOW**

Career management, like any pursuit, needs specialised tools. Most of these are obvious and self-explanatory, but here's my recommended list.

A6 NOTEBOOKS: As you pursue your career (or a specific job-hunt) get anything that you can out of your head and down on to paper. Buy a handful of these little hardback notebooks and keep one in your coat or handbag, one in your car, one by your chair, one in your desk. When anything of pertinence or curiosity comes across your attention, jot it down. A little factoid from a newspaper or magazine article, an item of interest on a radio chat show or on the evening news, a remark overheard in a restaurant, an item that a friend draws to your attention in a phone call.

It is always hard to recall your accomplishments when your annual review is looming. If you have been jotting down these details all throughout the year – compliments from customers or senior management, a project completed ahead of schedule or under budget, a target exceeded – then you can quickly prioritise them and highlight the big ones in your discussion with your boss. *Get this stuff out of your head!* Bang it down any old way on to paper (some people prefer a Dictaphone®) and then you can transfer the items into dedicated files on your PC – one for accomplishments, one for feedback, one for research that pertains to your current job, one for research for your next move, one for industries or sectors that you are curious about and another for those you have decided not to pursue, and so on...

YOUR OWN PC: You need unfettered access to a PC, 365 days a year. I do not recommend using your PC at work to conduct your job-hunt because Big Brother probably *is* watching you, but you can update research files and CVs on your work PC, as long as you don't leave them on the system. Use generic filenames, avoiding terms like 'CV', 'Résumé', 'Cover Letter' or the names of companies you are applying to; and password-protect your files and work-in-progress so that a casual scan will not detect them. You will also need recent versions of your key software applications and a really good working knowledge of how to use them (see page 94, CVs – Look and Feel).

A HIGH-QUALITY PRINTER: For text work, I always recommend a laser printer, operating at a minimum of 600 dpi (dots per inch – this is the measure of how densely and accurately a printer produces documents), as inkjet and bubblejet printers tend to be slower and not as crisp with the printed word. Lots of experimentation needed here – bring your CV on a diskette to your retailer and get him to print off copies of it on different papers at different resolutions on different printers until you are 100 per cent happy with your choice. A visit to any of the major computer magazine websites will usually give you a strong starting point as they review top- and bottom-end printers in comparative tests all the time (see page 94, CVs – Look and Feel).

INTERNET ACCESS: As vital as having a phone these days, so get your own. Internet cafés are a useful fallback if you have a breakdown, but there's no comparison with having your own computer, printer and connection in the comfort and privacy of your own home. There is such a wealth of information out there now, it would be a huge handicap not to avail of it (see page 32, The Internet). Experiment for a couple of months with a dial-up connection over the phone and see if a broadband connection is worth your while. It may be a bit more expensive, but it can save you a massive amount of time versus the thumb-twiddling that you have to do while you wait for sites to load over a dial-up connection. This all sounds quite costly, I realise, but there is no need nowadays for a large capital outlay for any technology hard/software – pay it off over three or four years and forget about it. It's a minimal monthly outlay and the advantage of 24/7 access to your own equipment set up the way that you like more than compensates for the spend.

A GOOD E-MAIL ADDRESS: manahanthemagnificent@hotmail.com may be an acceptable e-mail address for private use with your buddies, but it's not going to impress a potential employer. If you are starting out, a freebie e-mail address is just about acceptable; if you are in any way established, get and pay for a decent one. Keep a dedicated e-mail address for career management purposes – that way it won't get cluttered with spam or with pictures of your Aunt Mabel's new dog/cat/grandchild. DO NOT use your work e-mail for any e-correspondence relating to a job-hunt. It is unprofessional and immediately smacks of disloyalty and dishonesty to a potential employer.

A PHONE WITH VOICE MAIL: A mobile phone number is fine, but you should also include a home number for evening contacts – a mobile only smacks slightly of 'no fixed abode'. If it is a pay-as-you-go mobile phone, make sure you have plenty of credit before making any important call. Whatever type of phone you are using, always make sure that you personalise your voice mail message. Write your script, rehearse it a few times and lay it down. Listen back to it and make sure it sounds crisp, serious and courteous (see page 124, The Power of the Phone).

UP-TO-DATE PHONE BOOKS/YELLOW PAGES: The phone book is an obvious necessity, but the Yellow Pages is a marvellous resource for any job-hunter. You can quickly identify competitors, suppliers, wholesalers and distributors relating to your companies of interest. Moreover, if you are unclear about career direction, it can be very interesting to flick through the index of a Yellow Pages and find businesses, products and services that you never even knew existed – a great source of ideas and a strong starting point for research purposes.

CALLING CARDS: Even if you don't have a card as part of your job, you should get some. There is nothing more irritating than having to write down someone's name, address, phone number, mobile phone number and e-mail address on the back of an envelope at the end of a meeting. The exchange of business cards is a protocol dating back a *loooong* time. The quality of your card said a lot about you in Victorian times and it still does (especially if you use cruddy, cheap ones). Once again, if you are starting out, you *can* use those vending machine cards that are to be found in large shopping centres/malls; but beyond that, you should spend a few pounds on crisply printed cards of discernible quality. For meetings when you will not be leaving a CV behind, this is an essential tool. If you have never handed over a card before, it can feel a little strange the first few times, but you will immediately see its value and it will further distinguish you from the crowd.

RECORDING DEVICES: A Dictaphone®, a Walkman® with a microphone, an iPod® with voice recorder or a video camera; useful both as an aide-mémoire and as a tool that enables you to see and hear yourself as others see and hear you. Get a plentiful supply of tapes (so you can track your ideas/performance over time) and buy or borrow the hardware as you need it.

A REFERENCE LIBRARY: Invaluable and indispensable. The internet can only go so far: many magazines are not archived on the net; likewise regional (or some national) newspapers. Good municipal libraries will have clippings files on your target organisations – some of which will pre-date the spread of the internet. Access to the latest texts on generic business thinking or the thinking specific to your sector is of obvious value. This is not information you need to spend big bucks to get hold of – it is sitting on the shelf of your local library. If you live within a reasonable distance of your *alma mater*, you can use the university library and the resources of their careers and appointments offices. You may need to join an Alumni Association to gain access, but the fees are usually small and you can play the unemployment card, if that is your circumstance.

REFERENCE BOOKS: Get a really good dictionary. Be sure that the words you use actually mean exactly what you think they do. Also a good thesaurus – the ones that come with word-processing software are not bad, but most don't go far enough. Two other books I would very much recommend are Bill Bryson's *Dictionary of Troublesome Words* and Lynne Truss's *Eats, Shoots and Leaves*. Both give invaluable advice on the almost-lost art of good writing and the virtually extinct art of punctuation. You may be an absolute demon at text-messaging, but unless you are going to SMS your application to a reader who is under the age of 30, you need to be able to write concisely, clearly and accurately. (If that last sentence makes me sound like a grumpy old man it is because I have read so many lousy CVs that I have become one ahead of my time.)

PEACE AND QUIET: If you are sharing a house or flat with other young people, or if, like me, you are a parent, this is not always easy to get. My little angels (aged five and seven as I write) understand that Daddy is not to be disturbed when he is on the phone and, by and large, they adhere to this rule. But if one of them has a fall or is being teased by the other (perish the thought!), all bets are off and the wailing and gnashing of teeth can be heard from some considerable distance. Most parents will empathise with you at this point, but if you are in the middle of a delicate networking call and are trying to prise information or an appointment out of the person on the other end of the line, you can do without the added stress of, 'She stole my Barbie's® wedding dress daddy!' Put a comfy chair in your garden shed. Make sure your cordless phone works as you sit in the car in your driveway. Have a fallback plan and be prepared to flee the building when that vital call comes in.

Peace and quiet for discussions, research, writing or calls that you need to make from home should be planned for and/or negotiated. Whatever your circumstances, make the best arrangements you can for others in the house to be well out of the way, to avoid being disturbed.

Chapter 8

THINKING LIKE THEM...

> *If there is nothing very special about your work, no matter how hard you apply yourself, you won't get noticed, and that increasingly means you won't get paid much either.* **MICHAEL GOLDHABER**

The vast majority of job-hunters scour the papers and the web looking for job ads, assemble some sort of written representation of themselves (*Curriculum Vitae*, letter, application form or a combination of the three), stick on the stamp, pop it in the post box and really have little or no idea what happens next. I regularly meet clients who could wallpaper their entire house with rejection (PFO) letters but don't realise why they aren't getting past this oh-so-difficult first hurdle.

The most successful, the ones who make the whole process seem enviably easy, have learnt one vital skill. They don't think like a job-hunter – they think like the person on the other side of the table who will be hiring them. In some cases, they may have crossed the watershed and have gained some experience in hiring people, which puts them in a position to recognise the process of recruitment for what it is: a time-consuming, enormously expensive purchasing decision; and they go about the task of selling themselves with that perception constantly in mind. It is easy to think this way if you have ever hired another person, but more difficult if you have not. You must learn this skill.

To successfully promote yourself in today's marketplace, you must learn to step outside of your immediate viewpoint and think like the person who will be evaluating you.

Two adages from the gurus of Madison Avenue advertising which will give you the right sort of perspective as you start to think about the process of landing that next job:

ADAGE NO. 1
'ALWAYS REMEMBER THAT YOU ARE ABSOLUTELY, AND IN EVERY WAY, UNIQUE AND SPECIAL – JUST LIKE EVERYONE ELSE IN THE WORLD.'

ADAGE NO. 2
'IF I CAN SEE THE WORLD THROUGH JOHN SMITH'S EYES, I CAN SELL JOHN SMITH WHAT JOHN SMITH BUYS.'

WHAT DO THEY WANT?

Okay, so what are that person's fundamental concerns?

- Recruiters working with, or for, employers want to formulate effective recruitment strategies (that is what they get paid for) that attract top-drawer candidates to the organisation.
- Recruiters want to get through the initial screening process as quickly, efficiently and cheaply as possible and put forward a shortlist of candidates, any one of whom (on paper at least) could do the job.
- No recruiter wants to be associated with a bad hiring decision. Bad hiring decisions have a lingering odour and can louse up an otherwise healthy career...
- In short, recruiters/employers are all seeking the Holy Grail: A GOOD HIRE.

GOOD HIRES

The attributes exhibited by these near-mythical Good Hires are actually fairly basic stuff. Good Hires:

- Are flexible, healthy and honest.
- Don't make waves. (Good Hires always fit seamlessly into a new team or organisation.)
- Learn quickly (and inexpensively) or bring useful knowledge with them.
- Stay with the organisation for a meaningful length of time. (The duration varies by sector.)
- Progress within the organisation and pass their experience on to the next generation of Good Hires.
- Contribute *a lot* more than they cost (we're back to that magical term, 'return on investment').

LOOK REALLY CRITICALLY AT YOURSELF

It doesn't sound like a lot to ask, does it? But Good Hires are very elusive and tricky beasts, as any employer will tell you. Before applying for any job, you need to look at yourself in the cold light of day and ask, 'Am I a Good Hire for this position?' If you are not, don't apply. Full stop. Save yourself time, effort and heartache and DON'T APPLY. Clients frequently take exception to my saying this and ask, 'Oh come on! What's the worst thing that could happen?' Well, the worst thing that could happen is that they could HIRE YOU! They could hire you to do a job that you won't enjoy, aren't suited to and won't be any good at. You could be looking over your shoulder for the (probably short) duration of your stay with this organisation, wondering when they are going to realise their mistake...

THEIR THINKING AND APPROACH

If, however, you believe that you are a Good Hire for a job that genuinely excites you, you need to enter the Twilight Zone, put yourself in the recruiter's shoes for a moment and understand what they are thinking when they see your CV for the first time. (*Cue cheesy special effects...*)

A position needs to be filled in your organisation. Whether the position is newly created or filling a vacancy due to promotion, transfer, retirement or departure, it is your task to find the best person for the job. You assemble (or update) the job description and discuss specific experiential or educational requirements with the line manager. You then compose a recruitment advertisement, place it in an appropriate publication and wait to see what sort of response comes back. Typically, the response consists of a big (sometimes huge) pile of *Curricula Vitae*, most of which try to assure you that the applicant is the perfect person for the job. This pile can be 10, 50, 100 or 500 résumés high and it is *your* job to find the golden needle in this haystack of paper.

SHORTLISTING

Employers use a filtering process to beat the pile of paper down to more manageable proportions. They sift through all of the applications once and they do this *very* quickly. Skilful recruiters will give each application a maximum of 30 seconds of their time on this first pass. Thirty seconds. As they whiz through the pile, they are comparing each document against the check-list of requirements for the ideal candidate — education, training, personal attributes and professional experience. Applicants who do not score highly against this check-list are immediately binned, and the rest are divided into the **Possible** pile and the **Likely** pile. The Likely pile consists of the applications that are a very close match to the requirement list and this pile usually forms the basis of the all-important **Shortlist**. On the second pass, the recruiter will whittle down the Possible pile, critically evaluating each applicant against the standards set by the Likely pile and their own mental check-list. What is left is the Shortlist, which may or may not require further trimming. (*Special effects abruptly end.*)

'Thirty seconds for the first pass?' I hear you sputtering. 'That's OUTRAGEOUS! How can you possibly evaluate someone's entire professional existence in 30 seconds?' Harsh, isn't it? But excellent candidates can and do make their pitch on paper in that sort of time-frame. Advertisers do it with products ranging from ice cream to cars every day. All of those clever little vignettes that clutter up our television screens four times an hour are 30 seconds long. We are living in the era of the sound bite and, faced with a deluge of information, we have all developed these filtering processes. So get used to the idea of a very short Sales Pitch to clear these initial hurdles.

WHO MATTERS?

The final point in this section on thinking like them is to impress upon you just how little you matter. To them. Job-hunting is not about you, it is *entirely* about them. The first time it becomes remotely about you is when they offer you the job (see page 297, Negotiating Remuneration). Until that moment, you are just one of a (possibly very large) pool of candidates who have applied.

They are not interested in your family problems, your faulty car, your low bank balance, your dislike of formal clothing, or any of the myriad issues that matter a great deal to *you* as you advance through this process. So if you find it difficult to wear a stiff collar and tie and can give a much better account of yourself when you are comfortably dressed in casual clothes – tough. If you find it difficult to talk positively about yourself and flush to the roots of your hair in doing so – tough. If you have had dreadful experiences with bullying bosses in unfeeling companies in the past – tough. From the only perspective that matters, THIS IS NOT ABOUT YOU!

> ### UGLY FACT NO. 3
>
> ### JOB-HUNTING IS ALL ABOUT THEM, NOT ABOUT YOU.

The sooner you accept this and leave all your baggage, prejudices and negative past experiences behind, the better. Very easy for me to say, I realise. But if you want to be taken seriously and be in a position to choose between a number of offers for good jobs, rather than being forced to take the 'best of a bad lot' due to pure economic need, it is crucial that you don't lose sight of the simple fact that they just don't give a damn. You are the supplicant – they have the plum job. With a very few notable exceptions, employers have always been in the driving seat when it comes to the jobs market. You are the passenger. You cannot determine direction, speed or any of the other critical factors. Look again at the graph of control (see page 17) – your control begins only when you decide to apply.

So now you have some idea of how they think, and how tight their assessment criteria are, it's time to start applying that insight as you get yourself down on paper...

PART 2

APPLYING FOR THE JOB (BEFORE YOU GET TO MEET THEM)

Chapter 1

PUTTING YOURSELF ON PAPER

Trying to define yourself is like trying to bite your own teeth.

ALAN WATTS

It is a very unusual job-hunt indeed in which you do not have to produce a written representation of yourself and put it forward, at some stage of the process, to a total stranger. The *Curriculum Vitae* (or résumé) has to do a very tricky job – it has to catch the reader's attention and then hold that attention by speaking loudly and clearly on your behalf. And you will not be there to correct any little misconception or incorrect inference that the reader may draw from your document. There may be some minor thing on your document that you could clear up in *two seconds* if only you were there – but you're not. So, it is no surprise to discover that:

UGLY FACT NO. 4

9 OUT OF 10 CVs END UP IN THE BIN.

Why does this happen? Even allowing that a certain number of applicants for every position are just not suitable (irrelevant or insufficient experience, underqualified for the role, lacking key personal attributes, or just plain chancing their arm) that still leaves a significant percentage of solid candidates with relevant track records ending up in the bin at this first stage of the recruitment process. Why?

If you are suitably qualified, have experience that is immediately pertinent to the positions for which you are applying, but you are not getting invited to interview, then you are either pitching yourself out of your league or your CV is simply not doing its job. Look at the graph of control (see page 17) – the decision to apply or not apply for a given job and the quality of your written representation of yourself are key aspects of the job-searching process over which you have total control. That is worth repeating loud and clear – THAT YOU TOTALLY CONTROL. I recommend that you take the time and trouble to fully exercise that control. But in doing so, do not make the mistake that so many candidates make of including everything about yourself on your CV. It may be important or seem fascinating to you, but the simple fact is that NO recruiter cares about your life story at this early stage of the process (see page 54, Who Matters?). Therefore, you need to trim your written representation of yourself to (ideally) one or (maximum) two pages and make damn sure that it *grabs* the reader's attention.

UGLY FACT NO. 5

A BUSY RECRUITER WITH A LARGE PILE OF CVs TO WADE THROUGH IS GOING TO SCAN-READ EACH ONE FOR 15–30 SECONDS.

With no malice intended, she is looking for a reason to dump you in the bin and if you have not sold yourself in the first 30 seconds, that is where your CV (and by extension, you) will end up. No one has the time or inclination to plough through three, four or five pages of your professional history and education when they might have another 30, 100 or 500 documents to read after yours. (The exceptions to this are academic, scientific and medical CVs which can run to 50 pages of publications and references.)

RULE NO. 1
YOUR CV IS NOTHING MORE THAN A 30-SECOND
ADVERTISEMENT TO GET YOU TO INTERVIEW.

It should be as tightly written as the funniest and cleverest 30-second television advertisement you have ever seen, because 30 seconds is all your CV will get to sell you. If you were spending thousands of pounds to buy 30 seconds of prime-time television airtime to sell yourself to a potential employer, think how carefully you would choose every word. Seriously, try it. 'You should hire me because I...' in 30 seconds or less. (This is sometimes known as the 'Elevator Sales Pitch'. The term was coined in the US and means that if you bump into someone important in the elevator, you have a very short time, while they are trapped in there with you, to make your pitch.) Accordingly, keep your written represen-tation short, relevant and easy to whiz through. Your CV should reassure the reader of three things, and three things only:

- Yes, I can do this job. THIS job, not just any job, but *this* one
- Yes, I am a highly motivated person, and
- Yes, I will add value to your organisation.

In order to be able to write in this way, you need to follow Rule No. 2.

RULE NO. 2
WHEN WRITING ABOUT YOURSELF, THINK LIKE
AN EMPLOYER, NOT LIKE A JOB-SEEKER.

The poor unfortunate who has to plough through the large pile of CVs has a check-list of desirable *qualifications*, *training*, *experience* and personal *attributes*. If you can get yourself into that person's head and catch a glimpse of that list, it is much simpler to write the CV that will get you noticed by her.

Chapter 2

LEARNING CURVE 2 – RETURNING TO WORK, A SELLING CV

> *Alien tears will fill for him pity's long-broken urn; for his mourners will be outcast men and outcasts always mourn.*
>
> **OSCAR WILDE'S EPITAPH**

Alison, early 30s, qualified nurse, business diploma, separated, one child

Alison came to us to help her secure a position back in the private sector following a career break to start her family. Her first qualification had been nursing and she gained several years of general nursing experience. She then successfully made a transition into the healthcare industry, starting as a Sales Representative with a small company and working her way rapidly up to Sales Manager. She was successful in this role, generating good growth and share in the markets for which she was responsible as well as opening up new markets for her product range.

After four years, she resigned to start her family and also set about starting up her own retail venture, a fashion outlet on the high street in her small home town. Once this business was up on its feet, she appointed a manager to run the boutique and began to look for opportunities back in the private sector.

We collaborated with Alison to generate a strong, punchy, résumé-style CV and helped her compose a covering letter targeted at her desired part of the healthcare industry. This core CV highlighted all of her significant accomplishments and training, and granted Alison the flexibility to amend it according to the type of job for which she was applying. We also provided her with up-to-date research on the state of her target industry and indicated where she should look for further information.

Once Alison had secured some interviews, we further trained her in researching the companies prior to interview and gave her a quick brush-up on her already considerable interview skills. She declined two offers of employment and took up the third position which, happily, was with an organisation she had always hoped to work for.

LEARNING POINTS:

- Alison was extremely effective in face-to-face situations and needed no significant input for her interviews, but she was not particularly adept at **writing** and even less so at writing about her own accomplishments and track record. It is difficult to think of yourself in this light and even harder to write this way. **Elicit help** if you discover that you have this problem. Garner opinion on your CV – not necessarily on the layout and styling, but just on the raw content.
- She quickly realised the importance of a strong **written presentation** in a highly competitive sector – despite her strong background, she had not been invited to interview with her existing CV. She was applying for sales jobs and she simply wasn't selling herself on paper!
- Using your old **network** and getting back up to speed on movements in your industry. On our advice, Alison talked to industry bodies, reps, doctors, nurses, chemists and wholesalers, and was able to amend her CV and cover letter to reflect that knowledge (see page 168, Networking).
- The value of formal **research** – Alison received feedback that she had been very impressive at interview with her in-depth knowledge of the company, its products and its performance in the market (see page 162, Research).

Chapter 3

CVs – THE BASIC INFORMATION

> *Right now, I'm having amnesia and déjà vu at the same time – I think I've forgotten this before.* **ANONYMOUS**

ALL OF YOUR HISTORY

To begin the process of compiling your CV, write down everything about yourself, including the associated dates. Do this on your PC so you can edit and amend it over time. You may need to brainstorm with others in order to dredge up these data:

- Your career objectives – short, medium and long term
- A 50-word profile of yourself (the Elevator Sales Pitch, see page 61)
- Companies/institutions/organisations that you have worked for and their locations
- What the organisation did, provided or made and for whom
- Your boss/manager's titles for each of your jobs
- All of your job titles over the years
- Responsibilities and key functions of your jobs
- Promotions or extra responsibilities – why did you get them? Think about the job of work you were hired to do on day one and the full range of responsibilities you had as you left the organisation (see page 404, Appendix 2)
- Achievements on the job – any time you made a difference
- Education – full-time, part-time, distance learning. Include your results and qualifications here too

- Training – in-house, formal training with external organisations, and self-directed efforts
- Interests and extra-curricular activities (restrict this to current activities; unless you were a national champion at something this needs to be up to the minute – see page 133, Little Boxes – Application Forms)
- Achievements off the job – anything interesting from your life outside of work.

SECTIONS & HEADINGS

Then you can decide on your sections and headings – **Professional Progression** sounds much more impressive than **Work Experience** but would be an inappropriate heading for a series of summer jobs on a student's CV. Then decide the general order of your sections and whether you will place items in chronological or reverse chronological order. You now have the text of a Core *Curriculum Vitae*, which will be the foundation of all of your applications.

Your Core CV should not contain exactly the same information for every job for which you apply. For each new organisation, you will almost certainly need to do some tailoring of your CV and cover letter.

> **'If you can't explain it simply, you don't understand it well enough.'**
> **ALBERT EINSTEIN**

THE 'SO WHAT?' RULE

The best guideline on this is to read each sentence in your written application from a potential employer's perspective and apply the '*So What?*' Rule. Imagine that you are the busy employer/recruiter who is reading the document for the first time. You don't know the writer, you have never heard of the organisations they have worked for and you are not interested in their prowess at Scrabble in the inter-varsity championships. At the end of each line or sentence, say, '*So What?*' In other words, '*Why is this applicant telling me this? Does this point make my job of building a shortlist any easier? Does this statement apply to the job that I am trying to fill?'* If you cannot adequately answer the *'So What?'* for any item that appears on your CV, delete it.

FAQ

'I have been working for over 12 years now and I just can't get my CV shorter than 3 pages. What should I do?'

Presuming that you have not been in the same role for those 12 years, and further presuming that you are applying for a comparable or more senior role to your current one, read each sentence in your CV from a recruiter's perspective and vigorously apply the *'So What?'* Rule.

Too many CVs are nothing more than a re-statement of a series of job descriptions. In most instances, the job title tells the reader most of what they need to know about that period of your career. Don't waste space and the reader's time going into minute details. Give them the news headlines about previous positions – title, boss's title, special responsibilities, promotions, contributions that you made and/or what you took from the job.

Anything more than five or six years old is virtually irrelevant in today's market and should be reduced to a line or two. The reader is going to focus on what you are doing now and the responsibilities and accomplishments associated with that position, so you should put the bulk of your effort (and space) into that (see page 50, Thinking Like Them...).

CV TYPES

Chronological: The most common format used. This CV highlights your career starting from your earliest job and leads up to today, clearly demonstrating your progression along the way.

Upside: This is the format most employers expect to see and it is relatively simple to write. It is the best format to use if you are moving within your sector, and has the selling advantage of highlighting both your job titles and the organisations that you have worked for along the way.

Downside: All too often, chronological CVs start to look like autobiographies – too long, too much 'telling' and not enough 'selling'. This kind of CV also makes it hard for you to break out of your pigeonhole if you are thinking of changing career path. It is also of little value to you if you are applying for your first job or have a broken employment history.

Functional: This style of CV highlights your major skills, clustering your achievements and contributions regardless of when they occurred. For example, you may have done a small amount of account handling in three different jobs in your past; the functional CV allows you to clump all of the skills and experiences relating to those disparate times into one section of your CV.

Upside: Functional CVs are useful if you have a stop–start history of employment, or if you are trying to highlight particular activities that you want to undertake in your next job. They can also be useful if you are either applying for positions in a new sector or applying for your first job.

Downside: Because it is a less common format than the chronological CV, the reader may look askance at your application and wonder what you are trying to hide. Human Resources people in particular tend to shy away from wanting to meet candidates who apply in this way.

Combination: This format takes the best elements of the Chronological and Functional CVs, underscoring your major skills within the usual chronological flow. This is a potent combination, and if you discipline your writing style it can be a real winner.

Upside: Selling all the way.

Downside: The CV can start to run a little long if you are not very careful. This is fine for very senior positions, but catastrophic for middle management and below.

Text Only: Many jobsites require that you have a text-only CV and some employers will only accept CVs as part of the text of your e-mail rather than as an attachment.

Upside: Having a text-only version of your CV ready will put you ahead of the posse as most candidates rely on sending a word-processed document.

Downside: It is difficult to make a text-only document easy to read and, having no formatting capability, it is also more difficult to highlight the key elements of your professional life to the reader.

Bespoke: The CV that you write for one specific reader. Typically, this document will be the result of a great deal of meticulous research. You will be writing in the full knowledge of that reader's needs and concerns, and presenting yourself as a defined solution rather than just another potential employee.

Upside: In a word, potency. If you are well-matched to the organisation's needs and you do the spadework, this form of CV is very compelling. Applying this way, *via* the right person, can get you an interview even if you are lacking in one of the stated requirements for the job.

Downside: There are no downsides to this method, just the wish that you had the time and resources to do this for every application you make…

THE ORDER OF SECTIONS ON YOUR CV

The other aspect of the '*So What?*' Rule relates to the order in which you place the various sections on your CV. If you are just leaving formal education or if you have just completed a course of study as an adult that is leading you down a new career path, then by all means put your education section first. Otherwise, the reader is interested in seeing two things and two thing only for the first pass: (1) a thumbnail profile of you that tells him immediately if you are in the ball-park for this job and (2) what you are doing *right now*. Your education, training, contact details and hobbies can all come later in the document. Career objective statements should only be used by those going for their first job; after that, your profile (see page 110, Me... at a Glance) and experience should immediately tell the reader what your story is...

In all cases, you should *not* have a frontispiece on your CV – you know the sort of thing I mean:

CURRICULUM VITAE

ROWAN MANAHAN

House Name
Street Address
Town
Postcode

This is a pointless waste of paper and space. OF COURSE it's your *Curriculum Vitae!* What else was it going to be? Jump straight in and bring the reader with you:

ROWAN MANAHAN

PROFESSIONAL PROFILE

- Strategic, innovative Career Management professional with a track record of success from entry-level to boardroom
- Demonstrable counselling, analytical, presentation and writing skills
- Experience gained with job-hunters at all levels
- Married with extensive recruitment work on behalf of corporates and public service organisations

---

THE GRADUATE CV

If you are leaving university (or formal education at another level) for the first time, you should order your CV as follows:

1 Name
2 Career Objective Statement
3 Education (*most recent first and include results/thesis*)
4 Work Experience (*in reverse chronological order*)
5 Relevant Skills
6 Extra-curricular Activities
7 Referees
8 Contact Details

In many ways, the first CV you produce is the hardest. It is when you have the least experience, history and self knowledge to distinguish yourself from your peer group. Look at the section headings above – what distinguishes one, say, Electrical Engineering graduate from another in the eyes of the reader? You may have completed a minor thesis or project on some aspect of electronics that is relevant to the reader's business. Otherwise, your Education section is not much of a differentiator. Sorry.

The exception to this is if you are someone with a brain the size of a planet, who won every scholarship and came first in your class every year since you turned five; then most readers will sit up and take notice. Otherwise the beautifully produced page of educational accomplishments on your CV can be reduced to three words in the eyes of the reader: Electrical Engineering Graduate. Sorry. This is why, at graduate level, your *work experience*, your *skills* section and your *extra-curricular activities* can take on an importance that you wouldn't necessarily expect.

EXPERIENCE: A summer job that you took on to give you more beer money is now going to be scrutinised under a microscope! An internship with an organisation in your desired sector would be nice to have, but it can also raise questions. Why are you applying to another company now? Did you not get invited back? Did you not like (or fit in with) the corporate culture and decide not to return? What do either of those outcomes now say about you? The focus of your writing in this section must be on what you *learnt* from the jobs that you have done and, more importantly, what you *contributed* to those employers. Were you in any way special?

- Rank yourself against your peers under every heading you can think of.
- What did your customers, suppliers, colleagues and bosses really think of you?
- Were you placed in positions of trust (key holder, cash-handling, security)?
- Were any criticisms levelled at you?
- What about praise and compliments? Again, think about colleagues, customers, suppliers and bosses.

- Did you make any suggestions that were taken on board?
- Were you assigned extra responsibilities?
- Did you solve any problems or at least make valuable suggestions?
- What about contributions in a team setting?
- Did you complete tasks/projects working on your own initiative?

SKILLS: Once again, it's best to look for feedback here – you may have demonstrated a skill that you think is no big deal and which you therefore wouldn't think to include on your CV but which someone observing you thought was pretty special (see page 80, 360°).

- Maturity/sense of responsibility beyond your years.
- Customers just *loved* you.
- Computer literacy – sorting out problems for colleagues/management.
- Clean driving licence.
- A *real* facility with a foreign language.
- A *real* ability/knowledge of training people in a certain skill.
- Public speaking or presentation skills which may have been honed in a debating society or class representative role.

EXTRA-CURRICULAR ACTIVITIES: I cover these in some depth in the chapter on Application Forms (see page 133) but at graduate level, the key thing we are looking for is accomplishment, initiative, leadership potential and the ability to work with others. I was a Rubik's Cube® expert, a Frisbee® coach and a Martial Arts champion and instructor while I was in secondary school and college. Not exactly run-of-the-mill sports I grant you, but I was a winner and an achiever in all of these things. *All* of my interviews, post-graduation, focused in on what I had had to do to achieve the things I did in those wacky sports and you can be sure my answers painted me in a positive light. So, as long as your pastime of choice is legal, and as long as you are good at it, you should think about including it on your CV ('Well, I'm grand champion of the Universe at cow-pat tossing').

The other interesting detail I notice on graduate CVs is how calculated potential Bogeymen (see page 38) are in pursuing their extra-curricular activities. They are always the Editor, Auditor, Chairman, Treasurer or Elected Representative of any club/society they get involved with while still in education. It may be that no one else wanted these posts or that the Bogeyman in question had the other candidates kidnapped or ran a dirty campaign in advance of the elections, but one way or another, they always seem to end up on top. There is probably a nature/nurture argument here as to whether these people learn to ruthlessly pursue their goals or if they get it from their mother's milk; but one way or another they *do* start early. And if I've noticed this trend, you can be sure that the person who is going to be reading your CV has noticed it too...

UNDER 10 YEARS' EXPERIENCE CV

This order of sections will be useful in the early stages of your career. You could put Education up front if you have just completed a significant course of study that pertains better to the role you are applying for than your current job does. Otherwise, you are better off sticking with a brief profile and jumping straight into your current role.

1 Name
2 At a Glance
3 Career and Achievements
4 Education (*always most recent first*)
5 Training and Relevant Skills (*always most recent first*)
6 Professional Memberships
7 Extra-curricular Activities
8 Referees – on request
9 Contact Details

CAREER & ACHIEVEMENTS: The achievements or contributions section is the part you really need to spend time on. This is the transferable stuff that employers will want to talk about at interview. You don't need to get too far into the 'how' of your achievements; focus instead on the 'what' – this will invite 'how' questions at the interview which will allow you to really start selling yourself. More ideas on this section can be found in the 360° Exercise (see page 80).

You rarely need to get into the minute details of your job description and areas of responsibility. For example, if you are a Management Accountant, a simple phrase on the lines of 'In addition to the usual responsibilities' immediately enables you to delineate the special or expanded responsibilities that you have sought out or that have been devolved on to you. Every reader knows the 'usual suspects' list of responsibilities, so don't take up a lot of space on these, particularly for older jobs. To help you to do this, complete the exercise in Appendix 2 (see page 404) for each job you have held. This will quickly show you how/if you developed within the role in each position. Here is one way of laying this out:

Last point of your professional profile

CAREER AND ACHIEVEMENTS

August 200X to Present
Headhunted by Widgets Incorporated (UK) as Management Accountant, reporting to the Financial Controller. Widgets competes in the blah-blah sector, the local affiliate has a turnover of £XX million and has 350 staff. My brief encompasses:

- Preparation of monthly/quarterly/annual Accounts and variance based reporting.
- VAT analysis and reporting.
- Cash flow reporting.
- Liaising with banks, suppliers and debtors.
- Ongoing liaison with auditors and regulatory authorities.

Special responsibilities:

- Development, implementation and updating of all policies and procedures under my purview.
- Capital Expenditure projects from inception to completion.
- Collaboration on key projects – insurance, systems development, stock control.

Contributions:

- Migration from legacy system to SAP – project team member.
- Merger, Acquisition & Diligence activities from time to time.
- Conducting training in Finance for non-financial Management.

EDUCATION: A simple and clean way of presenting this information is in a table. You should work in reverse chronological order and only include those details that will be of interest to the reader. Once you are a few years out of education, no one really cares what subjects you took in second year or what results you got – unless it was something very impressive.

Last point of your Career and Achievements section

EDUCATION

INSTITUTION	QUALIFICATION	YEAR
College name, location	**Masters in Business Administration** Thesis: Implementing an ERP system in the multinational setting	2002
Institute name, location	**Membership Exams (ACA)**	1999
School name, location	**A levels**	1994

Make the table lines invisible and it is even easier to read:

Last point of your Career and Achievements section		

EDUCATION

INSTITUTION	QUALIFICATION	YEAR
College name, location	**Masters in Business Administration**	2002
	Thesis: Implementing an ERP system	
	in the multinational setting	
Institute name, location	**Membership Exams (ACA)**	1999
School name, location	**A levels**	1994

TRAINING AND RELEVANT SKILLS: *Veeeeery* important section. Training represents the investment made by your current and past employers in you, so if they aren't making that investment, it will be setting off alarm bells in the reader's head… This is why it is vital to put yourself forward for any training that is available within your organisation. You don't want to sound whiny and needy to your boss, but make sure she is aware of your commitment to personal development and lifelong learning.

'Job security' and 'take-home pay' have been listed as the two key drivers/motivators for employees in all the studies conducted since World War II – until recently that is. The latest studies are showing that ongoing 'training and development' has supplanted 'job security', probably because employees have finally recognised that job security is an extinct concept. If your employer is not developing you and investing in you, beware. It is the career management equivalent of strip mining – it looks bad on your CV, but more importantly it means that your skillset is becoming outdated.

You should present the Training section on your CV in the same way as Education – in an easy-to-read, tabular format. One other thing about training: just because you have been sent on a training course doesn't necessarily mean that you have to include it on your CV, particularly if the training has been 'corrective' in any way. This would be especially true if you have been sent on training following an unfavourable appraisal.

MEMBERSHIPS: List your professional memberships by way of reassurance, but also because your new employer will usually be picking up the tab for them.

THE EXECUTIVE/SENIOR CV

Order of the sections:

1 Name
2 Professional Profile
3 Key Accomplishments (*I have found it best to split these up and tailor them as appropriate for each application*)
4 Professional Progression (*focus heavily on promotions and achievements. If length is not a problem, you can give some detail of 'how' you made these things happen*)
5 Education and Accreditations (most recent first)
6 Other Training and Relevant Skills
7 Professional Memberships
8 Extra-curricular Activities
9 Referees – on request
10 Contact Details

These CVs are always the most difficult to write and, as you get older, involve an agonising process of compression – which elements do you omit and which do you highlight? An effective CV for a senior player in any sector is going to be dependent on heavy research and very tight positioning. There's more at stake here and the return on investment is far larger, so executives typically enlist help from a professional CV crafting service. My advice on this is to shop around and, if possible, to select your wordsmith on the basis of referral from someone you know and trust. The really good ones will offer a 'no quibble' policy – if you are not completely happy with the end result, you don't have to pay anything.

'How long or short should it be?' is the question that most senior executives think about when it comes to representing themselves in writing. My answer, as always, is, 'That depends.' First, it depends on how well known you are. In the unlikely event that he was applying for a job, Paul Hewson's CV could consist of the words, 'Howerya, I'm Bono.' He is a brand – instantly recognisable, memorable and indelibly associated with the work and events that he has been involved in. You may not have quite this degree of fame, but you might be very well known to some of the people that you are going to be writing to, in which case brevity will serve you well. Detail your history and your major accomplishments without delving too much into the 'how' of those accomplishments.

If, however, you are a relative unknown, you will need to provide more reassurance to the reader. Remember the massive job that your CV is doing here – it is taking the reader from an 'Oh no, not another damn CV' mindset to curious, to genuinely interested, to making a decision to set aside time from a busy schedule to meet the writer. When you have been in the hiring seat, how many times have you ever done that out of all the CVs that have crossed your desk? So when you are applying at this level, inform/reassure, and then persuade – that is your order of business. Any whiff that you are the supplicant will kill your chances dead. Any trace of neediness, haplessness or desperation on your part will likewise result in your efforts coming to nought.

Positioning, positioning, positioning. Get into the reader's headspace and give him a reason to want a get-to-know-you meeting with you. No one is going to hire you on the basis of your excellent CV, but if it is less than excellent no one is going to bring you to the next stage of the process.

So, you are a Bono. You're very well known in your sector and your reputation precedes you. I contend that you still need an outstanding CV simply because 99 times out of 100, you are going to be viewed by people (Board members, non-exec Directors, management outside of your area of expertise, young recruitment consultants) who have never heard of you and in the context of a bunch of other people with a similar background putting themselves forward for the same job. So take the time, do the hard analysis, do the soul-searching and get the document glittering!

Chapter 4

360° – THINKING OBJECTIVELY ABOUT YOURSELF

> *My sledge and anvil lie declined, my bellows too have lost their wind, my fire's extinct, my forge decayed, and in the dust my vice is laid, my coals are spent, my iron's gone, my nails are drove, my work is done.*
>
> **WILLIAM STRANGE'S EPITAPH (Strange was a blacksmith who died in 1746)**

WHY DO I NEED A 360° VIEW OF MYSELF?

If knowledge is power, then self-knowledge is the most useful force you can wield in your career and any job-hunts you undertake in that career. People who have gained insight into themselves are much more effective leaders, team members and employees, and are valued as such by society and employers.

It is very hard to write about yourself for your CV. To condense all of your experiences and accomplishments into a few succinct paragraphs in order to make the reader want to meet you is no laughing matter. We have already talked about all of the data that you need to collate, and about picking the essential components – the elements that address a specific reader's concerns. But a well-written CV is more, much more, than that. A winning CV, one that immediately grabs the reader's attention and pricks her interest, is a CV that gives that reader a flavour for the kind of person you are.

Take it to the next stage and put yourself (yet again!) in the boots of the interviewer. Let's say you have shortlisted 10 candidates for the job for which you are screening. Let's further say that two of them are just unprofessional clowns, two are arrogant creeps and the other six seem like reasonably competent, decent people. On probing deeper, you discover that two of the remaining six don't like themselves very much and another two are carrying chips on their shoulders from previous employments.

'The greater our knowledge increases the greater our ignorance unfolds.'
JOHN F. KENNEDY

So you have whittled it down to the final two – one of whom can talk about himself with great conviction, understands how he is perceived by suppliers, customers, bosses and colleagues and makes sure that he doesn't ruffle feathers with any of those groups, and has gained a reputation (when you do the background check) for having a Midas touch when it comes to dealing with people and getting the best out of them.

The final candidate is similarly qualified, similarly experienced (link sausages! see page 159) and has a comparable track record of success, but just doesn't provide you with the same level of reassurance as to his abilities in dealing with people. The technical term for this kind of hiring situation is a NO-BRAINER. Candidate No. 2 has just been beaten by a Bogeyman (see page 38).

So do the 360°. Do it on yourself and then get other people, whose opinions you value, to fill in the boxes for you. You can offer to do it as a trade with friends and family members or with old colleagues – 'I'll show you mine if you'll show me yours…' If you already know all of this juicy stuff about yourself and that it coincides with what the world thinks of you, lucky you (and why are you reading this book?). If you are not sure of this knowledge, get to work…

THE JOB THAT I DO

Current or most recent Job Title:

Your Boss's Title:

Type of Organisation:

Key areas of responsibility:

-

-

-

BREAKDOWN OF CURRENT/MOST RECENT JOB

What I do/did very well in my job (think of third-party evidence here – compliments from co-workers, customers or your boss, for example):

Areas of weakness in my performance:

The best things about my job are/were:

Aspects of my job that I hate(d):

ACCOMPLISHMENTS

A professional achievement is something which (a) you did well and enjoyed; (b) made a contribution that could be measured; or (c) would make you interesting to a prospective employer. Examples could include developing a new idea, service, product, process or procedure; exceeding a sales, profit or market share target; reducing inventory or other costs;

improving profit margins; streamlining an important part of your job; making some part of the business more efficient; being assigned to recruit, supervise and/or train other people or being assigned a broader area of responsibility on the job.

Look at the accomplishments you made in the past 10 years. If it goes back further than that, it will need to be truly earth-shaking stuff. The table below should help you come up with some good material. In each case, indicate exactly what you did, the immediate result and what it meant to your team or organisation.

MY INPUT	RESULT	OUTCOME
Turnover or other growth?		
Targets met/exceeded?		
Key new business gained?		
New processes/procedures?		
New product/service/idea?		
Streamlining approach?		
Significant problem solved?		

MY INPUT	RESULT	OUTCOME
Cost savings?		
Special relationships (internal or external) developed or fostered to a new level?		
Recruiting and managing staff?		
Training of new staff? Cross-training existing staff?		
Motivating staff with special incentives? Staff turnover reduced?		
Any initiatives, suggestions or other contributions?		

Pick the top five to seven accomplishments from your recent years and list them below in order of importance to the organisation you were working for.

1.

2.

3.

4.

5.

6.

7.

ME IN A NUTSHELL

Describe your professional self in one sentence. Imagine that you have just met a head-hunter at a party:

Give yourself marks out of 10 for the following:

Commitment	☐	Administration ☐
Urgency	☐	Multi-tasking ☐
Professionalism	☐	Crisis Management ☐
Flexibility/adaptability	☐	Event Management ☐
Learning curve	☐	Analysis/ability to evaluate ☐
Empathy	☐	Creativity/innovation ☐
Finance/numeracy	☐	Account Management ☐
Writing skills	☐	Fostering relationships/networking ☐
Selling	☐	Problem solving ☐
People management/motivating	☐	Interpersonal skills ☐

MY SKILLBASE

Talents are the special abilities that you are born with. Skills are learnt, honed and developed on an ongoing basis. Reflect on your full range of skills, those used both in and out of work.

IT skills? What packages do you use well?

```
┌─────────────────────────────────────────────────────┐
│                                                     │
│                                                     │
│                                                     │
│                                                     │
└─────────────────────────────────────────────────────┘
```

Recruitment, team-building/training skills?

```
┌─────────────────────────────────────────────────────┐
│                                                     │
│                                                     │
│                                                     │
└─────────────────────────────────────────────────────┘
```

The following list delves further into your skillset. The skills are broken down into four categories. Give yourself marks out of 10 for **how good you are** at each skill (we will look at the skills that you **enjoy** later).

ABSTRACT		PEOPLE	
Creating something from nothing	☐	Usefully assisting others	☐
Classifying/Categorising	☐	Supervising others	☐
Painting/Drawing	☐	Organising/Co-ordinating efforts	☐
Learning	☐	Counselling/Advising	☐
Using computers	☐	Teaching – getting ideas across	☐
Planning/Strategising	☐	Speaking/Presenting	☐
Teaching – explaining concepts	☐	Negotiating	☐

Researching/Finding out new stuff	☐	Listening	☐
Writing	☐	Empathising	☐
Mathematics	☐	Fostering relationships	☐
Exploring/Investigating ideas	☐	Selling	☐

INFORMATION   **PHYSICAL**

Reading	☐	Operating equipment	☐
Working with numbers	☐	Driving	☐
Following instructions	☐	Doing mechanical tasks	☐
Making decisions	☐	Cooking	☐
Seeing to the heart of the issue	☐	Gross motor skills – sports	☐
Learning	☐	Painting and decorating	☐
Noticing important details	☐	Using tools	☐
Using computers	☐	DIY – Building/Repairing	☐

Core skills other than already mentioned?

MY TOP 7 SKILLS

From the picture you have built on the previous page, list those skills at which you excel and which you think make you attractive as a potential employee in today's workplace:

1.

2.

3.

4.

5.

6.

7.

Now list the seven skills that you most **enjoy** using in order of satisfaction:

1.

2.

3.

4.

5.

6.

7.

How closely do the two skill lists correlate? Going back to basics, it is imperative that you pursue a career that you (a) are **good at** and (b) **enjoy**. You might be the best Widgeting Engineer on the planet, but if widgeting leaves you cold, you are placing yourself at risk. You are at risk because your health can suffer as a result of doing work that does not fulfil you. Also, if your morale is low, management will notice and, if they have to make tough choices about who they keep and who they let go, your name is unlikely to appear on the 'keep' list (see page 344, Turn-ons and Turn-offs).

MY STYLE

What is your **focus** on the job? (*rank if necessary*)	Customers	☐
	Quality	☐
	Profit	☐
	Results	☐
	Procedures	☐
	Winning	☐
	Cost control	☐
	Productivity	☐
	Keeping the team going	☐

Under what **constraints** have you operated? (*rank if necessary*)	Time	☐
	Budget	☐
	Targets	☐
	Multiple clients	☐
	Regulations	☐
	Laws	☐
	Corporate guidelines/ expectations	☐

Team player or solo flyer? (by preference)
Preferred team style?
Any experience with ISO9000 or similar?
Have you been given any particularly positive feedback over the
years? From whom? Any themes emerging in the feedback?

Describe yourself with five adjectives.

1.

2.

3.

4.

5.

What is your most significant professional *weakness*?

MY PERSONAL DEVELOPMENT

List the most useful training courses or programmes that you have ever been on:

COURSE TITLE	INSTITUTION/CO.	YEAR	USEFUL BECAUSE

What would you spend a £5,000 **personal** (not technical) training budget on this year?

Best moment in your career/life to date?

Who was your most difficult boss to work with and why?

How would your best friend describe you?

1.

2.

3.

4.

5.

Why does he or she value you so much?

What about your current boss/co-workers? (*or most recent*)

1.

2.

3.

4.

5.

Worst moment in your career/life to date?

```
┌─────────────────────────────────────────────────────┐
│                                                     │
│                                                     │
│                                                     │
│                                                     │
│                                                     │
└─────────────────────────────────────────────────────┘
```

Where do you plan to be in your professional life in 5 and in 10 years' time?

```
┌─────────────────────────────────────────────────────┐
│                                                     │
│                                                     │
│                                                     │
│                                                     │
│                                                     │
└─────────────────────────────────────────────────────┘
```

CANVASSING OPINION

So now you have your view-point and, hopefully, you have discovered a few useful things about yourself along the way. Time to start getting other people's input on some of the items – skills, loves and hates, accomplishments, weaknesses, great moments. ANY feedback you can get from anyone who knows you well could be useful.

And remember – their perception is *their* reality. Even if you vociferously disagree with something that they point out about you, take it on board. You may not have intended to behave or be perceived in that way, or they may have *totally* misconstrued what was behind your action; but it is real to them and they have had the courage and courtesy to tell you. Thank them.

You are looking for points of convergence (and disagreement) here. So you think you are very empathetic and that you are a good listener but what do the people in your 360° circle tell you? Does the feedback confirm or deny your assertion? What do you think, what do you know, what can you *prove*?

Chapter 5

CVs – LOOK AND FEEL

> *At Sony we assume that all products of our competitors have basically the same technology, price, performance and features. Design is the only thing that differentiates one product from another in the marketplace.*
>
> **NORIO OHGA**

Layout and styling can only be finalised when you have a specific job to apply for. There are no hard-and-fast rules for CVs – different people will inevitably like different things – but you won't go far wrong if you follow these eight rules of thumb:

1. WORD-PROCESS IT

Unless you are going for a job as a calligrapher, your CV should be crisply produced on standard word-processing software. If you are stuck with a legacy system or a little-known and not widely used application, save your CVs and letters in Rich Text Format (filename.rtf). This will allow you to transfer your files to different computers with little or no difficulty.

2. FONTS

Use appropriate typefaces – word-processing packages these days come with umpteen fonts, the majority of which are worthless for business use.

Save them for fun activities and use Times or a similar, serifed font. (Serifs are the little tails that stick out of letters. *Sans serif* fonts are cleaner and more modern-looking, but can also be a little soulless.) Most of what we read is produced in serifed fonts – newspapers, magazines and books – and we are accustomed to reading them and believing them.

If your CV is likely to be scanned, you may need to use a sans serif font like Arial, Verdana or GillSans and test it by OCR (Optical Character Recognition), scanning it to assess layout and legibility. Underlining can also cause problems for scanners. Don't use rare or specialist fonts, particularly if you are going to send soft copies of your CV by e-mail (see below) as the receiving computer may not have them installed and all of your careful formatting will be ruined.

3. LEGIBILITY

Allow generous margins and plenty of white space on your CV – this will make it easier to read. Your font sizes should also contribute to making life easy for the reader:

TIMES 14 BOLD CAPITALS
Times 12 regular
Times 11 regular
Times 10 – getting a little hard to read
Times 8 – way too small – typically used when you need to cram in more information than will comfortably fit.

GILLSANS 14 BOLD CAPITALS
GillSans 12 regular
GillSans 11 regular
GillSans 10 – still readable because it's *sans serif*

Another issue for font sizes – many placement agencies still fax CVs to client organisations, so your layout needs to retain its legibility when it has been sent to a crumbly old fax machine and the lettering becomes fuzzy. Once again, test it and see if it works…

Establish a protocol for your CV that makes the reader's job easier and stick to it throughout your correspondence. Unless you are sending a text-only document (see page 68) over the web or in the body of an e-mail, you have tremendous scope for drawing attention to the important elements of your document using the formatting tools in your word-processing application.

The reader who is scan-reading your CV for the first time is looking at job titles and the organisations you have worked for, and possibly an overview of your qualifications and training. Make it as easy as one, two, three. Put your **Job Titles** in bold as they are usually the most important thing to highlight. Put the *Organisation Names* in italics. When you are delineating training and education, you can continue the protocol – putting the names of the *Institutions* in italics and the **Qualifications** or **Courses** that you took in bold.

CAREER AND ACHIEVEMENTS

August 2001 to Present
Headhunted by *Widgets Incorporated (UK)* as the **Senior Management Accountant**, reporting to the Financial Controller. *Widgets* competes in the blah-blah sector, the local affiliate has a turnover of £XX million and has 650 staff. Along with the typical analysis, audit and reporting functions, my brief encompasses:

- Line management for 11 staff – 3 Accountants and 8 Clerks.
- Development, implementation and updating of all policies and procedures under my purview.
- Capital Expenditure projects from inception to completion.
- Collaboration on key projects – insurance, systems development, stock control.

Key Contributions:
- Migration from legacy system to SAP – project team member.
- Merger, Acquisition & Diligence activities from time to time.
- Conducting training in Finance for non-financial management.

May 1998 to August 2001
Joined *Fidgets Ltd.* as **Payroll Clerk**, reporting to the Management Accountant. *Fidgets* is a London-based manufacturer and distributor of yadda-yaddas. I rose quickly through the ranks following my qualification in January 2000. Progression:

Payroll Clerk	May 98
Accounts Clerk	Dec 98
Accountant	Feb 00
Management Accountant	Nov 00

July 1997 to May 1998
Following four rounds of interviews, *Gidgets Ltd.* in Surrey selected me ahead of 250 applicants for the role of **Job Title**, reporting to the Boss Title.

EDUCATION & TRAINING

INSTITUTION	QUALIFICATION	YEAR
SAP UK	Project Team Training:	2001
	Project Management	&
	Financial Accounting	2002
	Corporate Finance Management	
	Business Programming (JAVA)	
	SAP Supplier Relationship Management	
College name, location	**Masters in Business Administration**	2002
	Thesis: Implementing an ERP system in the multinational setting	
Fidgets Ltd. Training Division	**Leadership Skills I & II**	2001
	(I was also placed on the internal Mentoring Programme)	

Whizz-bang Mgmt. Institute	**Management Development Programme (12 week)**	2000
Institute name, location	**Membership Exams (ACA)**	2000
Whoopeedoo Training Ltd.	**Advanced MS Excel and Word**	1998
Gidgets Ltd. Training Division	Induction Training: **Time Management / Putting People First Presentation Skills / MS Windows & Office**	1997
School name, location	**A levels**	1997

4. WALK ON BY

Walk them through the document – think about what matters most to them and put that up front (see page 69, The Order of Sections). Demarcate your sections clearly using headings in a different font (or style) and lines or white space. Look at how the text in your favourite newspaper or magazine is laid out and get ideas there or talk to a friend in the design business.

5. PACKAGING

You don't buy products in the supermarket with cheap, dented, torn, rusty or faded packaging and, predictably, neither do employers:

- Use high-quality paper with a weight of 100 grams or heavier. Don't 'liberate' 80 gram paper from the photocopier at work: invest in a ream or two of decent paper for your job search. Human beings are fundamentally tactile and while you won't get any extra marks for using good stationery, if you don't it can indicate a less than professional approach.

- Print everything at high resolution (600 dpi) on a laser printer. Very few inkjets print text really well – if you have one, experiment with different resolutions on different papers until you are happy.
- Don't photocopy your CV for submission, unless you have access to a professional photocopier the size of a bus. (Anyway, why do you need dozens of copies of your CV? You are going to be tailoring it for each application you make.)
- If you are posting hard copies, send your CV flat (not folded) in a crisp white A4 envelope.
- Print your address label or envelope. Hand-write your return address clearly.
- Buy your own stamps – do not frank your envelopes at work. The reader *will* check and it *is* theft.

6. BINDERS

If you are submitting a hard copy of your CV by post, DO NOT BIND IT! Binders are a nuisance and always get torn off and thrown in the bin, to the accompaniment of a lot of irritation on the part of the reader. Binders make reading, photocopying, scanning and filing your CV more difficult, so DON'T. A paperclip or staple is perfectly sufficient.

If you are neurotic (like me) you can use a clear plastic slip cover – the kind that opens on two sides. (When I was in primary school, I firmly believed that you got an extra five per cent if you handed up your homework in one of these. I sometimes still do… if only life were so simple.)

7. SOFT COPIES

If you are e-mailing your CV as an attachment, you need to make absolutely sure that it arrives in as good a look and feel as you sent it. Word-processing software is inclined to foul up your beautifully formatted document (another reason for using standard fonts), so send it to a few friends' computers first to make sure it arrives properly. Get them to print it and then you should check every detail of its formatting.

The other detail you need to watch out for if you're sending soft copies is the 'Properties' of the file that you send. If you have asked friends to look at your CV or if you sought professional help in composing it, they may leave footprints in the Properties of the document. Save a clean copy of the CV on to your hard drive and open the Properties (generally found under the 'File' menu on your word-processing application). Make sure that it is *your* name in there as author and as the last person to save and print the file.

You can avoid all this hassle with layout and footprints by converting your file to the Portable Document Format (filename.pdf) using Adobe Acrobat®. (Some operating systems have this capability built in.) This ensures that the file will arrive with exactly the formatting you sent and also that no one can tamper with it – as placement agencies are wont to do.

AND ANOTHER THING...

> **'At BMW, design is treated like a religion.'**
> *FORTUNE* MAGAZINE

Two final points on look and feel: (1) it really helps if you can type and (2) your life will be immeasurably easier if you can actually use your word-processing software. If you are not already proficient, learn. Computer illiteracy is fast becoming as much of a hindrance and as professionally unacceptable as functional illiteracy. Don't rely on the good graces of others to do this donkey work. With the best will in the world, they won't care as much as you – even if you are paying them. Learn how to type and how to word-process.

The typing part is easy – there are a number of computerised tutorial programmes available which can literally 'talk' you through the training. There is also a multitude of computer courses available, but I would recommend that you identify a tutor (your network should be able to help here) and spend a few hours with him one-on-one, learning just those parts of the workings of your machine and of your applications that you actually need to know – you can always top up with another grind later as the need arises. This may cost you a bit more and you won't get a certificate from the process but, in my experience, far too many so-called computer courses are geared towards getting you through the course rather than giving you a clear understanding of, and ability to really use, your computer.

Chapter 6

CV VOCABULARY

> *Short words are best and the old words, when short, are best of all.*
>
> **SIR WINSTON CHURCHILL**

HEADINGS FOR THE SECTIONS OF YOUR CV

- Profile / Professional Profile / Overview / Summary / At a Glance / Thumbnail Sketch
- Core Competencies / Key Skills / Skillset / Principal Skills / Notable Skills
- Key Achievements / Major Contributions / Track Record
- Career to Date / Career & Achievements / Professional Progression / Career & Accomplishments / Relevant Career Details / Work Experience / Professional Background
- Education / Qualifications / Education & Accreditations / Education & Training / Professional Development / Training
- Publications / Presentations / Research Interests / Selected Publications
- Professional Memberships / Professional Associations and Development
- Extra-curricular Activities / Outside Interests / Interests / Hobbies / Pastimes
- Contact Details / Contact & Personal Details
- References / Referees / Supporting References / Professional References

DESCRIPTIVE TERMS TO USE ABOUT YOURSELF

- **Professional** / Conscientious / Specialised / Meticulous / Disciplined / Responsible / Reliable / Efficient / Diligent
- **Strong** / Adept / Sound / Effective / Successful / Thorough / Accomplished / Well developed / Above average / Confident
- **Excellent** / Exceptional / Outstanding / Superior / Highly developed / High capacity
- **Innovative** / Creative / Diverse / Inventive / Original / Resourceful / Ingenious / Imaginative
- **Strategic** / Pro-active / Clear / Astute / Measured / Cogent / Incisive / Shrewd / Coherent
- **Flexible** / Adaptable / Open / Versatile / Accommodating
- **Trusted** / Well regarded / Reputation gained with / Respected / Valued / Esteemed
- **Competitive** / Ambitious / Progressive / Tenacious / Market-driven / Results-driven / Goal-oriented / Performance-focused / Determined
- **Proven** / Demonstrable / Track record in / Comfortable with / Familiar with / Adept with / At ease with / Full knowledge of / In-depth knowledge of / Skilled in / Confirmed / Verified
- **Successful** / Consistent / Seasoned / Highly experienced / Effective / Senior / Dependable / Unfailing
- **Committed** / Motivated / Highly motivated / Dedicated / Staunch / Loyal / Enthusiastic / Keen
- **Tangible** / Concrete / Substantial / Material / Significant
- **Diplomatic** / Sensitive / Tactful / Judicious / Subtle / Prudent / Perceptive / Discreet
- **Blue-chip** / World-class / Industry leader / Market leading (*all of these would refer to the companies you have worked with*)
- **XXXXXX focused** (*e.g. Customer-focused, Quality-focused, Sales-driven, Target-oriented, Results-focused*)

THE SCOPE OF THE JOB THAT YOU DO/DID

- My remit included...
- My purview...
- Core responsibilities included...
- Highlights: (*followed by a pithy, bulleted list*)
- My central function was...
- My brief encompassed...
- My primary function was...
- I was tasked with...
- Along with the typical responsibilities of the role, I also had the following brief...
- My duties included... (*'duties' as a descriptive implies a relatively junior position – careful!*)

TOOTHSOME VERBS

Where possible, you should start your 'what I did' sentences with a good strong verb. It obviates the need for you to write 'I' and, if you present the 'what I did' material in list or bullet-point format, it immediately draws the reader's eye down the list. You will notice that all of the verbs here are in the past tense – this reinforces the sense of accomplishment.

- **Increased** / Grew / Developed / Expanded / Improved / Raised / Heightened / Enlarged / Broadened / Diversified / Accelerated / Optimised / Augmented / Delivered / Produced / Maximised / Accrued / Outperformed / Accumulated / Overcame / Exceeded (expectations or targets) / Surpassed
- **Won** / Beat / Succeeded / Achieved / Performed / Executed / Delivered / Accomplished / Secured / Anticipated / Compelled / Forced / Precluded / Prevented / Averted / Impeded
- **Reduced** / Minimised / Diminished / Saved / Lessened / Halved / Shortened (usually time or lead times) / Trimmed / Stemmed / Eliminated (usually waste) / Dispensed (with the need for) / Eradicated / Curtailed / Obviated (the need for) / Generated savings / Lightened

- **Initiated** / Started / Began / Launched / Founded / Activated / Instigated / Introduced / Set up
- **Developed** / Devised / Pioneered / Designed / Formulated / Originated / Discovered / Conceived / Generated / Created / Built / Commissioned / Formed (usually a team) / Assembled (a team) / Staffed / Established / Installed / Constructed / Planned / Composed
- **Instructed** / Ordered / Taught / Guided / Tutored / Coached / Piloted / Mentored / Appraised / Reviewed / Trained / Upskilled / Cross-trained
- **Deferred** / Put off / Pushed back / Postponed / Adjourned / Suspended / Extended
- **Led** / Drove / Directed / Spearheaded / Headed / Central role in… / Managed / Supervised / Oversaw / Presided / Project managed / Co-ordinated / Facilitated / Arranged / Organised / Monitored / Controlled / Assigned / Budgeted / Scheduled / Rostered
- **Supplanted** / Replaced / Displaced / Superseded / Succeeded / Overtook / Surpassed / Took over from
- **Represented** / Epitomised / Stood for / Characterised / Spoke for / Symbolised / Embodied
- **Supported** / Provided / Sustained / Buttressed / Strengthened / Fortified / Reinforced / Complied with / Encouraged / Motivated / Inspired / Assisted / Stimulated / Released management from / Lightened (the load of something or somebody)
- **Worked closely with** / Collaborated / Liaised with / Consulted widely / Interacted / Consulted appropriately / Consulted with stakeholders / Co-operated / Worked together with
- **Analysed** / Captured (information) / Examined / Identified / Probed / Highlighted / Studied / Diagnosed / Uncovered / Detected / Evaluated / Defined / Calculated / Researched / Investigated
- **Sold** / Marketed / Brokered / Negotiated / Persuaded / Influenced / Espoused / Publicised / Represented / Promoted / Gained approval for / Lobbied / Gained a foothold in / Broke into
- **Enhanced** / Improved / Developed / Streamlined / Standardised / Tightened up / Put shape on / Shaped / Structured / Edited / Reorganised / Updated / Renewed / Modernised / Redesigned / Modified / Revamped / Overhauled / Effected change / Rearranged /

Transformed / Restructured / Changed / Refined / Converted / Altered / Change managed / Revolutionised / Simplified / Revised

- **Disseminated** / Distributed / Allocated / Supplied / Circulated / Spread
- **Submitted** / Posited / Presented / Contributed / Tabled / Suggested / Urged / Served as / Pitched / Positioned / Illustrated / Related / Recommended / Advised / Counselled / Imposed / Steered / Outlined
- **Transitioned** / Moved / Shifted / Combined / Transferred / Relocated / Redeployed / Repositioned / Shuffled / Rearranged
- **Approved** / Endorsed / Permitted / Enabled / Authorised / Empowered / Consented to / Enacted / Sanctioned / Agreed / Concurred / Gained consensus
- **Implemented** / Brought to conclusion / Consolidated / Finalised / Resolved / Completed / Concluded / Settled / Firmed up / Ended
- **Recognised for** / Consistently recognised for / Praised for / Selected by management to / Singled out to
- **Gained approval for** / Suggested and implemented / Promoted / Identified the need for / Highlighted / Mounted a campaign for
- **Ensured** / Guaranteed / Made certain / Leveraged / Expedited / Gained advantage by / Forced / Eased
- **Administered** / Ran / Conducted / Undertook to / Processed / Maintained / Fostered / Handled / Dealt with / Implemented / Enforced
- **Recruited** / Selected / Hired / Interviewed / Enlisted / Attracted / Drafted / Appointed
- **Garnered** / Collated / Gained / Procured / Purchased / Acquired / Compiled / Attained / Obtained / Collected / Extracted / Removed / Took out / Pulled out
- **Utilised** / Made use of / Applied / Exploited / Employed / Operated / Exercised / Drew on
- **Mediated** / Interceded / Reconciled / Brought solution about / Brought together / Arbitrated / Unified
- **Verified** / Confirmed / Tested / Checked / Determined / Authenticated / Traced / Proved / Demonstrated / Audited / Inspected / Reviewed / Documented / Substantiated / Reconciled / Corroborated
- **Restored** / Remedied / Mended / Repaired / Stabilised / Reinstated / Corrected / Returned / Rebuilt / Fixed / Revitalised / Renewed / Revived / Breathed life back into / Rejuvenated / Rectified

- **Interpreted** / Translated / Deduced / Deciphered / Unravelled / Worked out / Solved
- **Criticised** / Assessed / Disparaged / Censured / Critiqued / Provided feedback on
- **Protected** / Defended / Preserved / Secured / Conserved / Retained / Safeguarded / Upheld / Thwarted (competitor) / Blunted (someone else's efforts) / Prevented / Stopped / Impeded / Forestalled / Hindered / Obstructed / Avoided / Evaded / Diverted
- **Decided** / Determined (the outcome) / Chose / Took the decision to / Fixed on / Opted for / Elected to (do something)
- **Specified** / Detailed / Stipulated / Denoted / Indicated / Delineated / Itemised / Insisted upon
- **Forecasted** / Foresaw / Predicted / Anticipated / Foretold / Envisaged
- **Prepared** / Readied / Made ready / Set / Made plans for / Laid out
- **Declined** / Rejected / Rebuffed / Refused / Turned down

QUALIFIERS

Adverbs give us more information about the words that we use, typically verbs (he went *quickly* to…) but also adjectives (the music was too *quiet* to hear) and other adverbs (*terribly* slowly.) Three *caveats*:

1 Don't **overuse adverbs**. It gets tiresome when everything you write is qualified in this way. If in doubt, pick a stronger verb and kill off the adverb.
2 It is still considered bad form to **finish a sentence** with an adverb – *He went there very quickly*. It reads better as, *He very quickly went there*.
3 Don't use **hanging comparatives** on your CV – *We completed the project more quickly*. More quickly than who or what? Advertisers use this technique all the time – *More music, less chatter*, trumpets the advertisement for the radio station. More music than who? Less chatter than who? Repeated often enough, catch-phrases like these become part of our vocabulary, but they are the kiss of death on a CV.

- **Quickly** / Rapidly / Swiftly / Promptly / Speedily / Briskly / Efficiently / Punctually / Without delay
- **Successfully** / Competently / Capably / Ably / Proficiently / Adeptly / Effectively / Responsibly
- **Cautiously** / Carefully / Judiciously / Prudently / Selectively / Discreetly / Tactfully
- **Consistently** / Constantly / Always / Unfailingly
- **Creatively** / Ingeniously / Resourcefully / Imaginatively
- **Decisively** / Resolutely / Definitely / Positively / Assertively
- **Flexibly** / Adaptively / Changeably
- **Enthusiastically** / Passionately / Earnestly / Keenly / Eagerly / Intensely / Ardently / Energetically / Vigorously
- **Slowly** / Gradually / Steadily / Progressively
- **Significantly** / Dramatically / Substantially / Radically / Considerably / Tremendously

STARTING OUT

Try to avoid the perpendicular pronoun 'I' when you are writing about yourself. Where possible, avoid writing, 'I moved to Widgets Incorporated as a Widgeting Engineer'; instead use 'Appointed as Widgeting Engineer for...' or one of the other phrases below. Repeated use of 'I' in writing is somehow less acceptable than using the same term in a verbal delivery. Start your paragraphs with:

- Appointed
- Headhunted as
- Joined XXXX as
- Approached by XXXX to become
- Invited to join XXXX as
- Gained position as
- Offered full-time post as
- Invited to return to XXXX as

NIT-PICKING

One of my personal bugbears is the humble apostrophe. No one seems to know when to use and when not to use these little fellas. Get this right, because if you come across a nit-picker, your CV could end up in the bin for this very silly reason. Apostrophes serve two major functions:

1 To indicate missing letters.
2 To illustrate the possessive case.

People *constantly* get these mixed up!

MISSING LETTERS:

Cannot	becomes	**Can't**
Do not	becomes	**Don't**
You are	becomes	**You're** (*your* means *belonging to you*)
Would not	becomes	**Wouldn't**
It is	becomes	**It's**

POSSESSIVE:

Belonging to that person – **That person's**
I worked there for five years – **I gained five years' experience**
The headlines for today – **Today's news headlines**
The most common mistake is the inclusion of an apostrophe in the possessive *its*. His, hers, its, ours, theirs, yours – these are known as absolute possessives and no apostrophe is required for any of them. If you write *It's* make damn sure you mean '*It is*'.

Chapter 7

ME...AT A GLANCE

FAQ

'How do you write a profile of yourself? I have heard that putting one of these at the top of my CV will really help my chances of getting to interview, but where do I start? What do I include or leave out?'

Many CVs now come with a profile or thumbnail sketch of the candidate at the top. In my experience, too many of these are stale, unsubstantiated, buzzword-driven tripe. Examples that I have seen:

- 'I am a dynamic, forward-looking sales professional.'
- 'I am a self-starter, brimming with enthusiasm.'
- 'I have highly developed people skills.'
- 'I am a blah-blah-blah, keen to apply my yadda-yadda skills in a blue-chip environment.'

'I cannot write five words but that I change seven.'
DOROTHY PARKER

So what? No, really – so bloody what? Look at those statements again from the perspective of a tired recruiter who is wading through a tall pile of applications:

- 'I am a dynamic, forward-looking sales professional.' (a) Says who? (b) Maybe I don't want a 'dynamic' Rep – maybe I just want someone who keeps her nose to the grindstone and gets on with the job. I want a persistent grafter who won't alienate my customers by spouting this kind of rubbish!
- 'I am a self-starter, brimming with enthusiasm.' Well, golly gee willikers, I suspect that if I meet you, the word 'perky' is going to spring to mind and, if your CV is any indicator, I am probably going to lose my lunch to boot.
- 'I have highly developed people skills.' What are you – a contestant in a beauty pageant? I bet you love to travel, and are kind to animals, old people and children too...
- 'I am a blah-blah-blah, keen to apply my yadda-yadda skills in a blue-chip environment.' Guess what, sonny? Everybody else in the pile wants to work here too...

PROFILING YOURSELF

Profiling yourself should be quite easy. You talk about what you do for a living all the time – to colleagues, your family, people at parties. But that is usually an **informative** discourse; you are not having to justify your existence *per se*. A thumbnail sketch at the top of a CV is a **persuasive** discourse. A tight, every-word-included-for-a-reason, selling statement. 'I am *exactly* what you need. I am making your life just a little easier here. Binning me would be a bad idea.' All useful impressions to leave in the reader's mind.

I recommend building a list of about 10 items for possible inclusion in your Professional Profile. The 360° profiling exercise (see page 80) should give you lots of ammunition, hopefully more than you need. You probably won't use more than five or six items from this embarrassment of riches for any one application. Now let's think about getting them into shape.

Point 1: Should be your one-liner about yourself. I know what *I* am. I am a '*Strategic, innovative Career Management professional with a track record of* *success from entry-level to boardroom.*' What are you? Clearly, this point needs to fit closely with their perceived needs. You might need to reach for a thesaurus to make that happen. Examples:

- Strategic Financial professional with a strong Commercial and Development record.
- Entrepreneurial senior Financial professional currently with a multi-billion-£ company.
- Seasoned Chief Executive with broad experience and proven track record of accomplishment.
- Blue-chip-trained Project Management professional with a background in high finance, M&A, green-field and multi-cultural deals.
- Business postgraduate with solid commercial experience gained in a large financial institution.

Point 2: A big attention-grabber. '*All sales and market share targets exceeded for the last five years*' would probably have been a better line for our Rep above. Now *that* is a person the reader wants to meet. She understands what selling is all about and isn't wasting the reader's time in any way. Examples:

- Comfort in building/changing/restructuring businesses for growth, finance or sale.
- Built six key brands to market leadership, exceeding parent company expectations.
- Breadth of financial experience includes: IPO, merger, sale of subsidiary and company.
- Disciplined Programme Manager, skilled at bringing teams in a focused direction.
- Demonstrable track record in managing complex, pressurised projects with large numbers of participants.
- Specialist in financial management and planning for diverse elements of a Group.
- Proven record of quality, relevant, timely reporting and contribution to robust decision-making and performance management.

Clearly, the points above are *very* specifically tailored to positions that the writers have extensively researched. If you know, *really know*, what you are going to be doing in the new job, then pitching your profile to it like this is a cinch. Without that depth of research, you are relying on woolly generalisations and your CV starts to look and smell like junk mail.

Point 3: The big, transferable and relevant (above all, *pleeeease*, relevant) skills. Have they been central to your success? Are they attested to by your referees? (See page 177, Managing Your References.) Have you enhanced them through training that you mention further on in your CV? Examples:

- Excellent analytical, leadership, interpersonal and change management skills.
- Strong event- and crisis-management and media-handling skills.
- Exceptional interpersonal, relationship management and presentation skills.
- Excellent analytical, reasoning, budgetary, writing and IT capacities.
- Strong abilities in recruitment, team-building and training for new and existing staff.

Point 4: Secondary skills, the competencies you have that get the job done. Your middle of the bell-curve stuff (see page 193, Interview Mapping). Again, these should be reverse-engineered from your understanding of what the job that you are applying for entails. *'Comfortable and effective with X, Y and Z.'* Examples:

- Effective team leadership with an open, collaborative style.
- Astute at finding creative, effective solutions within complex environments.
- Comfortable relating to technical/non-technical management and staff at all levels.
- High degree of computer literacy – familiar and effective with all key applications used by (the company you are applying to).
- Highly developed recruitment, team-building and training skills to positive outcomes.

- Reputation gained as a problem solver with strong strategic, logical and analytical capacities.

Point 5: What have you been recognised for? Promoted for? Singled out for? '*Consistently selected to deal with technical/sensitive/intractable deals*' would be a nice thing to be able to say if the job you are applying for involves a lot of negotiation. Examples:

- Consistently recognised for professionalism, management of complex, integrated projects, teamworking and results.
- Recognised by management for acquisition review and corporate finance projects.
- Selected by international management to trouble-shoot intricate, technical and sensitive projects.
- Recognised throughout my career for steep learning curve, professionalism and results.
- Consistently recognised for innovation, commitment, customer relations, flexibility.

Point 6: The clincher. Your focus on the job and the constraints that you are comfortable working under. '*I am not some kind of snot-nosed, starry-eyed naïf here – I know what matters and I understand how the world works*.' Examples:

- Commercially driven while working within regulatory and budgetary constraints.
- Customer-service- and quality-focused while working to corporate expectations and tight timeframes.
- Focused on profitable production within JIT system and to agreed targets.
- Customer-focused while working within time, budgetary and legal constraints.

BLINDINGLY OBVIOUS STATEMENT

You must be able to stand over every syllable in your profile and your referees need to be primed and ready to confirm these statements (see page 177, Managing Your References). I know that it can be very tempting to do so, but you really, really should not overstate the case – there is a *world* of difference between 'Strong', 'Excellent' and 'Exceptional' skills in any capacity.

A well-phrased profile does more than get you to the shortlist. It begins to set the agenda for the interview that follows. So don't go claiming that you can raise the dead and expect them to breeze past it when you are in the hot seat. You are planting seeds here – be ready for the drill-down that will inevitably follow.

BULLETS OR PARAGRAPHS?

I favour a bullet-point approach to profiling, probably because I spend so much time reading CVs and also because I am a firm believer that people are lazy dogs and won't take the time to read a four-line paragraph, where they might, just *might*, scan-read six tightly composed bullets.

Writing about yourself this way takes a lot of forethought and practice. But if you do it well, the tired reader will metaphorically beam at you for making his life just a little bit easier and you are far less likely to end up filed in the bin.

> 'Vigorous writing is concise. A sentence should contain no unnecessary words, a paragraph no unnecessary sentences; for the same reason that a drawing should have no unnecessary lines and a machine no unnecessary parts.'
>
> WILLIAM STRUNK JR,
> *ELEMENTS OF STYLE*

Chapter 8

SUMMING IT UP – THE COVER LETTER

The present letter is a very long one, simply because I had no leisure to make it shorter. **BLAISE PASCAL**

Your CV is an advertisement to get you to an interview. In that case, your cover letter is the first second of that advertisement, which will either cause the reader to sit up and pay attention or to reach for the remote control to change the channel… Your cover letter is the first thing about you that any employer sees and will therefore form the basis of her initial impression of you. A well-presented and structured piece of writing will always favourably dispose the reader to you, so give the cover letter the attention it deserves.

A cover letter should neither be a re-statement of your CV, nor should it be a cursory 'Here's my CV…' note. All too often, cover letters are just 'dashed off' and are nasty, generic documents. We all get 'Dear Occupant' junk mail in our homes and our e-mail inboxes are stuffed with spam and everybody *hates* it. Well hey, what a surprise! Employers feel exactly the same way about 'Dear Sir/Madam' or 'To whom it may concern' at the top of a cover letter. Spelt the person's name wrong? They've just been promoted and you wrote to them under their old job title? Welcome to the bin!

There is no excuse for sloppiness of that kind. Find these basics out and get them right! Whether your letter is in response to an advertised position or part of a cold-call process to an organisation that you would like to work for, it needs to address three things:

- Why you are writing to them
- What you have to offer
- What you would like to happen next

in three succinct paragraphs.

How hard could that be? Well, in today's competitive jobs market, just as there is no such thing as a 'one size fits all' CV, you need to take time, and be careful and attentive with your cover letters.

LAYOUT

You should create some stationery for yourself. No one expects you to invest in engraved letterhead on heavy linen paper, but a crisp and distinctive header and footer will always look more polished than a same-font-throughout, hastily-typed, cover note. Try putting your address at the top, centred in a different font. Tie this in with your CV – whatever font you have used for your body copy is your font for the text of the letter; and the font/style that you used for the headings in your CV can be your letterhead. Examples:

ROWAN MANAHAN
HOUSE NAME
STREET ADDRESS
TOWN
POSTCODE

ROWAN MANAHAN
HOUSE NAME
STREET ADDRESS
TOWN
POSTCODE

Or, you can right justify it and make it very discreet:

Rowan Manahan
House Name
Street Address
Town
Postcode

ROWAN MANAHAN
HOUSE NAME
STREET ADDRESS
TOWN
POSTCODE

Your footer should be a line extending across the whole page with your home phone, e-mail and mobile phone details underneath:

T: (CODE) 123 4567 • **E**: rmanahan@yourisp.com • **M**: (CODE) 234 5678

This is crisp, neat and something *very* few people bother to do. What does it say about you? '*I am polished, I am professional, I pay meticulous attention to detail, and I am not run of the mill.*'

Make sure you date your cover letter and, if it is in response to an advertisement, put a subject header (plus any reference number) up at the top:

Rowan Manahan
House Name
Street Address
Town
Postcode

10th Month, 200X

Mr Joseph Brown
His Title
Widgets Incorporated
Address
Town
Postcode

RE: Operations Manager (ref no. 123 XYZ)

Dear Mr Brown

Further to your advertisement in the *Paper Name*, I am applying for the above position...

GETTING IT RIGHT

Once again – put yourself in the shoes of the person who will be reading this document and question the value of and impression cast by every word that you include. Every aspect of your CV and letter needs to be targeted:

- Right industry for your qualifications/training and experience (they may also be looking for use of appropriate terminology).
- Right organisation for you (public service *vs.* private sector, indigenous *vs.* multi-national, relaxed *vs.* uptight, people-focused *vs.* overtly profit-focused).

- Most importantly, sent to the right person – the person who is capable of actually giving you a job (see page 24, Routes of Entry).

BANG BANG BANG

Your opening paragraph says that you want the job and why you are suitable for it (*'My extensive track record of accomplishment and contribution in the area of Operations Management renders me a suitable candidate for the vacancy in your team'*).

Your second paragraph expands upon that, delineating in broad strokes those elements of your qualifications, training, experience and personal attributes that pertain to the job. You can do this with a series of bullet points or in *very* punchy sentences. For advertised positions, you can frequently reverse-engineer back from their stated list of requirements: duration of experience, qualification level, must-have skills and nice-to-have extras.

Your third paragraph says something along the lines of, *'I enclose my current Curriculum Vitae which will expand on the above. I trust that this will be satisfactory to you and I look forward to discussing my candidacy further with you at interview.'*

You can sign off 'Yours faithfully' if you have never spoken; 'Yours sincerely' if you have (see below); and 'Best regards' if you know the addressee quite well. Leave a space for your signature and print your name:

Yours sincerely,

_____

Rowan Manahan

/ Encl

T: (CODE) 123 4567 • **E**: rmanahan@yourisp.com • **M**: (CODE) 234 5678

WARMING UP A COLD CALL

An unexplained piece of correspondence arriving on someone's desk is never as powerful as a piece of correspondence that has some context or recognition value. It is a great help if the reader can put a voice and background to your let-

'Letters are expectations packaged in an envelope.'
SHANA ALEXANDER

ter/CV, and so you should always consider making a quick call to better position yourself in his mind:

'Mr Brown? Rowan Manahan is my name. I saw your advertisement in the *Daily Blah-Blah* and I'm interested in the position. I just wanted to get a sense of how the Operations role fits into the Widgets organisation chart. I currently report to the Managing Director of my company – to whom does the Operations Manager report there at Widgets?'

You can then engage Mr Brown in a two- to three-minute dialogue (carefully scripted – see page 124, The Power of the Phone), impressing him with your approach and planting seeds in his head. Your letter can then open with, 'Further to your advertisement in the *Daily Blah-Blah* and our telephone conversation, I am applying...' For a solid candidate, this is a sure-fire approach. For an oddball candidate, or one making a transition into a new career, it is even more essential.

Sometimes, with the best will in the world, you just *can't* succinctly convey in writing the reason why you would be a good candidate for a job. A picture paints a thousand words? Well, a chat is always going to paint a better picture than a cover note. The body of a good, tight cover letter will be 200–300 words in length or roughly 1½–2 minutes of talking time. If you have done some thinking and role-play, you will always be more engaging and convincing on the phone (or better yet, in person – but these appointments are almost impossible to get) than you will be in writing and you will be able to say more and expand upon your points in a way that you just can't in writing. So make that call!

SPECULATIVE LETTERS

What if you desperately want to work for *Widgets Incorporated* but they haven't advertised for a very long time and your research is not giving you any sense that there are likely to be positions arising in the near future? First port of call – your network. How is business going at *Widgets*? Are they on target? Growing versus last year? Holding their margins? Who are the new entrants and threats in their space? Have there been any regulatory changes in this sector in the recent past? Globally, have there been any significant changes in the way that *Widgets* does business? New faces? New strategic approaches? New products/services launched? Mergers or acquisitions that have affected the business?

Second port of call – the HR department in *Widgets*. Talk to the most senior person you can get to and determine: (a) Are there jobs coming up? (b) In what department(s)? (c) How do they usually fill those jobs – agencies, headhunting, bounty-hunting, website ads, trade magazine ads, newspaper ads? (d) Who are the players in the department you want to work in? During the course of this dialogue, you can subtly let the HR person know how well informed you are about the state of play in *Widgets* by dropping some of your big pieces of knowledge into the conversation. This is why you need to talk to a senior person – young HR people rarely have this breadth of knowledge and insight and, as such, they are usually not worth having this sort of conversation with.

Once again for those of you who haven't been paying attention: DO NOT WRITE TO HR LOOKING FOR A JOB. They have no power to create a position or to finally decide who gets that job. Write to the person who knows what is going on in the relevant department (typically the head of that department) and who can cajole extra money out of the budget to support a hiring decision that he sees paying a dividend for the organisation.

From the reader's perspective, speculative letters are the most tedious ones to receive. In many cases, there is a standing instruction to the administrator who handles the post to pass these letters on to HR. So it is of the essence that you position yourself in advance, and the phone is the simplest way of doing this. When your letter *does* arrive on

Mr Player's desk, it needs to address one thing only – that you are aware of a difficulty/problem/issue facing the organisation and that you are (or have) the solution. That approach *might* get you a 15-minute meeting.

Chapter 9

THE POWER OF THE PHONE

> *Telephone. Noun. An invention of the devil which abrogates some of the advantages of making a disagreeable person keep his distance.*
>
> **AMBROSE BIERCE**

I hate the phone. HATE it. I refer to my mobile phone as my '*damned umbilical cord*' – as long as it is turned on, I am never out of reach. The phone is impersonal, yet somehow callous, always relentless and I *detest* using it. Nevertheless, I recognise its value as a business tool and I very much recognise its worth as a job-hunting tool. If you feel as I do about the phone, you are going to have to go on a crash course in getting past those feelings, because you are inevitably going to be spending a lot of time talking to people who matter on this 'invention of the devil'.

MOMENTS OF TRUTH

Every time you talk to someone new on the phone it is a Moment of Truth. They very quickly form a strong and lasting impression of you (under all the usual headings) and if that impression isn't particularly favourable, you are going to have a very hard time persuading them to do whatever it is you want them to do.

Your disposition at the moment of the call is irrelevant; to the caller that is. Hangovers, outrageous deadlines, screaming children, too much caffeine, marital tiffs, winning the lottery – it doesn't matter what it is that has altered your mood; you need to project an aura of confidence and positivity as you answer the phone. Snarling, 'Whaaat?' and immediately and profusely apologising won't recover the image cast in the Moment of Truth.

VOICE

The person on the other end of the line has nothing to go on but your voice. Right from your greeting onwards, your tone must be appropriate and measured. One technique that has constantly proved its worth in tricky phone situations is to stand up as you say your piece. I am not quite sure what this does to your voice; perhaps it gives it more depth because you are able to breathe more fully (see page 390, Breathing), but it definitely works.

Ring your own answering machine and have a conversation with it for 30 seconds to one minute. Do you like how you sound? If you are not *delighted* with the impression you are conveying, start playing with it. I am not proposing that you develop a 1950s faked 'telephone' voice ('*How nice to hear from you, Vicar!*') but if your normal mode of expression on this medium is not doing the job, get working on it.

Greeting: A cheerful 'Hello' or 'Good morning/afternoon/evening' is always a good start. Most people like it when you include your name in your greeting too – 'Good morning, it's Rowan here.' Not too bouncy or effusive, but personable and upbeat nevertheless.

Pace and Emphasis: Most people speak far too quickly when they are on the phone. Remember the listener has no cues other than your voice to work with. In a face-to-face conversation, that listener would be taking more than 50 per cent of your meaning from facial expressions, gestures, posture, disposition and eye contact. And people take the wrong meaning a *lot* of the time in face-to-face conversations! Give your listener a chance and slow it down quite a bit. Again, listen to yourself and get others to do the same. How does your opening pitch sound? Intelligible? Rushed? Overly slick? Are you placing emphasis on the right words? If your delivery is too speedy, not only does it drive down understanding, but your listener may also take the inference that you don't want to be interrupted and you might start to sound like a fast-talking snake-oil salesman.

Sign-off: Have you ever found yourself saying, 'Oh! Just one other thing...' to the phone after the other person has hung up? For career management calls, always let the other person hang up first. Keep it controlled and err on the side of formality as you sign off. Develop three or four phrases to end your calls and rotate them:

'Thank you and good-bye now.'
'Thanks again for taking the call.'
'It was nice to make your acquaintance. Good-bye for now.'
'It's good to hear your voice. See you later.'
'I look forward to meeting you.'
'Good to catch up. See you soon.'

POSITIONING YOURSELF

Regardless of the purpose of your call, you need to position yourself in the recipient's mind very quickly. Once again, we are back to *forethought*, *rehearsal* and *structure*. If you get a call back from a busy executive, leaving them hanging on while you rummage around for your 'script' is not going to win you any favours. Be ready.

Silence on the end of the phone is akin to silence on the radio – awkward and awful. If you are taking calls on the phone at home (or in a working situation), it is useful to have your speaking points and questions jotted down on 3x5 inch cards. Have your materials clearly labelled and arrayed in front of you in small stacks – one for placement agencies, one for live prospects, one for someone who is doing you a favour, and so on. If you need to take the call while you are out and about, you simply transfer the stacks to designated pockets, so there is no pregnant pause while you try and remember what it is you wanted to say. Just reach into the appropriate pocket and pull out the relevant stack of prompt cards.

Make sure that the person calling you doesn't get an engaged tone. At the very least, put call waiting on your home phone and make sure that it diverts to voice mail after just a few moments. (If at all possible, it is very useful to put in an extra phone line reserved just for career management calls.) Likewise turn on the appropriate diverts on your mobile phone and, mobile or landline, check your voice mail religiously. Final finicky point here – make sure you have paper and writing implements right beside the phone. The 'Hang on a second, I'll just find a pen' line gets stale very quickly for the listener. Thirty seconds of waiting time can seem like an eternity… If, for some reason, you *do* have to root something out, keep talking to the other person: 'Okay, I've got the laptop. I'm just booting up now.'

VOICE MAIL

BIG Moment of Truth here. Personalise your voice mail message and rehearse it a few times before laying it down:

> 'Rowan Manahan's phone. I'm sorry that I am not available to take your call at present, but please leave a brief message along with your name and contact details and I will call you back as soon as possible.'

For added professionalism, you can update this on a daily basis:

> 'This is Rowan Manahan on Monday the 10th of XXXX. I am in (insert location) today and I will be unavailable/in meetings/away from my phone/unable to take calls from 11.00am to 12.30pm and from 2.15pm until 4.00pm. Please leave a brief message along with your name and contact details and I will call you back as soon as possible.'

Polished, switched-on and mindful of the caller's needs – all good impressions to be casting from the outset.

NETWORKING AND RESEARCH BY PHONE

Where you can, save yourself a trip and make that call. You can frequently elicit the kernel of information that you need without having to do a face-to-face meeting. If you are courteous and to the point, most of the people on the other end of the line will be grateful for your clarity and professionalism. I would warn against (a) overdoing this – sometimes the face-to-face is worth *way* more than you realise and (b) making this a one-way street. If you are calling an old college chum on whom you haven't clapped eyes in eight years, don't expect him to be enthusiastic about giving free advice on a specific issue. If, however, your call comes in the context of a regular ongoing contact and the last three calls you made were to provide information/congratulations/advice or even to just stay in touch, then call away…

CALLER ID

One of the few things that makes using the phone bearable on an on-going basis. Turn yours on and use it to the hilt. Advantages:

- You know who's calling before you answer the phone and you can screen calls and only answer those that you deem to be important.
- Most modern phones allow you to have a directory list of recent callers for easy access to phone numbers of the people who have called you.
- Caller ID also allows you to see who has called even if they don't leave a voice mail message.
- On your home phone, if you see that the call is not for you, you can safely ignore it and not end up stuck in a conversation about Aunt Mabel's new dog.

SCRIPTING

Do you have words at will or do you will your words to come? Even if you are fluent by nature, I would recommend at least thinking through the possibilities in advance of any important call and jotting them down on paper. What is your objective in making the call? If you get X are you going to ask for Y, and if the person on the line offers you X and Y before you even ask, are you going to ask for Z? Be ready for both generosity and objections. Be ready to get through to the person in charge, even if you thought you were going to be speaking to an assistant (this happens most often at lunch time and after hours when the assistant has gone home. Accordingly, these are both good times to call if you want to speak to the person in charge).

Draft out your thoughts and hone them down. You may not want (or need) to slavishly write out every word that you wish to say, but a few polished phrases on paper will give you a road-map for the call. This will also help you eliminate apologetic or equivocal terms, flowery phrases or insider jargon from your delivery. You should also notate everything that is said in an important call. You may prefer to record it, for the purposes of minuting it afterwards, but don't let important details slip for the want of a bit of paper and a pencil. If there are action points arising out of the call, transfer them on to the To-Do list in your diary system and you may need to follow up in writing to the person you were speaking to as a gentle reminder of action agreed or promised.

HERE BE DRAGONS!

The dragons I am referring to are, of course, Personal Assistants and Receptionists:

'May I say who's calling, sir?'
'And what is the nature of your call, madam?'
'Will she know what your call is in connection with, sir?'
'I'll put you through to her secretary, madam.'

All you need is three minutes of the King or Queen's time, and here you are stuck talking to the dragon outside the castle! And that dragon's sole purpose in life is to stop people like you from getting an audience with the King/Queen.

Do you know the name of the person you are calling? Always try and find this out in advance. Call the organisation on Friday and ask for the MD's name and the name of his PA. Check the spelling/pronunciation, then thank the receptionist and hang up. Then when you call on Monday, you can confidently start with, 'I'd like to speak with John Brown please.' If you get put through to the PA, you can start with, 'Josephine? It's Rowan Manahan here. Is John in today? I need him for about three minutes.' Josephine, at this point, is wondering who you are, but is unlikely to challenge you too harshly in case she has spoken to you before and forgotten you.

Dragons are there to make the boss's life easier. They are *not* there to thwart you in particular, just anyone whom they deem to be an unnecessary waste of the boss's time. So start thinking about how you are going to get past these tiresome watch-dragons:

- Do not directly lie! Even if you get through to the boss, you will look snake-oily and the dragon will lose face for having let you slip through.
- Talk about providing 'feedback' to the boss on the basis of something recent or topical.
- Say that you want to register a complaint right at the top and that you don't feel that you have been taken seriously by the lower ranks (this would be true, for example, if HR keep sending you rejection letters).
- 'He's in a meeting.' The classical defence, along with holidays, out of the office or similar. Ask what would be a good time to catch the boss in person, as you would prefer not to leave a message (dragons always offer to take a message).
- If it doesn't look like you are going to get to the boss, try and engage the dragon — be more than usually pleasant, courteous and cheerful. Explain that you always start at the top and work your way down (appeal to the dragon's empathy) and then inquire if there is anyone else the dragon would recommend you speak to…

- If you don't get past the dragon, or if you get sidelined off to someone else, make sure you get the dragon's extension number for future calls.
- If you are sidelined or diverted to talk to someone of a lower rank, start with, 'I was just talking to Josephine in John Brown's office and she said that you are the person to talk with…'
- Call at odd hours when the dragon is not likely to be there. You never know your luck.
- If you *do* get to the decision-maker, or if you get some sort of result from your efforts (information, a lead, insight, a next-stage meeting or whatever) make sure you get back to, and thank, the dragon.

The business of getting to the people that you want to speak to is frustrating and nerve-racking at first. Practise. Call Michael Dell, Carly Fiorino or Steve Jobs to thank them for the marvellous product that you have just purchased and don't give up until you get the message either into their ear or on to their desk. Then use the same techniques to get past the dragons in your target organisation.

TELEPHONE INTERVIEWS

This is an ancient protocol that has been modernised in recent years from an 'informal chat' to a highly structured, time-saving, money-saving step in the screening and selection process. On rare occasions it will be you that has initiated the contact only to suddenly find yourself being grilled by the decision-maker. Most of the time, you will be notified well in advance that the first stage after the CV submission is a phone interview of 20–45 minutes' duration.

If you are facing one of these, all of the usual conventions highlighted in the sections on interviews pertain (with the exception of your dress sense) but are made a little more difficult because you have to rely purely on the *words* you use and your *voice* (see page 125, Voice and page 129, Scripting) to convey the right impression and meaning. By now, you have probably realised that I am a demon for meticulous preparation. Here, yet again, is an opportunity to separate wheat from chaff. Are you going to be polished (relatively), at ease, fluent and interesting to listen to or are you going to be humming and hawing your way through a series of makey-uppy-as-you-go-alongy answers? The interviewer is going to be working *very carefully* to a pre-determined script – why would you do any less?

(I am reminded of the hilarious confrontation between Kevin Costner and Nick Brimble in the otherwise execrable *Robin Hood, Prince of Thieves*. Brimble (Little John) is beating the hell out of Costner (Robin Hood) in the ubiquitous quarterstaff fight by the river. Robin looks to the Saracen, Azeem (Morgan Freeman) for help or advice. *Move faster! Hit harder!* is all Freeman gleefully shouts. I *know* you know these simple, simple things and I know you're hoping that there is a short-cut. Believe me – there isn't one. Do the spadework!)

FOLLOWING UP

It shouldn't have to be noted, but just in case… If you undertake to do something on the phone, DO IT! Don't go to all this trouble and then blow it for the want of a bit of follow-up. And yes, it happens every day. It's also a good idea to keep the ball in your court wherever possible, rather than relying on the other person to revert to you.

LITTLE BOXES – APPLICATION FORMS

Employers in certain sectors just *love* application forms and, for the hirer at the coalface, they do have a number of advantages:

- There is nearly always a declaration which you (the applicant) have to sign stating that all of the information furnished is true, followed by a warning statement from the employer that 'falsification can lead to summary dismissal', or words to that effect.
- Hirers can compare like with like more easily by using a standardised format and can get through the tedious business of initial screening more rapidly.
- You are frequently required to include information which you would normally omit from your CV, such as health status or sick leave record; reasons for leaving your current and previous employments; precise remuneration details for each position held (and remember that 'falsification can lead to summary dismissal'). They also typically require you to indicate month and year for commencement and termination of each employment, which can expose gaps that you might otherwise prefer to gloss over.

APPLICATION FORMS – THE ABSOLUTE BASICS

You would be astounded at how many candidates disqualify themselves from consideration by making careless, fundamental mistakes in completing application forms. At the very least, you should do the following:

- Get extra originals or make copies of the form for trial runs.
- Very carefully check through the instructions section and any instructions in the accompanying letter – employers can be very specific (e.g. block capitals in black ink).
- Read all the questions on the form thoroughly, making notes on a pad as you go. Do this at least twice.
- Draft your preliminary answers on paper and then sketch out a draft on one copy or a spare original.
- Read it through several times and note any improvements that you might make. Then read it again with the employer's hat on and make sure that you have addressed all of their principal concerns.
- Fill in the original. In many instances now, you can do this online. If it has to be handwritten and your calligraphy is not up to scratch, get a friend with really nice handwriting to do it for you.
- Compose your covering letter (see page 116).
- Proofread everything carefully – get friends to help you do this to ensure accuracy.
- Copy everything for your records.
- Deliver by registered post or by hand and get a receipt.

SPECIAL SECTIONS THAT CAN MAKE A DIFFERENCE

Some of the boxes on a standardised application form do allow for a measure of individuality:

The Extra information/Supporting statement section. This is usually the last section to be filled on the form and it is one of the few boxes in which you can really express yourself well. So it is vital and can make all the difference to your application.

- Tailor each word that you include and make sure that every sentence highlights your potential *value* to the organisation. Human beings buy benefits, not responsibilities. Your level of responsibility in previous jobs indicates your maturity and reliability, but many other candidates will have broadly similar experience. Responsibilities provide reassurance to the reader; contributions and achievements on the job make them want to meet you…
- Try and stay within the confines of the box provided – impress the reader with your tight writing style.
- Make certain that you have included everything that you would normally put on a CV.

The Interests section. Keep this section as short as you would on your CV. You can use it to further identify yourself with the personal attributes the employer is looking for. Employers look to the interests section of a CV or application form for a number of reasons:

- To see how you round out as a person.
- To allow for some 'relaxing' questions if the interview gets too hot and heavy.
- To identify conflicting interests which may make large demands on your time and interfere with your ability to meet deadlines, stay late at work, etc.

For both your CV and any application form, you should consider including current interests under the following broad headings:

- *Physical* – some level of physical activity will reassure the reader that you are not a total slob with all of the associated keeling-over-at-your-desk health risks of slobdom…
- *Cerebral* – do you do anything to improve your mind or keep it active? Reading (tell them what kind of books, papers, magazines), cinema, theatre and music (again, tell them what kind) are all examples of cerebral activities.
- *Social* – many jobs will require you to talk over food with suppliers and customers, or to work effectively with other people in teams.

If you enjoy cooking, certain types of food, going out to dinner, or anything that demonstrates an ability and comfort in this area, you should mention it.

- *Altruistic* – if you are involved in fundraising, local charities, your residents' association, your children's school, you should mention it ('I am a decent, involved human being…').

Okay, so you now know what kind of job you would like and you have your written representation of yourself all ready to go. Where and how are you going to send it? Your route of entry into your desired job is vital (see page 124, Routes of Entry) and there are some fundamental errors that you should be aware of…

Chapter 11

LEARNING CURVE 3 – A CASE STUDY IN BLUNDERS

> *Experience – that most brutal of teachers. But you learn, my God, do you learn.* **C.S. LEWIS**

A client company in the multimedia sector forwarded this one to me. An unsolicited application for a Graphic Designer position arrived clumsily folded into a small brown envelope. The stamp was applied crookedly and the letter was addressed to the '*Personnell* (sic) *Manager*' of the company. There was no return address. My client runs a medium-sized multimedia company; as such, they have no Human Resources Manager – the MD and the person who handles the accounts fulfil that function between them.

The cover letter was produced on nice bonded paper, but was not addressed to the target company, was not dated, and opened with '*Dear Sir/Madam*'. It then continued with: '*I am writing to you in appilcation* (sic) *for any vacancy which should arise in the next few months, for which you feel I may be qualified.*'

Any professional reader would have stopped reading by this point, because they would now know everything that they needed to know about this poor fool: that he is *careless* (indicated by the crooked stamp, the folded application, two typos so far and no addressee); he is a *bulk-mailer* (that crooked stamp is a giveaway, the letter was not personalised in any way, plus both the letter and the CV were photocopied); and he is *not optimistic* about his chances (clearly expects to be unemployed for a 'few months'). Even if your organisation was *crying out* for staff, would you call this half-wit back?

The cover letter continued with, '*I have recently been made redundant from a position as a Multimedia Designer with Company Name. My duties at Company Name included W, X, Y and Z...* (lots more information about the range of responsibilities, all of which were detailed again in the CV that was attached). The cover letter was signed in ink, 'Yours sincerely', despite the lack of an addressee. (I suppose that we should have been grateful that the signature wasn't photocopied too.)

The CV was a photocopied two-pager which gave information but no detail and highlighted responsibilities but gave no sense of accomplishment. There were no particulars of projects worked on, awards gained or even of the range of computer applications that the Designer was familiar with. He listed web design as a key responsibility, but did not have a website of his own that the reader could visit to view samples of his work.

Furthermore, the applicant had held 11 jobs in a nine-year period and offered references from only the most recent and from another of four years previously. The applicant also enclosed the most recent reference document, which gave us some insight into the redundancy – the company had experienced a '*sharp downturn in market conditions*' and had to '*with great regret*' terminate his employment.

Just about every mistake that you can make, encapsulated in three sheets of paper. (I did have one other beauty recently where the applicant attached insufficient postage and the receiving company had to shell out the difference – nice!) If this poor idiot ever got another job, I would be pleasantly surprised. Moreover, his ability to *hold* a job for any length of time should make for interesting reading.

I encounter this kind of thoughtlessness all the time and it makes my life easier on two counts:

- When I am in the hiring seat, applicants of this nature make the shortlisting process *so* much easier for me. (I use a wide-topped bin for this kind of work, because CVs are not particularly aerodynamic. They do, however, make a *very* pleasing fluttering noise as they fly towards my dumping ground.)
- Without people this inept, there would be little need in this world for the Career Management profession and I could be out of a job.

IMPROVING THE ODDS

So what could this person have done to improve his chances? Let's take it a step at a time.

1 On being told that you are being made redundant, negotiate to make it seem as though you are still in the job for longer. Redundancy has become so prevalent there is no stigma attached to it any more; nevertheless, it has one major disadvantage. Don't tell the marketplace that you are redundant until you have to – it drastically impairs your ability to negotiate remuneration. Make sure that the referee you are using from that organisation is genuinely on your side and will say that you worked there longer than you did. This could give you up to six months' more breathing space.

2 If you are taking your career seriously, you should have your target list of organisations that you would like to work for already completed. If you don't, a few days of hard work with the Yellow Pages, the internet, the local library and the phone should provide you with a solid list of prospects and suspects (see page 162, Research).

3 NEVER write to Personnel/Human Resources unless you want a job in that department. Find out who the decision-maker is. Get a name. Check the title and the spelling. Always write (a) to a person and (b) to the person who has real decision-making authority.

4 If at all possible, don't write cold. Telephone first and have a short (pre-scripted) chat. Then write to follow up (see page 124, The Power of the Phone, and page 116, Summing it Up – The Cover Letter).

5 Focus on how good you are – not on what you have been required to do in previous jobs. Your CV should not read like a personnel file; it should be a glittering list of wins and accomplishments.

6 Tailor, tailor, tailor. The only photocopy should be the copy for your files.

7 Accuracy – if your spellling and grammur aren't up to scratch, enlist help. Spell checkers on computers only go so far. Look at this sentence: *Eye have a knew PC that cheques my spelling and eye trussed it too do it's job.* Not a single mis-spelt word, but garbage nevertheless. The grammar checker in your word-processing application may pick up on these mistakes, but there is nothing like a fresh pair of human eyes…

> **'Proofreading is more effective after publication.'**
> PHIL BARKER

8 Don't include references unless they ask you to. It is like showing up for a first date with your entire family by your side (see page 177, Managing Your References).

9 Follow up. Don't expect them to call you (see page 116, The Power of the Phone).

PART 3

FACE-TO-FACE 1

(GROUNDWORK

FOR INTERVIEWS)

Chapter 1

BEFORE YOU EVEN GET STARTED

> *The law west of the Pecos.*
>
> **JUDGE ROY BEAN'S EPITAPH**

You've been invited to interview? Congratulations! You have just passed one of the toughest examinations of your life. There are very few exams out there that require an 85–95 per cent mark to pass; but you have done it – you have made it from a huge pile of CVs down to the shortlist.

Let me start by reiterating one of the oldest clichés in the book: as you sit there, *you already have the job*. If you have been invited to interview it indicates, at the very least, that someone out there thinks you can do the job. In these tough times, NO ONE is going to give you an hour of their time unless they think you can answer their problems and fulfil the role.

And yet many people face the interview process with a sense of absolute dread – why?

- 'I'm well qualified, I have good experience and yet I never get hired after the interview. I don't know what I'm doing wrong...'
- 'I hate talking about myself.'
- 'I always prepare well for interviews, but then I can never remember what to say.'
- 'You always have to lie to get through interviews and I'm a rotten liar.'
- 'I find it very hard to talk about my career without sounding like I'm boasting.'
- 'I've never done anything special, so it's hard to sell myself at interview.'
- 'They never gave me a chance to sell myself.'

Do any of these sound familiar? If you are thinking this way, you have lost sight of the fact that you've already beaten 85–95 per cent of the opposition to get this far. Time to re-evaluate in a positive frame of mind.

- Do you know why you got the interview?

- What do you think impressed them on your CV/application?

- Re-check everything you know about the sector, the organisation and the role itself, and start listing where you match their requirements – and where you don't. Keep researching right up to the last minute.

- Remember – **they think you can do this job!**

- What makes you a solid candidate for this position? Start to build a list of likely questions and think about how you will deal with them.

- Decide on your clothing and make sure everything is immaculate well in advance of the interview itself.

- If you have been foolish enough to tell an outright lie on your application, then you are right to be nervous about the interview process.

- If you have been honest so far, you really don't have anything to worry about.

So, calm it down, take a deep breath, and let's get to work…

Chapter 2

LEARNING CURVE 4 – INTERVIEW FATIGUE SYNDROME

Experience is not what happens to you. It is what you do with what happens to you. **ALDOUS HUXLEY**

Linda, early 20s, single, science degree
Linda's parents heard of *Fortify* through a discussion programme on the radio and asked for an urgent appointment for their daughter. Linda had attended 11 interviews for entry-level laboratory jobs over a seven-month period and had been unsuccessful each time. A last-minute appointment for the night prior to her 12th interview was arranged.

Linda walked through the door for her practice interview with her head bowed and wearing unflattering clothes. She was obviously very nervous in the interview and switched back and forth from monosyllabic to over-long, waffling answers. Her responses revealed a very negative self-image and she conveyed a strong sense of being daunted by the prospect of entering the workforce.

We began with the things that were easy to fix. We coached Linda on appropriate body language for an interview setting, starting from the initial handshake; then moving on to her deportment, giving concrete advice on hair, make-up, suit style/colour and accessories. (Linda ended up with a comprehensive shopping list and purchased her new wardrobe with her mother the following morning on the way to the job interview.)

We then provided feedback on Linda's answers to the practice interview questions. She had heard most of these questions before in her 11 interviews, but had not grasped the subtext behind them. When we explained the 'reasons why' for each of the questions, we were able to start building a new approach on the key subjects of ability, motivation and teamworking. Linda's answers had been honest for the most part, but had been occasionally evasive or contradictory – in each case when she had been trying to paint herself in a positive light. Overall, the impression that she gave was of a diligent, pleasant and intelligent young woman, but with such low self-esteem that she would be difficult to motivate, hard to manage and virtually impossible to work with.

Linda was moved to tears by this feedback and it transpired that she was feeling tremendous family and peer pressure, as all of her classmates were now employed. Her confidence had taken an enormous battering each time one of her friends got a job and she got yet another rejection letter. Linda was a classic case of **Interview Fatigue Syndrome** whereby her performance deteriorated with each interview she attended to the extent that her most recent meeting had lasted only 18 minutes!

The discussion then moved on to long-term career and personal aspirations and Linda showed signs of enthusiasm for the first time in the consultation. In the light of the rosy pictures she was painting for her future, the looming interview began to look less ominous and Linda's demeanour brightened considerably. We suggested that this attitude would be far more constructive than her current, somewhat hangdog manner and Linda left the practice session with a renewed sense of confidence and just a slight degree of 'To hell with them' in her attitude. She succeeded at interview the following morning, securing the job ahead of 58 other applicants, and has since been promoted. Linda's mother is my biggest fan.

LEARNING POINTS:

• Linda **learnt nothing** from her early failures and did not get **feedback** on her performance at interview so she continued to make the same mistakes over and over again. Organisations, particularly in the private sector, can be slow to give meaningful feedback to unsuccessful candidates. If you don't succeed at a number of consecutive interviews, you must get *something* out of the wretched process, so go digging (see page 307, After the Interview).

- Over time, Linda slipped into **clichéd** answers to the old 'standard' interview questions. Interviewers don't care if you have heard it all before, they want a fresh, enthusiastic approach (see page 41, Fanatics).

- Linda sought **advice** only from friends and family – none of whom were employed in her desired sector. Talk to **useful people** about your desired industry. Advice taken solely from the web and from friends on interview technique tends to be, at best, clichéd and, at worst, contradictory and counter-productive (see page 162, Research, and page 168, Networking).

- Be aware of the phenomenon of **Interview Fatigue** – which can be a particular problem for graduates on the so-called 'milk round' or people facing a large number of interviews with different organisations following a period of training. Pace yourself between interviews, develop a routine and bring yourself to a peak just as the interview begins – much like an athlete in training for an important race. Treat every interview as though it were your only chance and prepare accordingly (see page 204, Countdown to the Interview).

- If you find yourself **depressed** or very **anxious** about the prospect of an upcoming interview, don't attend it. You are wasting their time and your own. Take a break from the process and re-energise. De-stress – take up a new hobby, go for a short break, give yourself a treat. If you find your mood shifting dramatically again coming up to the next interview, talk to a career management professional (if you are a recent graduate, your College Careers Service can be a tremendous help in situations like this).

Chapter 3

WHAT'S REALLY GOING ON...

> *To achieve the impossible, one must think the absurd; to look where every-*
> *one else has looked, but to see what no one else has seen.*
>
> **ANONYMOUS**

FAQ
'Why do they ask those weird questions at interview?
What are they really trying to find out about me?'

As far as any interviewer is concerned, the entire recruitment process
can be distilled down to these three questions:

1　Is this candidate capable of doing this job? (*Competency/Track record*)

2　Will this candidate actually *do* the job?　　　　　　　(*Motivation*)

3　Can I work with this person?　　　　　(*Manageability/Team fit*)

Competent interviewers will examine the following five areas to tease
out as much information as they can to answer those three questions.
Knowing this, you can anticipate a significant percentage of the questions
that you will be asked and prepare your answers accordingly (see page
193, Interview Mapping).

EXPERIENCE

Questions on this address issues of both competence and motivation.

- Have you a track record in the area you are applying for? If this move is a change for you, how can you reassure the interviewer that your experience is germane to the new job?
- Does your track record demonstrate an ability to take on greater responsibility and succeed?
- Do you really have 10 years' experience or do you have 1 year's experience repeated 10 times?
- Has anyone ever taken a risk (that paid off) by hiring or promoting you?
- Have you learnt from your mistakes?
- To what extent is your approach governed by your upbringing or your current corporate culture?

QUALIFICATIONS/TRAINING

This is of greatest relevance when you are starting out, but it can also be of interest if you are changing direction later in your career. Your attitude to lifelong learning (sometimes referred to as K-80) may also be probed. The key areas are your **self-discipline** and **learning curve**.

The other significant factor about training is that it represents an investment in you made by someone else. Sharp recruiters will closely examine the Training section on your CV to see if you have been 'groomed' by your current or previous employers. It can also reveal weaknesses – if you joined an organisation and, a year later, you were sent on Time Management or Assertiveness training, it is a strong indicator that a problem was identified in your first annual review. Careful!

ENTHUSIASM/PROFESSIONALISM

Motivation all the way. Firing someone (even a slacker) is an expensive nuisance and can be very difficult to do these days, so interviewers will be looking for a professional, enthusiastic demeanour during the screening and selection process, which (they presume) will be carried through into your daily work.

Research (see page 162) is the key here. If you have really done your homework on the organisation or industry, it displays both professionalism and a high degree of interest. Don't be surprised if interviewers use industry-specific terminology or discuss hot issues to determine how well you have prepared.

Another big indicator as to the quality of your preparation is the questions that *you* ask during the interview (see page 219, Asking Them Questions).

PERSONALITY

This is key in reassuring them as to your manageability. The interviewer(s) will also examine whether or not you will 'fit in' with the culture – many organisations now use assessment centres to probe this area on a formal basis. If the department you want to work in currently comprises a bunch of testosterone-charged, A-type, misogynist, chest-thumping, fighter-jock types, there's not much point in management trying to slot in a delicate flower of femininity who shies away from conflictual situations... nor would dropping some knuckle-dragging Neanderthal into a tightly knit group of socially adept women strike me as a recipe for success.

BACKGROUND

Partially answers all three areas of concern. Your upbringing is perceived by some interviewers as having a bearing on your work ethic and can obviously have an impact on your interaction with your co-workers. Again, assessment centres may probe into this area. Questions regarding your background and personal circumstances will have to be very subtly framed, as employment equality legislation prohibits employers from poking about in your private life. This is sometimes worked around by including a social gathering as part of the recruitment process. If the recruiter starts talking gregariously about her friends and family, it can be difficult for you to avoid doing the same.

Chapter 4

EARLY PREPARATION

A friend to honesty and a foe to crime.

ALLEN PINKERTON'S EPITAPH

FAQ

'I'm well qualified. I have great experience. I'm a hard worker and I'm good at what I do. I'm even a nice person! WHY WON'T ANYONE HIRE ME?'

I hear this kind of plaintive cry on a regular basis. If this sounds familiar, chances are you are doing one or two simple things incorrectly at interview. The hiring process is also called *Screening and Selection*. This is a misnomer – it should be entitled *Screening and **Elimination***.

Suppose there are 100 applicants for a single position, 90 of whom are screened out at the CV stage. For the remaining 10, do you suppose that the interviewers are looking to find out the absolute best points of each candidate or the chinks in their armour? Which takes less time? Which is easier? Which is *cheaper*? The old cliché tells us that if you've got the interview, you've got the job. That should be true, but never lose sight of the fact that the interview is all about identifying which of these people, all of whom are *Possibles*, is the real thing.

UGLY FACT NO. 6

THERE IS A WORLD OF DIFFERENCE BETWEEN THE CANDIDATE WHO IS GOOD AND SOUND AND THE CANDIDATE WHO MERELY SOUNDS GOOD...

Herewith, my all-time list of things to do if you *absolutely* don't want the job:

• Turn up late, sweating and out of breath, because you didn't bother to scout out the building and you couldn't find a parking space.

• Dress inappropriately, because you don't care about the impression you make on your own (or anyone else's) behalf.

• Don't really listen to the questions asked and prattle on nervously, laughing at your own hilarious jokes and regaling the interviewer with a stream of irrelevant stories and examples.

• If that tack doesn't work, try answering with monosyllabic grunts and hostile stares.

• Tell the interviewer how she *should* be running the business and how you're going to change *everything* when you are in charge.

• Admit to perfectionism, overworking or not suffering fools gladly when asked about your weaknesses. Alternatively, reveal your major flaw which significantly impairs your ability to work effectively on a daily basis: *'Does not play well with others.'*

• Contradict yourself as the interview progresses, because you can't remember which lie you told to whom and in response to which question... Or better yet, claim credit for significant achievements on your CV and then be completely unable to supply any detail as to how you accomplished these feats.

- Divulge that you have applied for *loads* of jobs in the last year, because your current job is a bore, your boss is a bastard and you can't wait to get out of 'that rotten company'.

- Ask trite, naïve, self-serving questions at the end of the interview because you haven't researched the industry or the job and you're only really applying because you want a bit more drinking money.

I sincerely hope that none of those sound familiar to you. Right, so we all know (or think we know) the obvious things not to do, so let's look at some positive measures you can take to dramatically improve your chances in the face-to-face stages of the hiring process:

- Getting comfortable talking about yourself (page 155).
- Really knowing who you are and what you have to offer (page 80).
- In-depth research – knowing what is going through their heads (page 162).
- Building and using your career management network (page 168).
- Managing your references (page 177).

Chapter 5

GETTING READY TO TALK ABOUT YOURSELF

> *No one can make you feel Inferior without your consent.*
>
> **ELEANOR ROOSEVELT**

FAQ

'I hate talking about myself and I always find it difficult when they ask me about my strengths. How do I tell them my good points without seeming to blow my own trumpet too much?'

Common problem. Very few of us are raised in an environment that encourages a boastful, swaggering attitude and yet you will be asked to do *exactly* that in almost every interview. Bear in mind that what *you* feel is utterly irrelevant to the interviewer(s) (see page 54, Who Matters?). If one candidate muttered and mumbled through their answer to a question on strengths and the other pondered for a moment and then confidently and fluently listed off a series of pertinent gems about themselves, who would you hire?

A television continuity announcer, stuttering and stumbling through a link piece because the AutoCue is broken, is irritating (albeit hilarious!) and lacks credibility. You will be too if you don't practise delivering your answers with eloquence and force. '*Eh, eh, emmmmm, well I'm eh, I'm a very, eh **clear**, yes, I'm a very **clear** communicator...*'

SALES SPEAK

You use an alien language in the selection process, one that you have no occasion to call upon outside of the job interview setting. On a day-to-day basis, you utilise three vocabularies:

* The vocabulary of **Profession** (the specialised language of your job or course of study).
* The vocabulary of **Acquaintance** (small-talk, light conversation, social lubrication).
* The vocabulary of **Intimacy** (that special lexicon that you reserve for your family and closest friends – usually a sort of short-hand, peppered with in-jokes and odd expressions).

The words that comprise these vocabularies are your '*Active Vocabularies*'. These words are frequently used, easily remembered, and flow effortlessly from your mouth – they are locked into your Vocal Memory. Your '*Passive Vocabulary*' consists of those words that you recognise and understand, but don't use yourself on an ongoing basis. You need to dredge some unfamiliar words up from this Passive Vocabulary and get comfortable using them. They will become your fourth vocabulary as you prepare for an interview. I call this the '**Vocabulary of Self Promotion**'. (It's the kind of self-laudatory phrasing that would get you a clip round the ear from your mother if you used it in her presence, no matter what age you are.)

BEING READY

An interview is an exercise in public speaking that calls heavily upon this fourth vocabulary and, as such, it merits a great deal of rehearsal. If you don't have good, honest and fluent answers to these predictable old interview questions, then you are in trouble from the outset:

* 'Tell us a bit about yourself/take us through your CV.'
* 'Why do you want to leave your current job/organisation?'

- 'What attracted you to this job/sector/organisation?'
- 'What are your strengths?'
- 'What are your weaknesses?'
- 'How would you describe yourself?'
- 'How would you approach this job?'
- 'What interests you most in your work – what motivates you?'
- 'Do you prefer to work in a team or on your own?'
- 'How would your workmates describe you?'
- 'Where do you plan to be in five years' time?'
- 'What do you regard as your greatest success/failure to date?'
- 'What particular quality(ies) do you feel you will bring to this job that other candidates won't?'
- 'I'm sure you must have some questions for us...'

Not having a ready answer on these is like turning up to an exam when you have been given advance access to the questions, having done no study at all. Simplistic questions of this nature will not be used in today's more complex interviews, but the vocabulary that you need to answer them will form the heart and soul of your approach to the face-to-face stages of any recruitment process. Self knowledge is vitally important here, as is practice. List what you think makes you stand out from the crowd. Then compare your list with what your colleagues, friends and relations tell you (see page 80, 360°). The most valuable person you can talk to for this kind of feedback is someone you used to work for – past bosses *love* to be asked for advice relating to your future career.

Once you have the list, pick and choose the strengths that are going to be useful in the new job and practise citing them out loud in advance of the interview. Psychologists call this process **desensitisation** and use it to help people overcome phobias. Use a Dictaphone® and practise your answers to these stock interview questions over and over. Better yet, use a video camera and watch and listen to yourself. Get feedback from your network on the content and delivery of your answers.

If you are consistently failing at interview, you are probably doing something very basic very badly. A blind spot, by definition, is something that you can't see in yourself. Your friends and family may not notice it either.

Or may be too polite to tell you. Or you might not be listening to what they are telling you. The information is there. Have the courage to look for it.

SELF BELIEF

This is another major issue with regard to talking about yourself at interview – I continually get the sense that many interview candidates just don't believe in what they are saying about themselves. The hackneyed 'You've got the interview, you've got the job' axiom is all very well, unless of course you talk yourself out of it. Which is *precisely* what most unsuccessful candidates do.

Candidates talk too little. They don't expand on their strong points. They use qualifying language – '*I believe…*', '*I think…*', '*I feel…*' – which utterly devalues everything that follows. There's a reason why you have never heard a newsreader say, 'I *think* this is the Nine O'Clock News'.

Candidates hide their lights under a bushel and expect the interviewer to go looking for them. You didn't tell them about your ability to walk on water? 'Well, they never asked me…' Remember Ugly Fact No. 3? Of course they didn't ask you! They don't give a damn about you! If you don't put it in front of their faces, don't expect them to come looking for the information.

This is, in part, a cultural issue. We are not encouraged by our upbringing or education to trumpet our achievements. 'Self praise is no praise at all' has a very familiar ring to it for most people. But this negativity goes deeper than the cultural overtone. In the English-speaking world, we use a language that has remained fundamentally unchanged for hundreds of years. Subtract all of the modern slang and techno-babble and we still speak like characters in a Jane Austen novel. And that mode of expression is very demurring and self-deprecating. Victorian English was all about understatement.

Take a look at any good dictionary. It is chock-full of negative terms for which there are no positive opposites. You can be disastrous, discarded, discommoded, disconsolate, dismal, distracted, inadvertent, inane, uncouth or unctuous, but remove the prefix and you aren't their opposite. Have you ever met anyone who was gruntled or kempt? Corrigible? Ept? Sipid? Illusioned? A family that was functional? The American slang expression 'dissing' (talking negatively about someone or something) has finally made it into the *Oxford English Dictionary*. The problem is, you cannot use these 'dis', 'un' and 'in' words about yourself in a job interview – you need to shed that skin when you walk through the door.

If you are applying for a job, remember that the employer is effectively making a purchasing decision. As you come into the room, you have a price tag hanging around your neck and the employer is picking you up, shaking you, looking at you from all angles and wondering, 'Is he really worth that much?' Never lose sight of this fact:

> ## UGLY FACT NO. 7
>
> ### AN INTERVIEW IS A SALES PITCH.
> ### YOU ARE SELLING A PRODUCT.
> ### THE PRODUCT IS YOU.

This would be fine if you were the only item in the shop, but in most interviews, unfortunately, you are being measured against candidates so similar, you might as well all come in generic yellow packaging. I have heard employers rather unkindly refer to the candidates in a recruitment drive as being 'as indistinguishable as link sausages coming out of a machine'. Same education, same suits, same fake smiles plastered on, same clichéd answers. Many interview candidates are so afraid of standing out that they become almost paralysed by their conformity. They are virtually impossible to tell apart. Or remember. Or like. DO NOT fall into this trap.

You cannot please all of the people all of the time and you will almost certainly betray yourself if you try to fudge on who you really are. If you are a square peg, there is no point in applying for round hole jobs. If you somehow manage to get hired for one, your boss is going to spend a lot of time bashing you on the head with a hammer until all of the corners have been knocked off you. More to the point, if you fail at interview while lying or concealing one of your rough edges, it is likely to be *that very thing* that caused them to reject you. Much better to tell the truth (with a positive slant on it, of course) and be rejected for who you really are. What are you afraid of?

MANAHAN'S MANTRA
IF YOU HAVE TO LIE TO GET IN THE DOOR,
THIS PROBABLY ISN'T THE JOB FOR YOU.

PROVIDING REASSURANCE

In a professional interview setting, the name of the game is reassurance. 'Hiring me represents no risk to your organisation', should be the foundation of your delivery. Give them any reason to think otherwise and they will be drawing a line ~~through~~ your name instead of <u>under</u> it. It is fair to say that most candidates are totally unaware of their self-deprecation and of the feeling of unease that it engenders in the listener. Well-trained interviewers will be able to pinpoint exactly why they are uneasy – they will pick up on hesitations, changes in the pitch of your voice, inappropriate vocabulary, conflicting non-verbal cues or other indicators that betray your lack of self belief. Your common-or-garden interviewer will not be quite so scientific in his analysis, but will 'just have a feeling' that you are not the right person for the job…

BACK TO THE DRAWING BOARD

If you have failed at interviews for jobs that you felt you were well suited to, you need to go back to the drawing board. Winning interviews are not about answering questions ('*I hope I told them what they wanted to hear…*'); they are about delivering a carefully prepared personal agenda (see page 193, Interview Mapping). This requires self knowledge and confident delivery, neither of which come without a lot of hard work.

Stage actors spend *weeks* working with the rest of the cast, honing their delivery. They are not focusing on the *substance* of the play; most principal actors arrive for day one of rehearsals with their lines already memorised.

> 'Lead the audience by the nose to the thought.'
> LAURENCE OLIVIER

Rehearsal, then, is all about *style*, establishing credibility and making each performance a memorable experience for the audience (see page 41, Fanatics).

To succeed at a job interview, you have to overcome your upbringing, the overly modest language of your forebears and your natural human dislike of the process itself. And all without straying over the line into arrogance or pugnacity. Do you seriously think you can make all of that up as you go along?

Chapter 6

RESEARCH

> **Research is what I am doing when I don't know what I am doing.**
>
> **DR WERNHER VON BRAUN**

You need to do a lot of spadework before you show up for a 21st-century interview. In some cases, you need to have this work done before you even apply for the job – because some of the other candidates will have completed extensive research and will refer to it in their CV and cover letter (see page 38, The Bogeyman).

Why all this effort? Very simply, organisations use interviews to see how hard you are willing to work on your own behalf. This is a very useful indicator for them – we *know* that you care about yourself, so if you are careless and sloppy in preparing for the interview on your own behalf, why would we expect you to behave any differently on *our* behalf after we hire you? So, start digging:

- First port of call – the organisation's website. Download and devour the whole site, including press releases, earnings statements and company reports. Go back several years if you can. If the CEO said she was going to focus on initiative X three years ago, did that happen? If not, why did they abandon it? If yes, did it make a difference?

- Share price – how has the organisation's price fared over the long term? Look at a five-year graph and compare it to the five-year graph of the exchange that the organisation is quoted on. How has the share price responded to announcements by the company? To new product launches, competitor initiatives or merger and acquisition activities? Track the share against key competitors and also look at analyst comments – they tend to be much more pithy than the overblown statements made by the CEO.

- Then you should look up the organisation on Google (www.google.com) and see what the wider world thinks of them.

- You can also 'Google' any names you know (or discover) of people who work in the organisation. Put them in quotes and put the organisation name beside them (e.g. "joe bloggs" widgets incorporated).

- It can be worth checking to see if your target organisation has been mentioned in the corridors of power. Check on the Government's website – have they been the subject of a debate? Have they been used as a shining example of how things should be done (environmental issues, investment in the local community) or are they held up as the epitome of vice and loose corporate governance practices?

- If you want to get really serious about checking up on them, go to the Companies Office and look them up on that – Directors, returns, other branches of the company. You can track the number of employees, their stated turnover and margin figures and a number of other valuable gems of information here. The Companies Office is of little or no value for a large conglomerate or group of companies, as they will typically have only a consolidated return and you may not be able to access the P&L (profit and loss) or balance sheet for the section of the group that you are interested in.

- Follow up a Companies Office search with a credit check on your target organisation. You probably won't be able to get that for free, but it can unearth some very interesting details – particularly for Small to Medium-sized Enterprises (SMEs).

- The larger public libraries often maintain clippings files on organisations and sectors. Get in there and read them – new products, expansion of facilities, advertisements, pending and old legal actions, union issues – they'll all be there.

- If you can't find a clippings library, many large newspapers maintain excellent searchable archives. In most cases, it won't be free, but it can be well worth the price if you are having no luck using other resources. (Your local library may have a corporate subscription – ask your friendly Librarian.)

- Public libraries (and most university libraries) usually have a journals section where you can read three years' worth of the trade magazine(s) for the sector you are going for. Find out what magazine(s) to read from your network (see page 168). There will be lots of mentions of the organisation(s) that you are interested in. There may be articles by or about the person you end up working for...

- Find out which advertising agency handles your target organisation's account and go and talk to them. (If they are reluctant to talk with you, send a young relative who is 'doing a project' to do the digging for you.) Get hold of old advertisements, promotional pieces, corporate reports. Find out how much they spend and on what. What have been the big strategic shifts in their communications strategies in the past few years? Advertising agencies maintain a 'Guard Book' of all of their clients' press clippings and advertisements and they will also have a show reel of any TV appearances or advertisements.

- Is there a representative or trade body for the sector you are about to enter? Look up their website, buy the Chairman lunch, read their publications – this will give you a big picture on the sector and allow you to talk much more forcefully and knowledgeably at the interview.

3-D RESEARCH

The organisation you want to work for does not exist in isolation. Even if you don't know anyone (who knows anyone, who knows anyone, who knows anyone...) who works there, your target organisation has suppliers, distributors, wholesalers, competitors (find them in Yellow Pages) and customers. And *someone* in your network knows *someone* on that supply and competitive chain...

Take a three-dimensional approach to your research. The Y axis is the supply chain, the X axis is the competitive environment in the sector and the Z axis is the wider economic and social environment in your territory. The more senior the position you are going for, the more comprehensive your research needs to be. They will expect this of you, but more importantly, digging like this will improve your chances of making a good decision on the organisation(s) you decide to join or not to join.

So find people on these three axes and go and talk to them (see page 168, Networking). Really – take the time and trouble to make a phone call, pay a visit to, or buy a coffee for someone who can give you a tiny little crumb of information. As always, you run the risk of coming up dry in your search – but at least you can talk to the interviewer(s) about the efforts that you have made and the opinions that you have heard expressed.

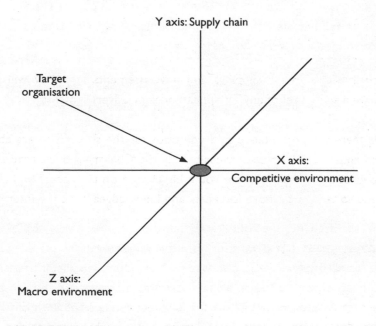

Chapter 7

LEARNING CURVE 5 – ARROGANCE

Nobody can be so amusingly arrogant as a young man who has just discovered an old idea and thinks it is his own. **SYDNEY J. HARRIS**

James, early 20s, single, business degree and Masters business degree
James was having difficulties getting a job in his desired sector – consultancy. He had applied to all of the major international consultancy companies during the 'Milk Round' in his college and he had been called for interview with five of them over a three-month period. The first four had rejected him after the first round of interviews. He came to see me prior to the fifth interview, looking, as he put it, 'for pointers on where I might be going wrong'.

James was an exceptionally bright young man, with a very strong academic record from his early teens through to his Masters degree. He was well-spoken, fairly well-presented and had obviously given the interview process a lot of thought. However, it rapidly became apparent that James thought he was something pretty special and a certain arrogance and pomposity crept into his manner during the course of the mock interview.

It was also immediately obvious that he had not conducted any meaningful research into the consultancy industry – he had a very shallow and somewhat naïve perspective in his answers to questions on this topic. The overall impression he gave was that he would be difficult to manage and that he would need to be very carefully monitored in the presence of clients/customers, lest he put his foot in it to his employer's cost.

After the practice interview, I provided objective feedback, along with action plans as to how James might remedy the poor impression that he was making. As is often the case, James was *appalled* to hear the answers he had given when they were reiterated *verbatim* and when he was shown the motives and subtexts behind the questions and what his answers revealed to a trained interviewer.

James was not successful in his attempt with the fifth consultancy company – he simply had too much ground to make up in too short a time. However, he did secure a good position with a consultancy firm in New York several months later and moved three times in two years, each time to a more senior role.

LEARNING POINTS:

- A **positive mental attitude** is vital at interview. '**Attitude**' is the kiss of death. You might be the brightest person in your whole family and among your entire circle of acquaintances, but that intellect is (a) not an accomplishment and (b) nothing more than a minimum entry requirement to get your foot in the door. James kept coming back to how bright he was in questions about his assets. When I finally said to him, 'A high level of intelligence is taken as read here, what else have you got to offer?' he was completely stumped!

- Skimming, **surface-level research** is virtually a waste of time (see page 162, Research). The person on the other side of the table lives, sleeps, eats and breathes the business you are about to enter, so you can't get away with reading a few news headlines and hoping to bluff your way through on that. To be fair, very few candidates these days chance their arm like that, but with the plethora of information that is available out there, they are going to expect you to really know your stuff – not an unreasonable expectation, in my opinion.

- **Self knowledge** is central to success at interviews, superseded only by an **awareness of your impact** on others. No matter how special you are, how clever you are, how solid your academic track record is, these are nothing more than minimum entry requirements for a hotly contested position in a competitive sector. All of the above merely get your foot inside the door. Then you need to be able to talk about what else you really bring to the party… (see page 80, 360°).

Chapter 8

NETWORKING

Networking is my mantra!   **TOM PETERS**

Old-boy network's power exposed.   **NATURE MAGAZINE**

Education – 'old school tie' still a factor.   **BBC**

Boardroom old-boy network in firing line.   **OBSERVER**

Computer networks, media networks, wireless networks, fibre-optic networks, network marketing – the term gets bandied about a lot these days. Networking for career-management and job-hunting purposes is no longer a necessary evil, nor the province of Public School or Ivy League alumni – it has become a basic survival skill. Why?

1 The market has changed. Employers (particularly in the Small to Medium-sized Enterprise sector) are circumventing expensive newspaper advertisements and even more expensive placement agencies where they can and are networking to find new employees. This is an (a) cheaper and (b) more reliable method of recruiting talent.

2 Talk to any outplacement or career management company in your locality. They will give you the hard statistics on the number of their clients who find employment due to some level of personal contact. The figure will vary, but it will *always* be 50 per cent or more.

3 The rising tide of Bogeymen (see page 38) have learnt the value of networking and have set the bar very high for you to compete with them.

BUT BUT BUT...

'But I'm just as good as that guy!'
'But I have brilliant references'
'But I don't know anyone'
'But that's not fair'
'But that's *nepotism!*'

Let me tell you the sole 'but' that matters in the midst of all this bluster. It's this: BUT from the only perspective that counts – the employer's – going out to the grapevine and using the network is (a) cheaper and (b) more effective. So get ready to compete this way, because the conventions have changed and *no one* – not employers, not placement agencies, not educational institutions, not your opposition – is playing by the old rules any more.

Of course, any employer is going to be happy to take on someone who is a (somewhat) known quantity and who has been referred by someone who is (in some way) beholden to that employer. But also, *of course*, no employer is going to take on some sub-literate, incompetent clown just because he happens to be someone's nephew. Very few businesses can afford to carry that kind of dead-weight on their payroll these days. There are exceptions to that statement no doubt, but do you want to work for that kind of organisation?

> I remember standing in the print room of a newspaper listening to some old-hand print workers discussing the recent appointment of the newspaper owner's son. 'What's his job?' asked the first guy. 'Good question. I dunno,' replied the second. The third (and oldest) printer thought for a moment, chuckled indulgently and said, 'I'll tell you what his job is. He's the boss's son, *that's* what his job is.'

Don't have a business to inherit? I'm bleeding for you. Family not well connected in the sphere in which you want to compete? Cue the violins. *Most* people don't start out with a network. This is ammunition that you have to acquire and tenderly nurture.

A BLANK PAGE

Let's start from the assumption that you don't know anybody who is immediately useful for the job-hunt or career move that you are about to make. Second assumption: you have started to gather publicly available intelligence about the sector that you are interested in and the organisations that compete within it. Third assumption: you are prepared to pursue this hunt fully and aggressively.

One picture that you really do need to start to fill in is the Organisation Chart for the institutions or companies that you are interested in. Senior management will frequently be mentioned on the organisation's website. Less senior players are usually harder to identify and you will probably need to resort to your network and to the media to find them. How old are they? Educated in what and to what level? How many years on the job? Are they near retirement? Are they any good? Are they at risk of being downsized?

> 'Knowledge is a process of piling up facts; wisdom lies in their simplification.'
> MARTIN HENRY FISCHER

Any data that you gather at this stage can be turned into knowledge later. Remember the chain (the acronym, appropriately enough, is DIK) – **Data** is given a context and becomes **Information** which, in turn, is confirmed and fleshed out into **Knowledge** (see page 162, Research). Diligent investigation of this nature can only take you so far, however; you must talk to people in order to find out what is really going on. The media can be a useful resource and will bring more morsels of data your way, but you have to be careful about relying on it as a source.

THE MEDIA

A typical television news broadcast is virtually useless to you in gathering information for a job search, but it may give you a broad-strokes direction in which to look. Newspapers, magazines and radio talk shows tend to be more valuable – you will get more depth and context, and these sources will raise questions and issues for you to explore further. If you can't make the time to listen to the radio or read everything you should, delegate the tasks to close friends and family (who listen or read anyway) on a rotating basis. Ask them to notate or clip *anything* that relates to your specified subjects, no matter how tenuous the connection.

The big limitation on using the media is this: pick a subject that you really know well and review the accuracy and reliability of the media's reporting on it. Nine times out of ten, you will be scratching your head and saying, 'Well *that's* wrong for a start.' I don't know about you, but I constantly find myself foaming at the mouth as I read/see/listen to the media.

> 'Stories about banks robbing people cannot be made as entertaining as images of people robbing banks.'
> CHET HUNTLEY

If you accept that the mainstream media are concerned more about ratings and circulation than they are about precision – and copper-fasten that belief with the certain knowledge that they constantly get things wrong about the subjects you have in-depth knowledge of – then you arrive at the inescapable conclusion that you have to take *everything* you see, hear and read from these sources with a great big chunk of salt. So, use the media as *part* of your research armamentarium, but don't go betting the farm on anything you glean there unless you can independently verify it.

You have to talk to people who are in the know, lest you end up in a role you hate, working for a boss you detest in an organisational culture you can't stand. Case in point: most young people seem to think that the world of Public Relations is glamorous and exciting, consisting largely of beautiful people in exquisite clothes exchanging sparkling conversation over cocktails. Five minutes talking turkey with someone in the business would disabuse any green PR-wannabe of this sort of twaddle very quickly.

I recently came across a study of 12th Graders (18–19 year olds) in the United States, all of whom had already decided on a career path. For the purposes of the study, they were given the opportunity to shadow someone in their career of choice for a week. After five working days, almost two-thirds of the participants had changed their mind about working in that sector. The grass is rarely greener on the other side of the fence (or on the other fella's grave). TALK to people!

CLASSIFYING YOUR NETWORK – EVERYONE IN A BOX

Classify the people you are going to call on as follows:

- **Sounding boards** – people whose opinion you value to run ideas by.
- **Wise old owls** – mentor figures for life, love, work, job-hunting.
- **Power-brokers** – those rare few who can get you inside an other-wise closed door.
- **Telegraph poles** – people who know everyone.
- **Greenhorns** – the next generation (sometimes they have insights or connections, sometimes you can become a mentor to them).

Create a Word document with a table like the one below – you may have other headings that you want to consider your network under.

PERSON	HOW MUCH DO THEY VALUE ME?	CLASS	SPHERE(S) THEY MOVE IN	NAMES THEY HAVE DROPPED

EXPLOITATION

Build a list of 25–40 People Who Matter (see page 372, Stress) and start thinking about them callously in terms of their 'usefulness' and 'connectedness'. If you have a circle of people who care enough about you to take a call, or better yet, *make* a call, you are immediately able to tap into their networks. If the anthropologists are right and we all have a circle of about 30 people, that means with a little humility, a little planning and a little schmoozing, you have an extended network of 800+ people (allowing for some repeats and cross-overs) to make the most of. And that's just going one degree of separation...

> 'A lie can travel half-way round the world before the truth has even put its shoes on.'
> MARK TWAIN

One reason that so many people shy away from networking (and from being networkees) is that it is, all too often, a one-way street. Most people don't like to ask and ask and ask; and *very* few people like to give and give and give, so be prepared to return favours and to exchange information. You might not be in a position to do this at first, but if you are playing the game in any way well, you should be in that position fairly quickly. In the meantime, if you are the supplicant, make sure that you are suitably courteous and get ready to send *lots* of thank-you notes.

MOVING BEYOND THE IMMEDIATE CIRCLE

Everybody you know and meet is a potential networkee:

- School friends, college friends
- People you met on training courses or at seminars/conferences
- Lecturers/trainers/teachers
- Old bosses/colleagues
- Old boy/girlfriends
- Neighbours

- Members of the clergy
- Gurus, journalists, pundits
- Club members — you think that that many people in the world really love golf?
- Professional association members and officers
- Parents of your children's friends
- Everyone you meet at parties/dinners/the pub
- Suppliers, distributors and customers
- Your doctor, dentist, vet, lawyer, hairdresser, plumber, handyman, etc. etc. etc. etc. etc.

Someone you have met knows a person who can be useful to you in every stage of a job search. Notate them — do this in a structured way in an easily located, central file, preferably on your PC. Phone them. Meet them. Extract the information. Send the thank-you. Return the favour (it goes without saying that your integrity must be spotless throughout this process…) Keep the lines of communication open. Build on the relationship. Knowledge is power.

This process will not bear fruit overnight, but it will bear fruit. Stick with it and the loops will start closing — people you have networked with will talk to other people you have networked with. *Example*: If you meet a player who enlightens you on some obscure, but useful, aspect of the sector you are targeting, send the thank-you note the next day as per usual. But then try and take it further — if you come across a morsel that you think might be of value to that player, send it on immediately. Don't plague them with e-mails, but one or two carefully chosen jewels will be (a) an appropriate thank-you and (b) useful to position you in the person's mind.

Play the game this way and your reputation as a person who has their finger on the pulse will grow. People will start coming to *you* looking for information or opinions. In these uncertain times, with the job-for-life covenant consigned to the history books, it is imperative that you position yourself in this fashion. Job security today no longer lies in what organisation you work for, achieving targets or how well your department is doing; it lies in **employability** (transferable attitude, skills and knowledge), **connectedness** and real **insight** into the workings of your sector.

WHAT A NETWORK IS NOT

It is useful to define your boundaries here – just how much are you pre-pared to exploit the people in your circle? More to the point, how much are they prepared to be exploited by you? First off, your network is *not* going to be a list of people who have the authority to hire you. Forget that idea right now. For the most part, a job-hunter's network is a data-gathering cooperative and, if you manage them well, a group of individuals, some of whom may do some degree of marketing on your behalf.

> 'Inside every working anarchy, there's an Old Boy Network.'
> MITCHELL KAPOR

So, rarely, your network will directly procure you a job, but it should be aimed at giving you access to the knowledge that can ultimately lead to a choice position. It can mean that you'll find out (ahead of the curve) that a certain organisation is expanding, examining a new technol-ogy or considering entry to a new market or territory. That means you can get your CV (highlighting just the germane aspects of your experi-ence, accomplishments, qualifications and personal attributes) on to the right desk at the right time. You have to be plugged-in like this to know what is going on in your sector(s) or organisation(s) of choice.

You must tread very carefully here – never place anyone on your net-work in an invidious position. If some kind soul has called in a favour and arranged a meeting with a power broker they know, DO NOT whip out your CV half-way through. If they ask to see your CV following the meeting, then it's happy days; but you should never make the networkee feel discomfited in any way. NEVER be so gauche as to put someone in the embarrassing position of having to say, 'No' to you in your network-ing efforts. Persistence is important but subtlety is the key.

ONE LAST THOUGHT

For the majority of jobs in public service, the phrase 'canvassing will dis-qualify' will appear on the advertisement and/or application form. This kills off the kind of last-minute efforts that most job-hunters employ as

they play catch-up with those who are actively managing their careers. If you are ahead of the evolutionary curve in your career (or if you have decided that you are going to be from this point on) then all of your information-gathering and canvassing will be complete by the time the post is advertised. Not in keeping with the spirit of the rule, I realise, but very much to the letter and, regrettably or otherwise, a *very* necessary part of managing your career in a public service environment. Get to it.

Chapter 9

MANAGING YOUR REFERENCES

> *I don't care what you say about me, as long as you say something about me, and as long as you spell my name right.* **GEORGE M. COHAN**

Because most people speak well of us most of the time, referees are often treated as little more than an after-thought by many job-hunters and so they trot out the names of a couple of old bosses and some retired college professor. If it were such a trivial part of the process, why do you think every letter of offer in the world includes the phrase, '...*subject to satisfactory references*'?

The people whom you need to say nice (and true) things about you are a very important facet of your preparation. Some placement agencies and almost all headhunters will do this kind of background checking on you before they consider putting your name forward. If they go beyond the few names on the list you provide to them (and again, a good check will go *way* further than this) they had better not be hearing anything that contradicts what your preferred referees have said about you or any other unpleasant surprises...

The same holds true for your new employer. Just because you tell them to talk to the three people on your list, it doesn't mean that a potential new employer isn't going to ask around about you. Staying on top of this is all part of effective career management. That is not to suggest that everyone out there thinks you are Mary Poppins ('*practically perfect in every way*') but even those who patently do not like you should have some degree of professional respect for you. Being liked is an overworked concept and is of far less value to a potential employer than being, in the main, *respected* for your effectiveness.

How you handle your referees is dependent upon how private you want your job-hunt to be. With the best will in the world, people *do* talk and even diplomatic, senior-level players may have one drink too many and get into an 'I see young Manahan has itchy feet again' discussion. So who do you ask, how do you handle them and when and how do you produce them as witnesses for the defence?

WHO TO ASK?

Unless you have a *very* open-marriage relationship with your current boss, his name should be kept off the list. A *very* trusted colleague who can vouch for your current successes and activities can be useful. Someone who left the company recently and who is happy to talk about you would also be a very useful reference. A major customer, with discretion as the watchword, or a key vendor As a rule, unless you are stepping out of formal education for the first time, all of your referees should be directly work-related.

If you are out of work, then as far as the market is concerned, all bets are off and they can ask to talk to *anyone* from your past. This is why it is so important to agree what the 'Exit Statement' is going to be when you are being made redundant or fired. (Incidentally, many organisations in these litigious times won't give a detailed reference, no matter who asks. They will give your start and finish dates and the title you held as you left the organisation and no more. If the reference they would otherwise give you is positive, they *may* be inclined to go beyond the very limiting scope of this policy; if the reference would be negative, they are more likely to stick to the letter of the procedure.)

For those leaving college, a head of department or tutor (who really knows you and remembers you) is okay, but bosses from part-time or summer jobs are of much greater value, unless your next job is going to be in the groves of academe.

If you are returning to the workforce after a long interval, your old referees may not be available any more. Track them down where possible, but you should also start looking up old colleagues, who may now be in positions of authority and ready and willing to stand up for you.

If you are changing your career path, you will need to very carefully brief your referees on your new ambitions and start putting words in their mouths about how your previous experiences (which they may have entirely forgotten) relate to the new role.

SUBPOENA OR INVITATION?

Build your wish list of referees and then start contacting the least important ones and work your way upwards – that way, you will be more skilled in the discussion and in getting what you want/need from the key referees. The last thing you want to happen is for a crucial player to express doubt about speaking up on your behalf. You are looking for whole-hearted buy-in here. *Any* reservations need to be dealt with immediately and well. Remember, the more helpful and open you can be in enabling your potential new employer to scope you from head to toe, the more reassured they will be that there are no unpleasant surprises lurking in your past.

As part of your networking activities (see page 168) you should be fostering your referees. Contact with old bosses, colleagues and subordinates for an exchange of information, leads and ideas can very easily be brought around to the concept of providing references for each other. For very senior roles, employers will frequently talk to subordinates as part of the overall picture, so you can offer to stand up and be counted for an old boss, even as he is standing up for you…

SPLASHDOWN!

When you get to that all-important stage of the final interview process, your level of contact with your referees will naturally go up – you may be discussing tactics with them, or garnering ideas for the optimal approach to the new job. All of this has the obvious benefit of reminding your referees of your skills and accomplishments from the past. You *can* provide them with an *aide-mémoire* list of the attributes you want mentioned or the successes you want to highlight from that time in your career, but this is usually perceived as being somewhat crass and your referee could well end up sounding like a parrot reciting the list. Better for these elements to 'come up' in conversation and then the referee can put his words on it when the phone call comes.

Many advertisements require you to include details of your current remuneration and references as you apply. I would not recommend doing this at the outset, unless the position you are applying for is in public service and you will be disqualified from the shortlisting process for failure to comply. For a private sector role, you can enter 'excellent references will be furnished upon request'. See the section on Negotiating Remuneration (page 297) for my thoughts on mentioning salary at this stage. Unless absolutely necessary, I don't like including references at the written stage for two reasons:

- It is like showing up for a first date with your whole family by your side. It smacks of an over-eager approach, rather than the 'let's see if we really like each other' style that I would recommend every job-seeker to adopt.
- If the reader recognises one of your referees at this stage in the process, he may either (a) think that referee is a clown/snake/louse and tar you with the same brush ('Well if that cretin Jones is one of this guy's references, we **certainly** don't need to meet him!') or (b) contact said reference too early in the process and start hitting you at interview with insightful questions based on the conversation.

CLEARING THE FINAL HURDLE

The final hurdle is not the basic reference check. It is the reference that your new employer seeks from your current employer *after* you have resigned. It may even happen after you have started work in your new position. This is why I am such a nag on the subject of managing your career rather than merely job-hunting. Someone who is maintaining a degree of control and fully bringing that control to bear throughout their career will rarely have to worry about being damned with faint praise (or being damned outright) during a reference check.

If you are not thinking this way, problems from your history *will* come home to roost. Your new boss will bump into your old boss at a conference and, over an informal drink, your predilection for ignoring instructions, or going over your boss's head, will come to the fore. You may have been (or thought that you were) justified in doing this at the time; but now it is severely colouring your new boss's perceptions of your actions. And you are still on probation…

Career management is, at its most fundamental level, all about survival. It is about carefully building and nurturing your reputation. Inevitably, there will be begrudgers who resent your success, but the quality of your contributions and the tenor of your reputation should be sufficient to more than drown out those few dissenting voices. If that is not the case for you, start paying heed to this aspect of your career *right now*. Making your professional way in this world is hard enough without this kind of handicap. Take the high road – cultivate your reputation and cultivate those who will attest to that reputation.

Chapter 10

LOOKING THE PART

> *I've had enough of being perceived as a gloomy Goth casualty.*
>
> **ROBERT SMITH OF THE CURE**

(Well, maybe you should stop dressing like one then, Robert…)

Ask any interviewer who has just made a good hire when they knew they had found the best candidate for the job and nine times out of ten they'll say, 'As soon as she walked through the door.'

WHAT DOES YOUR APPEARANCE TELL THEM?

As interviewers, we are constantly on the look-out for patterns of behaviour (both good and bad) that will serve as predictors of your likely behaviour once we hire you. Let us go back for a moment to square one. The one assumption that any interviewer can fairly make about you is this: **You care about yourself.** In the selection process, if the indicators are that you are lacking in professionalism/attention to detail on YOUR OWN BEHALF, what possibility is there that you will display professionalism or attention to detail on behalf of your employer?

Therefore, the old line about only getting one chance to make a good first impression is never truer than when applied to the interview situation. Treat this first face-to-face meeting as a fantasy first date and you won't go far wrong.

UGLY FACT NO. 8

YOU HAVE FIVE SECONDS TO MAKE A POSITIVE FIRST IMPRESSION. FIVE.

Think how many potential dates you have rejected in social situations on the basis of first impression... from across the room... before they even opened their mouths! Do you seriously believe that interviewers are capable of switching that mode of thinking off? And by the way, the less trained the interviewer is, the more likely she is to rely on this kind of gut feeling.

TAKE IMPARTIAL ADVICE

You MUST look the part – clothing, posture, facial expressions, body language – everything must be impeccable. To some extent, most people dress either for comfort or to make some kind of statement. Like it or not, you will be assessed from the outside in, so if you are unsure of the impression that you are making with your appearance or if you want to improve that impression, you should consider a professional once-over. This does NOT mean asking for clothing, grooming or make-up advice from salespeople in shops – they are not objective and they have a very obvious personal agenda which rarely coincides exactly with yours. (We have all seen brides going up the aisle resembling a cross between a lacy toilet-roll cover and a meringue as a result of some fast talking by a flinty-eyed salesperson.) Before you spend your budget on clothing, go and see a reputable style consultant (don't rely on advertisements – use your network to find a good one if possible). These people depend for their living on making clients look their absolute best. There is no agenda other than making an appreciable difference to your image.

If you are still unsure as to what you should wear for a specific interview, loiter outside the organisation's premises at five o'clock some time before the appointed day and see what the norm is. Then go 5–10 per cent better in your clothing for your first meeting. Conformity is obviously the key – unless you are going for a very way-out job. At an absolute minimum, you should follow these basic guidelines:

- Be freshly showered/bathed – not a hint of body odour. If perspiration is a problem for you, make sure your clothes are well laundered/dry cleaned in advance and think about how you are going to arrive at the interview as fresh as a daisy.
- Take the time and trouble to have perfectly groomed hair.
- Have clean, dry hands, with nicely manicured nails. No nibbling on your nails and make sure that they are spotlessly clean.
- Be conservatively dressed in a suit that 'works' for you – good colour, good cloth and flattering style.

Teaching granny to suck eggs, I know; but time and again I see candidates come into the interview room apologising for their very existence by their mode of dress and carriage.

GOD IS IN THE DETAILS

The style gurus tell us that the suit is the canvas and what people notice are the accessories, so spend your money (or call in your favours) here. Shirt, tie and shoes are the important points for men. Top, scarf, handbag and shoes for women. A vital thing to get right (for both sexes) is the colour that you wear **under your chin**. Make sure that this is covered in your style discussion or, at the very least, go shopping wearing your interview suit and audition various shirts, ties, blouses/tops and scarves in different colours.

Other accessories that may be noticed are your car, coat, umbrella, glasses, belt, pen, notepad and briefcase. The comedian Billy Connolly jokes about always carrying a good pen in case he is asked to sign an autograph – because if he signed with a BIC®, people would presume that he had fallen on hard times. It is worth taking time over these details, no matter how tiresome they might seem. What would you think of a salesman who drove up to your door in a 12-year-old filthy rustbucket of a car with the side bashed in?

If you are going to do it at all, do it right. Follow these two final rules of thumb and you won't go far wrong:

1 You should look like a television newsreader – that is what professional people expect other professional people to look like (this is particularly true for women).
2 You should be one of the best-dressed people in the room. If you are sitting in the waiting room and someone with the dress sense and panache of Grace Kelly wafts by, you should NOT be thinking, 'I hope she's not going for the job.'

I am constantly amazed at the percentage of interview candidates who start off at a disadvantage because they didn't make an effort with their appearance. This can happen in two ways:

1 Grace Kelly floats into the waiting room and you start to feel inadequate, get the jitters and blow the interview.
2 A poorly trained interviewer can take one look at you and mentally say, 'Not our type of person.'

Either way, this really is a bone-stupid reason to be eliminated from the selection process (and yes, it happens all the time.) There is no excuse for shoddy dressing; beg, steal or borrow what you need. Remember, they expect you to treat the interview as a dream date, so groom yourself accordingly. There are people out there who think that they can know someone by the cut of their suit, the grip of their hand and the look in their eye. Now, we know that these people are fools, but it would be a pity to miss out on an opportunity for a really great job because you met one of them and you weren't looking your absolute best.

'The best clothes are invisible – they make you notice the person.'
KATHERINE HAMNETT

WITHDRAWN FROM STOCK

Chapter 11

DRESS CODE DOs & DON'Ts

> *Fashions fade. Style is eternal.* **YVES SAINT LAURENT**

DOs (WOMEN)

- Professional first and always, presentable second, fashionable a poor third, in terms of priority.
- Co-ordinated, elegant clothes are a must, preferably (sorry, please don't shoot the messenger) a skirt suit.
- Trouser suits are becoming more acceptable – make this judgement for each different interview (loiter outside the building in advance).
- A little make-up to accentuate your strong features. Be careful not to over-apply. Reputable, professional advice (not from a cosmetic sales-person in a department store!) can really help here.
- Immaculate, low-heeled, 'sensible' shoes. Wear flats if you are very tall. I don't care what the current fashion is – wear classic shoes.
- Quality accessories only – shoes, handbag, belt, scarf, gloves, glasses, pen, briefcase, diary, etc. Spend your money here; it is where most people will notice your effort.
- Wear neutral tones (darker by preference, unless it drains your face) in natural fabrics.
- The colour that you wear under your chin (blouse, top, jewellery, scarf) is vitally important. Experiment with different shades while wearing your interview suit – some will light up your face and some will just look *awful*.

- Carry a briefcase only if you must, and if you do, do not bring a handbag – the only people who carry briefcases in the office environment are outsiders.

FAQ

'I heard somewhere that you should only wear light-coloured tights to an interview. Why?'

- Dark tights are associated with evening wear. You are presenting yourself at a professional interview, not going to a cocktail party, and you should dress accordingly. If you have nice legs, dark tights will highlight them more effectively – but do you really want a male interviewer to hire you for the way your legs looked at the interview?

DON'Ts (WOMEN)

- Distractions – gaudy or dangling jewellery or very long hair. Hair falling into your face that requires constant flicking back. No dark hair roots either.
- Very open necks or bare legs. Nothing too revealing.
- Visible designer labels.
- Cardigans and twin-sets.
- Perfume. (Allergies. Worse yet, you might smell like someone's ex-wife and he won't know *why* he doesn't like you, but he *won't* like you…)
- Multiply pierced ears, or visible piercings anywhere else.
- Mobile phone/pager. Don't bring it with you, or at the very least, turn it completely off.
- Too much jewellery and/or too many rings is regarded as a sign of insecurity. Wear understated, classy pieces with no more than one ring finger on each hand.

THE OVERALL LOOK (WOMEN)

You want to look like a TV newsreader (this is now what the world expects a professional woman to look like), but that look can be a little 'sterile'. Feminise it with one strong accessory. You must be comfortable that you can wear the look and also that you can walk, talk and sit comfortably in the look. Practise. If you are in a business where you don't need to do the 'suit thing' for interviews, then make sure it's *very* smart casual.

DOs (MEN)

- The overall impression that you should want to convey is professionalism and presentability – not trendiness.
- Wear neutral tones (darker is usually more Impressive) in natural fabrics. No loud, shiny suits.
- Make sure that your suit is perfectly cleaned and pressed. It must not be at all threadbare or shiny. It doesn't need to be expensive, but it must be in *perfect* condition. If it is a new suit, break it in carefully well in advance of the interview, so that it doesn't look too stiff on the day.
- Spend *serious* money on your shirt. White or cream is always safest. Check which colours work best under your chin.
- Likewise, spend money on your tie and protect it carefully from rain, food and liquids on the day of your interview (some people carry a spare).
- Sensible, immaculate lace-up shoes and good socks (save your Fred Flintstone® socks for when you've got the job).
- Be perfectly shaven, well in advance, so your skin has time to settle.
- Quality accessories only – belt, glasses, pen, briefcase, diary, note-pad, etc.
- Carry a briefcase only if you have to – the only people who carry briefcases in the office environment are outsiders.

DON'TS (MEN)

- Long hair – have it cut a week before your interview so it has time to settle.
- Facial hair has been consistently shown in studies to deter interviewers.
- Blazer and trousers.
- After-shave. (Allergies. Worse yet, you might smell like someone's ex-husband and she won't know *why* she doesn't like you, but she *won't* like you…)
- Mobile phone/pager – don't bring it with you, or at the very least, turn it completely off.
- Too much jewellery is regarded as a sign of insecurity. Lose the chunky gold necklace and any bracelets you accumulated in your nightclub years, and stick to a maximum of one ring on each hand.
- Big clumpy watches. You are *not* James Bond. Get over it.

THE OVERALL LOOK (MEN)

Somewhere between a newsreader and Mr Big from *Sex and the City*. If you are in a business where you don't need to do the 'suit thing' for interviews, then make sure it's *very* smart casual – you should look like an extra from a Ralph Lauren advertisement.

THE VITAL PREPARATION FORM

> *Luck is a matter of preparation meeting opportunity.*
>
> **OPRAH WINFREY**

You should complete this simple two-page form for every interview you ever attend. Much of the information will be common across a variety of situations – maybe as much as 90 per cent – but it is that final few points that can make all of the difference. Even if you are applying for apparently *identical* roles in three competing companies, the internal structures, the focus of the companies and the corporate cultures may be surprisingly different. If tailoring is essential at the written stage of the job-hunt, then it is life-or-death at this stage. So make lots of copies and get writing (see page 193, Interview Mapping, to complete the exercise fully and effectively).

Current Position: Reporting to:

Position Sought: Reporting to:

How does the new position relate to your current (or most recent) job – similarities/differences?

What are your real strengths in relation to this particular job?

What are your real weaknesses in relation to this job?

What is your personal agenda – why do you want this position?

What track record (if any) can you demonstrate that qualifies you for the new role?

Why do you want to leave your current organisation and what **really** attracts you to this new one?

How will you approach the new role? What do you hope to accomplish for them? (five-year plan?)

Think of an interview that has gone well or badly for you. Can you pin down why it went well/badly? How did you think you had done? Were you surprised that you got the job or second interview or that you didn't?

In this interview, what will you say your strengths and weaknesses/disappointments are?

At what kind of interview do you perform best (structured, psychological, biographical, casual)?

What aspects of the interview process make you most nervous? How are you going to deal with your nervousness before and at this interview?

INTERVIEW MAPPING

> *To map out a course of action and follow it to an end requires some of*
>
> *the same courage that a soldier needs.*
>
> **RALPH WALDO EMERSON**

Mapping out your intentions for the interview is not just a technique for ensuring that there are no holes in your preparation; it should become the heart and soul of your line of attack. The Map starts with *Their Approach* because, without a clear understanding of that, you are very unlikely to succeed at any interview. Only when you complete the two sections devoted to their concerns, issues and likely approach can you start thinking about which of your skills and experiences you should include or omit in your pitch.

(1) OBVIOUS QUESTIONS (see page 201)

The nature of the role and of the organisation will largely inform your approach for this box. Make sure that you address the 'chestnut' questions and the core Competencies that the role will require. You can often get a clearer picture of these identified Competencies (sometimes called Job Standards) by phoning the Human Resources department and asking them to send you a job description for the role for which you are applying. Changes, shifts or trends in the industry/sector would also come under this category of questions.

(II) QUESTIONS I HOPE THEY DON'T ASK... (see page 202)

If you have found out anything about the people who are interviewing you or, even more usefully, the style of interview they tend to use or areas they focus in on, it can help you to anticipate a dirty question. Likewise, if there are *any* skeletons in your closet, start with the assumption that an interviewer is going to raise one of them and determine your best line of answering to quickly kill this subject off and move back to your sales agenda. Interviewers can use this technique purely to put you on the back foot and shake you up a little for another line of questioning and, if it catches you by surprise, this can be a very effective approach. You should also be ready for any and all of the awkward and nasty questions listed in Chapter 4 of Part 4 (see page 227).

(III) NUGGETS – ALL THAT GLITTERS ABOUT YOU (see page 203)

The 360° exercise (see page 80) provided you with an abundance of good stuff to say about yourself, but which aspects of your shining brilliance are going to be most attractive to *this* employer? Ideally, there should be two to three items/attributes/experiences that *really* distinguish you from the herd and a few more at which you are perfectly competent without necessarily being anything really special. For an interview that is going to last 45–60 minutes, I would recommend delivering no more than five to seven of these Nuggets. If you are stuck because you have too much good stuff to talk about, start ruthlessly applying the '*So What?*' rule and whittle it down.

Your Nuggets are your agenda for the whole interview. They are the reasons that anyone would want to meet or hire you, so GET THEM ACROSS! If you are going to bring a notebook into the interview (and you should), write this agenda – just five to seven words – at the top of the page in faint pencil so that the interviewers won't be able to read it. That way, you have a constant visual mnemonic as the interview unfolds.

In today's job market, if you walk out of the room having delivered only half of your Nuggets, don't expect to get hired.

PANNING FOR NUGGETS

'*Which Nuggets should I use?*' This can be a difficult choice and requires more objective thinking about yourself – but you should be getting used to this kind of self-centred (if somewhat tiresome) methodology by now. Back to school-level Mathematics for this one. Remember the bell curve? Pretty much anything that you can measure in this world comes out on a bell curve distribution – height, weight, visual acuity, intelligence, intimate measurements, whatever.

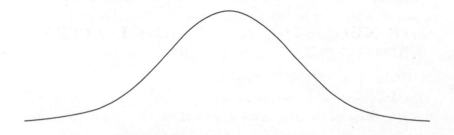

Most measurable things gravitate towards the big bulgy bit in the middle (a small confession here: I was never much good at maths – could you tell?) and you have extremes at the ends. So a bell curve for height in 500 randomly chosen males in the Western world would have a centre point of, say, 172 cm (5' 9") and extremes of 148 cm (4' 11") and 202 cm (6' 9").

SMORGASBORD

You have already identified your Nuggets. The final selection process comes when you have built up a strong picture of what the job you are applying for actually entails. Then you can start superimposing the Key Points (Nuggets) you want to make on to that picture. Employers frequently outline their menu of requirements when they advertise a position. Or they may send you a detailed job and person specification in advance of the interview. If they don't, you should ask for one.

A combination of insider knowledge, research and common sense will quickly allow you to determine the biggies – the Minimum Entry Requirements for the role and the Nice-To-Haves that the employer is hoping to find in the marketplace.

Rate yourself for each of the items – do it crudely and simply with marks out of 10 or 100. If there are 10–15 items on the list, you should be showing as average to strong average on more than half of them. What are your top three? These are the pertinent Nuggets at the right-hand side of the bell curve and they form the crux of your sales pitch for the interview. The 1–2 items on the left are the weaknesses that you will need to be ready to address and to provide reassurance on.

WHICH WAY TO THE EGRESS?

If one of these weaknesses is the core function of the role, you might want to revisit your thinking about this job. Similarly, if one of those core functions is a major Turn-off (see page 339, 'I Hate My Job') for you, it's back to the drawing board.

Example: if you are going to be spending more than 50 per cent of your time influencing others (colleagues, management, customers or suppliers) and you are a strong average in terms of skills for that, no problem there. However, if you have the aptitude, experience and training (you may even have a strong track record in sales) but derive little or no satisfaction from making a sale, that's a great big warning light.

The exception on this would be if you were taking a job as a stepping stone and could put up with the aspect that you are good at, but don't really enjoy, for a couple of years. Fine and dandy. Just make *sure* that the promotional prospects that the company is (no doubt) dangling in front of you are real and verifiable.

HONING

Throughout your preparation and rehearsals, you should be deciding which Nuggets to drop in response to which line of questioning. Guidelines:

- Drop one into your opener (something juicy like being headhunted, a promotion or the fact that you have been consistently singled out for responsibility all your life) and maybe mention another in passing (see page 209, Introducing Yourself Well).
- There might be an opportunity to drop another into your answer with regard to why you want to move on from your current organisation and why you want this job.
- If they get into questions about your strengths, it's open season – include at least three Nuggets, and you can also mention some of your lesser, common-or-garden qualities.
- Weakness questions – you can talk about a particular attribute that you applied to overcome a weakness (see page 215, Talking About Weaknesses).
- Specific competence questions (see page 228) – the theme to your answers is built around your Nuggets.
- 'What do other people say about you?' – it's like shooting fish in a barrel.
- 'Successes you are proudest of?' – pull up a chair and tra la la…

MAFIA HITMEN

Thinking about yourself in this clinical way takes some getting used to. But be assured, this is *exactly* the way that any potential employer will be thinking about you, so get used to it. The idea of waltzing into an interview with an agenda of Nuggets that you are going to deliver (no matter what) is bizarre the first few times you do it. So take a lesson from the Estate Agents and Mafia Hitmen of this world. Whether you are selling a house or disposing of a body, it all comes down to location, location, location. For you in the interview setting, it's all about presentation,

presentation, presentation, and that means rehearsal. Big time. An excellent way to do this is to apply for a few jobs that you don't really want just to get some interview practice. Take an interview for a job that you would actually like, except for the location, or because you have discovered that the organisation's culture is oppressive. This kind of dry run, combined with effective debriefing (see page 307, After the Interview) will quickly iron out any kinks in your delivery.

MAKING PERFECT GRAVY

Once you have pre-determined your approach in this way, it becomes second nature to apply it. The key in your practice is to distil out all of the flim-flam and get to the juice. Great chefs recommend 'reducing to concentrate the flavour of your gravy' – let it bubble away gently until its volume is reduced by half. This is the '*So What?*' rule applied (magnificently) to cookery.

In the course of a 45–60 minute interview, they are going to ask you a lot of questions; frequently up to 20. Do the sums – this doesn't give you a lot of time for any one answer. Twenty to forty seconds for list-type answers ('*What are your strengths?*' '*How would you describe yourself?*') and one to three minutes for meaty, essay-type answers. Save the longer answers for the questions that give you an opportunity to make the sale. Wasting eight minutes on '*Take us through your CV*' is just that – a waste (see page 209, Introducing Yourself Well).

Your practice must focus on distillation. Do a dry run and tape yourself. Play it back and start thinking about where you need to expand and where you can make cuts. Keep that tape. Repeat the process and keep refining. When you have produced your 'perfect gravy' answers, listen to the original tape again – I *guarantee* that it will make you cringe. Writers do this all the time. Whether they are writing *War and Peace* or the blurb on the back of a cereal packet, they constantly re-draft.

(IV) SUPPORTING EVIDENCE
(see page 203)

By evidence, I'm not referring to the Perry Mason, startling-discovery-just-in-time-to-win-the-case type of evidence. I'm referring to the kind of evidence that our old mate Louis Pasteur would pay heed to. Scientific research and discovery is based on the big empirical questions:

MEANINGFUL EVIDENCE
WHAT DO I THINK?
WHAT DO I KNOW?
WHAT CAN I PROVE?

If you had to stand up in front of a bunch of hard-nosed business people and recommend that they allocate a capital spend of £5,000,000 on some colossal new piece of machinery, you wouldn't be doing it on the basis of what you *think*. *No one* is going to bet the farm on what you *think*. You should be looking to provide a very high level of reassurance – as much empirical evidence as possible. Your core data needs to be irrefutable. Your conclusions have to be based on easy-to-follow, logical steps. No leaps of faith here!

An interview is exactly the same. There is no point asserting that you can walk on water, unless (a) you actually can and (b) you have *hard* evidence to back that assertion up. Water-walking was a core element in your last job description. You have been sent on three courses in Advanced Water Walking. You got the annual award two years running for Excellence in Water Walking in your last company. All of your referees will spontaneously mention your skills as an aquatic pedestrian.

THE 3 LEVELS OF OCCURRENCE
I MADE IT HAPPEN.
I WATCHED IT HAPPEN.
I SAT THERE WONDERING, '*WHAT HAPPENED?*'

Using the SPOUT model (see page 228, Competency-based Interviews), you can build your portfolio of evidence to corroborate your Nuggets.

We all like happy endings, so start from your accomplishments, wins and triumphs and work your way back through how they happened (i.e. how you *made* them happen) to the starting situation. Very few interview candidates arrive with this kind of structured mindset and, if you play it right, the interviewers will *love* you for making their job easier. If you play it too hard (*'Me Lud, may it please the court…'*), you will just intimidate or irritate them.

A carefully framed approach of this nature is relentless – you demonstrate that you understand their worries, that you have thought deeply about them, that you have what it takes to excel in this role, and, through the course of the interview, lead them to the inexorable conclusion that hiring anyone else would just be a needless risk.

If you can't do this, if you don't believe that it is true, if you're not *sure* that you have what it takes – why have you applied for the job…?

THEIR APPROACH

(I) QUESTIONS THAT I CAN ANTICIPATE

1.

2.

3.

4.

5.

6.

7.

8.

9.

10.

THEIR APPROACH

(I) QUESTIONS THAT I CAN ANTICIPATE

11.

12.

13.

14.

15.

16.

17.

18.

19.

20.

(II) QUESTIONS I HOPE THEY DON'T ASK

1.

2.

3.

4.

5.

6.

MY PITCH	
(III) NUGGETS	**(IV) MY SUPPORTING EVIDENCE**
1.	1.
2.	2.
3	3.
4.	4.
5.	5.
6.	6.
7.	7.

Chapter 14

COUNTDOWN TO THE INTERVIEW

Steel true, blade straight.

SIR ARTHUR CONAN DOYLE'S EPITAPH

Athletes pace their training so that they are 'peaking' on the day of a race. Soldiers are put through 'live fire' exercises to do the same coming up to a battle. You must develop a routine in the days and weeks counting down to an important interview. Negotiate with your loved ones and get their agreement on this. I have seen candidates get up from their desk and walk down the corridor to an internal interview. They don't look their best, their heads are full of the task they were just working on and they seem to treat an interview that could affect their career, life and standard of living as little more than a nuisance. Okay, I'll grant you – that's an extreme example, but it equates to an athlete showing up for a race having just eaten a heavy meal and wearing wellington boots.

You need to be as focused, calm and perfectly groomed as possible when you step through the door of the interview room. You have very little control of pace, approach or line of questioning once you are into the interview proper, so make sure everything that you *can* control goes smoothly.

THE DAYS BEFORE

- Collate your research on the organisation and the role, and review it over and over again. Make your last few phone calls to fill in any gaps. If there *are* still significant gaps in your knowledge of the organisation, decide how you are going to address them at the interview.
- Complete your interview preparation form (do a new one for each job you apply for, see page 190). Map your Nuggets against the questions you have anticipated (see page 193, Interview Mapping).
- Practise your answers to the key interview questions over and over. Keep doing this **out loud**, so you get the terminology and phrasing into your vocal memory.
- If possible, find out how many people will be interviewing you and what their names, titles and ages are.
- If you have never been to the area or the specific building where the interview will be taking place before, check it out a day or two ahead of time.
- Get your clothing cleaned and pressed well in advance. Lay it out the night before – run it by someone you trust for final approval.

THE DAY ITSELF

- Telephone to confirm that you will be attending and that you are looking forward to meeting the interviewer (do this the day before if your interview is in the morning).
- No strong-smelling foods in advance of the interview. A garlic-laden meal the night before can leave your breath smelling for more than 24 hours.
- Arrive five to ten minutes early. Allow plenty of time for traffic and parking. Sit and wait in your car or in a nearby café with a book or newspaper if necessary.
- If at all possible, get rid of your coat and umbrella in reception.
- Ask to use the facilities. Then: check your hair/accessories/make-up; clean your glasses; make sure that your shoes (including the backs of the heels) are immaculate.

- Wash your hands in warm water and dry them thoroughly.
- Adjust your clothing for the final time. Button your suit jacket, if appropriate.
- Review your Nuggets one last time. (If you are bringing a notebook into the interview, you should have them written at the top of the page in very faint pencil – see page 193, Interview Mapping.)
- Sit up straight, facing the door in the waiting room – do not pace around and do not read magazines, newspapers or company literature.
- Don't accept tea, coffee or a cigarette once you are in the building, no matter how badly you might want it. A glass of water is okay in the interview room, unless you are prone to very shaky hands.
- If your palms tend to get cold or sweaty when you are under stress, try and keep your right hand warm and dry for the initial handshake – long, slow, deep breathing will help here (see page 390, Breathing).
- Smile, firm handshake with good eye contact, and off you go…

Different people do different things to get 'into the zone'. If you are not sure how to do this for yourself, think of the last time you were really proud of a huge concentrated effort you made at something. It could be something physical or something mental. When you finished, your head came up and you sort of 'swam' back to reality. Women are forever complaining that men seem to live in their own little world when they behave like this – doing DIY, playing sports, reading the manual for the new DVD player. It goes back to the hunt, when man needed to be able to focus in this way in order to be an effective provider of fresh meat. Find out what works for you and start to develop your routine. The calming unit described in the chapter on Breathing (see page 390) is an excellent starting point. An interview or presentation is comparable to a hunt, so get it right and you won't go hungry…

PART 4

FACE-TO-FACE 2

(FROM THE

HANDSHAKE

ONWARDS)

Chapter 1

INTRODUCING YOURSELF WELL

One of a kind.

BUDDY RICH'S EPITAPH

> FAQ
>
> 'I hate the "Tell us a bit about yourself" question at the beginning of the interview. Where do I start? How long should I talk for? How much detail should I include?'

Getting off to a good start at a job interview is vital. Interviewers rely on first impressions as heavily as the next person, so if you come across as being overly nervous, inarticulate or a rambling, shambling speaker you are in big trouble. This chapter should more accurately be titled, *'Introducing yourself without boring them to tears'*. At the beginning of 99 per cent of all interviews, you will have to do a 'This is who I am and this is how I got here' speech. Interviewers will lead with a question reminiscent of the ones below:

- 'We've got a flavour for you from your CV/Application, but maybe you could give us a brief overview of your career to date.'
- 'Take us through your CV. In particular, we are interested in the reasons you had for making the choices that you did.'
- 'Take a couple of minutes please and bring us through your background and career.'

WHY DO THEY ASK THE QUESTION IN THE FIRST PLACE?

The whole idea of the Opener is to slide you into the process with an 'easy' question, but interviewers have a reason for *everything* they do and everything they ask and this question is no exception. Let's assume for a moment that the person who asked you the question *does* know what she is doing. Your answer to the Opener allows her to very quickly assess your:

- Level of confidence
- Overall intelligence
- Preparedness
- Ability to string coherent sentences together

This question equates to the 'What I did on my holidays' essay from your primary schooldays – it's predictable and it's easy. Or at least it should be. In many cases, I get the feeling that this question is an enormous effort for the candidate and that they have never really thought about summarising themselves and their career before.

It is also a Moment of Truth (see page 15). This is the first time you open your mouth and speak to your prospective new employer – apart from 'It's nice to meet you' – so you need to do this well. You also need to get through it quickly, and move on to the more useful elements of your Sales Pitch. You can't really sell yourself in response to this question; indeed many interviewers don't really listen carefully to your answer – they just want you to loosen up your vocal cords and get your backside comfortable on the chair.

CHIPMUNKS

So, if you *do* answer this one fluently and favourably, it nicely sets you apart from the pack at the outset and establishes the climate for the whole interview. Because this one is all about *you* and what goes on in *your head*, many candidates stutter and stumble their way through it. That is unforgivable! 'Oh, I hate talking about myself, I'm much better at talking about what I do,' is something I hear from a lot of clients. Tough, get over it. Remember that interviews are built around three questions:

- Can you do this job?
- Will you do this job well?
- Will you fit in here?

The last question is the most difficult to judge and, at interviews for senior positions, is the deciding factor more often than not. Being able to talk comfortably about yourself is a minimum entry requirement; as far as any interviewer is concerned, it's as fundamental as being able to read and write. So, get the chronology down on paper. Include all the big high points and moves from your education and career. Trim, trim, trim. Tailor the pitch to their areas of interest. Decide finally what to include and omit. Practise, practise, practise. Deliver. We are not talking rocket science here!

I would recommend that you have a 90-second version of this Opener and a 2-minute version. If you are going for a senior post, you can stretch that out to three or four minutes, but no more than that. Once again, tape or video yourself. How many words per minute do you speak at? Most people will use 170–190 words per minute in day-to-day conversation. JFK once addressed an audience at an extraordinary 327 words per minute in a speech, but very few people can speak anything like that quickly and portray themselves as being in any way reassuring and confident. Most of us would sound like a helium-voiced cartoon chipmunk going at that rate – hardly the sort of first impression you want to convey. Take it slowly – aim for 130–160 words per minute in your drafting. Write out a long version, including everything you want to say about yourself. Then you can start putting shape and discipline on it.

STRUCTURE

Beginning, middle, end. Pick your start point and work your way forward from there. Think about the reasons why you have done the things you did. Go back to your 360° exercise (see page 80). Review the compliments and feedbacks; one or two of them slotted into your opener will give it much more weight. Likewise your accomplishments – what were you good at, what got you noticed? What got you promoted? Were you ever singled out for extra responsibility? So:

- Why I made the choices I did
- Nice things that have been said about me
- Concrete stuff I did/accomplished
- 50–60 per cent of your allotted time spent on the last five years
- Spend that time on the last two years if you are coming out of formal education.

NO PRISONERS!

If there is something you want or need them to know about you from the outset, tell them. This is no time to be coy. Don't expect them to read between the lines – put it in between their eyes. If you were selected ahead of 999 others for a job and someone took a real risk in appointing you, a risk that paid off – *tell them*. Use simple words in short sentences and TELL THEM!

Many interviewers will not have scrutinised the beautifully phrased CV, which took you *hours* to finalise, in any depth. Some of them will be seeing it for the first time as you walk into the room. So be ready to talk really well about your history. No irrelevancies ('So what? Why is she telling me that?'), no weird tangents ('That was when I was into Satan worship'), no jumping back and forth in time ('Oh, and another thing about my first job…'). Logical, concise, articulate.

The other factor you need to avoid is the use of passive terminology – 'And then I found myself doing…' If you made a move, have a reason for it. It may not have been part of a Master Plan at the time, but if it sounds like you were being swept along with the tide, things will not go well for you as the interview unfolds.

DO THEM A FAVOUR

The second question asked in most interviews is either 'Why do you want to move on from your current role?' or 'Why do you want to work here?' I recommend that you round off your Opener with one or both of these answered and obviate the need for them to ask the second question. Clearly, they are concerned as to your motivation for leaving and, more importantly, for joining them. From the perspective that matters (i.e. the interviewer's) there are only a small number of legitimate and acceptable reasons for moving jobs:

- This is a better job/better organisation. (*More money, greater responsibility, better promotional prospects.*)
- My current job is temporary/contract and my time is nearly up. (*So why aren't they renewing your contract? Careful!*)
- My current job location is **seriously** inconvenient. (*This is becoming an acceptable answer as commuting becomes more and more of a nightmare.*)
- Lack of security in my current job – impending closure, take-over or similar.
- I was made redundant. (*Just you or everyone in your department? Local problems or international restructuring? Think about the inferences that the interviewers will draw from your statements.*)
- I got fired. (*This should be fun to try and explain.*)

The reason that no one *ever* states for wanting to move on is: 'I am experiencing a clash of personalities with my boss/a colleague.' This is frequently the root cause of a career move (see page 40, Silverbacks), but it is an absolute can of worms. Even if this is true in your situation, I do not recommend going down that road.

Reasons for wanting to join a new organisation are as widely varied as the stars in the sky. Do you have a real reason or is it just because they advertised? Slipshod, poorly prepared candidates typically witter on at interview about how wonderful the new company is – what I refer to as the 'Ooh, you are so big and brave and strong' answer. This approach will not score you very many points.

'Why do you want to join *us*, rather than the organisation next door?' would be a more accurate way of wording the question – it gives the interviewer some indication as to the depth of your preparation for the meeting. How you frame your answer to this question is going to be dependent on your real motivation and on the quality of your research. You could work for Apple, Dell, IBM or HP doing *exactly* the same work but only be really happy in the organisation whose corporate culture and values match your own. Do not fly blind on this oh-so-crucial issue.

There is no advantage in getting bogged down on the opening questions. An overview of your career and discussions on your motivation for moving on don't really give you any opportunity to sell yourself, so you should closely examine your real reasons and think very carefully about your approach to this one – your 'exit story' reveals a great deal about your attitudes and motivations to a skilful interviewer. The opening questions are an important element in the mix for them, but they just want reassurance. They are a relatively unimportant element in the mix for *you* as all you can offer is reassurance rather than a big chunky selling point.

IN CONTROL

Some version of the Opener happens at almost every interview. You know it is coming and they know that you know it is coming; so a bad start really is reprehensible. For a few brief moments, you are totally in control in the interview room (see page 16, The Graph of Control). Do not look that gift horse in the mouth. You can demonstrate that you are a logical, concise and articulate person with sound motivation – wouldn't that be a nice first impression to plant in their heads? If you have laid your groundwork and developed the agenda that you want to put forward at the interview (see page 193, Interview Mapping), then you can set the tenor and really start to bring control back on to your side of the table.

Chapter 2

TALKING ABOUT WEAKNESSES

FAQ

'What the hell am I supposed to say when they ask me what my weaknesses are?'

The subject of personal quirks, weaknesses, past failures, regrets and disasters is one which most candidates would prefer to gloss over during an interview. Which is precisely, of course, why interviewers *love* to home in on it:

- 'What are your weaknesses?'
- 'List your three biggest failings.'
- 'What do you regard as a failure or disappointment in your career to date?'
- 'How will you spend your personal training budget this year?'
- 'If you could change something in your life, what would it be?'
- 'What developmental needs were addressed at your last appraisal?'
- 'If I asked your colleagues what your biggest weakness is, what would they tell me?'

All essentially the same question, all homing in on everything that is worst about you – what a ghastly process! There you are in your newly purchased interview suit, with your shiniest shoes on, doing your best to sound credible, professional and enthusiastic, and all the interviewer wants to do is lift up stones and see what crawls out. Why? What are they really looking for when they ask this question? They don't *seriously* expect you to reveal your darkest secrets, do they?

RESORTING TO CLICHÉS

No, not really. Some naïve candidates *do* bare their souls in response to this sort of questioning (especially with sympathetic, genial interviewers) but most people skirt around the issue or trot out a clichéd response that they heard in the pub or read in an article:

'Oh, I suppose I'm a bit of a perfectionist.'
'I'm a workaholic and that can irritate my workmates sometimes.'
'I don't suffer fools gladly.'

WHY DO THEY BOTHER ASKING?

Interviewers hear these answers about as often as the police hear 'Is this really a 30mph zone, Officer? I didn't realise…' and a well-trained interviewer will take a very dim view indeed if you have the temerity to come out with this sort of rubbish. So, what do they expect? What are they trying to find out about you with this question? In a nut-shell:

- Do you have self-knowledge?
- Are you sufficiently confident to admit to a weakness in this professional setting?
- Have you listened to criticism in the past?
- Are you open to it now?
- Are you smug or complacent about your failings?
- What have you learnt from your mistakes?

KNOW THYSELF...

> 'People learn from their failures. Seldom do they learn anything from success.'
>
> HAROLD GENEEN

Nearly every job these days is going to require some level of communication on your part. In order to communicate effectively in the workplace, win the respect of your colleagues and be an effective member of the team, you have to (a) know your job and (b) know yourself. The weaknesses probe begins to assess whether or not you are a self-questioning sort of person, whether or not there is any depth to you and, ultimately, whether or not you know what's going on inside your own skull.

If you have an interview coming up shortly and you don't have a strong answer to this question that is based on fact, you need to do a little soul-searching. Failing that, ask your partner/spouse. Spouses are *always* ready to point out your failings and need very little encouragement to do so. Talk to friends and family. Ask them to tell you three strong points and one weakness about yourself. Tell them to do you the favour of being brutally honest. Do the same with colleagues from past jobs, or better yet, an old boss of yours (see page 80, 360°). Psychotherapists charge a *fortune* to help you along this sort of voyage of self discovery; the information is there for free, if you have the courage to ask for it.

ACHILLES' HEEL

Look at those things you prevaricate on. Items you consistently shy away from doing. Those parts of your job that you just don't enjoy, feel inadequate performing, or know in your heart of hearts that others do better. What about something that you would love to get training in to make that sense of inadequacy go away? Build a list of these Achilles' heels. Think about things that used to be a problem for you in the past, but that you have gained a measure of confidence in now. Look at how you gained that confidence or redressed the problem. These insights will form the nucleus of your answer on this most awful of topics.

The weakness question also assesses your open-mindedness, your willingness to accept constructive criticism about your professional performance and, by extension, where you lie on a scale of smug to driven. Many candidates have some degree of insight and are sufficiently confident (or cocky!) to admit a failing at interview, but will then smile at the interviewer and wait for the next question. ('Weaknesses? Well, I suppose I *do* have a bit of a big mouth and people do frequently misunderstand me.') BIG mistake.

HEAL THYSELF...

The unspoken heart of the weakness question is this: 'What are you doing about it?' If you fail to address this to the interviewer's satisfaction, it is *extremely* unlikely that you will be offered the job. So be prepared to open up a bit. No matter how catastrophic your performance has been in the past, if you can demonstrate that you learnt from a mistake and that you are now more effective because of it, the interviewer will be more inclined to mentally put a big tick next to your name.

Research indicates that human beings make poor decisions up to 60 per cent of the time. You do it, I do it and interviewers do it every day – we get things wrong. The key, in a professional setting, is to retrieve or amend the bad decision before it turns into a disaster worthy of a based-on-a-true-story, made-for-television mini-series. And if you can't fix it, you'd *damn* well better learn from the ensuing cataclysm.

I attended a martial arts tournament some years ago and overheard a venerable Chinese gentleman watching two black belts sparring. One of them was totally outclassed and was being hit every few seconds on his left cheek. The old gentleman sighed and said, '*There are three kinds of people under Heaven. Those who never learn from their mistakes, those who learn from their own mistakes and those who learn from the mistakes of others.*' If you owned the organisation, which kind of person would you hire?

> 'Anyone who has never made a mistake has never tried anything new.'
> ALBERT EINSTEIN

Chapter 3

ASKING THEM QUESTIONS

> *Questions are never indiscreet. Answers sometimes are.*
>
> **OSCAR WILDE**

FAQ

'They always ask if I have any questions at the end of the interview, but I'm afraid to get too pushy, so I usually just say, "No". Is it okay to actually ask them questions?'

At some point in the interview process, someone inevitably smiles at you and says, 'I am sure you must have some questions for us?' Most candidates *hate* this part of the interview, regard it as being very difficult to do at the end of a tiring, stressful process and just trot out one or two trite little questions that utterly fail to impress the interviewer(s). And that last point is the key – if you have intelligent, well-researched questions to ask, you have yet another chance to impress the powers-that-be and distinguish yourself from the herd.

BOO-BOOS

The most common mistakes made at this juncture are:

- Having no questions to ask at all (either due to memory loss, tiredness, lack of preparation or because they answered any concerns you had as the interview progressed).
- Asking self-serving questions about salary, benefits, working hours, training, holidays, etc.
- Asking clichéd questions.

It is inappropriate to bring up remuneration at a preliminary interview, unless the interviewer does so first. If you are not supposed to bring up salary, then asking how big your company car is going to be is NOT a good idea. Likewise training – if you are going for an entry-level position straight out of formal education, your research should have answered any basic questions you have about induction and training. If you are going for a more senior role and start harping on about training, you will position yourself as (at best) self-serving or (at worst) needy.

WHY DO THEY INVITE QUESTIONS?

So, how should you play this one? The starting point is to look at it from their perspective – why do they ask *this* question of *all* candidates? It would be understandable if they just asked it of those they were about to hire, but they don't – *everyone* gets asked this one. So clearly, it tells the interviewer(s) more about you which can help them in the weeding-out/selection process. What, then, does it tell them?

- Baldly and simply, it signifies that the back-and-forth part of the interview is over.
- It allows them to cross-check your answers as to why you want to work for the organisation in the first place (usually asked very early in the interview).
- It helps to identify (or confirm) self-serving candidates who are look-

ing to join the organisation, extract as much training and good experience as they can out of it for their CV and then quickly jump ship.

- Likewise ill-prepared candidates. This question helps the interviewer to assess the level and quality of your preparation for the interview – very important these days. If you won't work hard in preparing for interview on your *own* behalf (and here, we again make the not unreasonable assumption that you do actually care about yourself), what chance is there that you will prepare well for an important element of the job on *their* behalf? This is an obvious question. You know they are going to ask it. What do you mean you don't have some decent questions ready to ask? You *obviously* don't care whether or not you get the job – what else are they supposed to think?

- If you are being interviewed for a mid-ranking or senior position, the questions that you ask enable the interviewer(s) to assess your professional mindset. Are you a general or a foot-soldier. Do you have management potential? In other words, are you a player?

ARCHAEOLOGY

Your research (see page 162, Research) in preparation for this key question should, as always, be comprehensive.

- Company literature, websites, advertising and annual reports are all easily obtainable. Unfortunately, your competitors for the job will also be able to get hold of this information, so you *must* go further.
- You should also obtain the same sort of material for the organisation's key competitors.
- At the next level comes promotional material, articles about the organisation, broad-based industry articles and legislation or regulatory changes affecting the sector and/or organisation.
- Personal contacts – someone you know knows someone who is useful. Ex-employees, competitors, suppliers, industry figures, journalists, representative bodies. Track them down and talk to them (see page 168, Networking).

All too often I hear, 'Oh, I couldn't find anyone who worked for them to find out what sort of organisation they are...' Not good enough. DIG! Talk to *anyone* you can get hold of on the supply chain in your chosen sector: from providers of raw material/data, through the organisation itself and its competitors, through the distribution channel to customers/clients.

Prior to compiling your questions, you should re-assess your reasons for wanting the job in the first instance. Is it a stepping stone for you or a long-term career move with solid development prospects? Balance your ambitions against what you now know of the organisation. Do they genuinely try to attract and retain the brightest people or do they, in reality, operate a 'revolving door' policy? Type up your questions and keep them handy, so that when the inevitable moment comes, you can smile back and say, 'Yes, I do have some questions...'

A *caveat* here – some poorly trained interviewers ask this question as a *pro forma* exercise and don't expect you to have any meaningful questions. You will need to gauge the response to your first question before deciding to plough on.

POINTS ON ASKING QUESTIONS

- Keep it short. Remember who is interviewing whom...
- LISTEN to the interviewer's response. Amazingly enough, many candidates fail to do this.
- Don't ask thorny, issue-driven questions of placement agencies or personnel staff – it is unlikely that they will know the answers and you may just make them feel uncomfortable.
- If you have listened during the interview, they will probably have already answered some of your questions. Tick them off and don't go over old ground, unless you need further clarification.
- If they *have* answered your questions in the course of the discussion, this can be an opportunity for you to demonstrate your listening skills and learning curve – mention the item that the interviewer covered earlier on and follow up with a question on it.

- Watch the interviewer's body language as they ask if you have any questions. If they are shuffling their papers and have broken eye contact with you, the interview is over and they want to go home. Hitting them with a string of issue-driven questions at this juncture would be a bad idea. If, on the other hand, the interviewer has his pen poised to take notes and is sitting forward expectantly, you had better have some juicy issues to raise (see page 288, Body Talk).

SAMPLE QUESTIONS TO ASK

- Home in on new strategies, markets, products and technologies. If the organisation doesn't seem to have any, ask why, or mention from your research that a competitor seems to have the edge now and what is the organisation doing about it?
- If you *are* talking to a line manager – issues, issues, issues. Legislative or regulatory changes. New industry bodies or watchdogs. Impending mergers/take-overs. Big changes in the marketplace. New entrants to the sector. All good, meaty stuff.
- How has the vacancy arisen? Is the job newly created or has the incumbent been promoted, left the organisation (why?) or retired? (It is obviously to your advantage to have answered this question in advance of the interview. *Then* you can see if the interviewer(s) tell the truth when they answer you…)
- Evaluations and measurement – what method does the organisation use to measure performance and/or productivity? What constitutes success in this organisation/role?
- Ask the interviewer what he thinks makes the organisation a good place to work – ask him, without being smug, why you should come and work for them and what you can expect. The themes of career progression and personal development also come in here.
- '*I see from the newspapers/your literature/annual report/website that you are expanding/contracting/evolving into* (whatever it might be). *How will this affect the* (job or department) *that I am moving into?*'
- Finally, you can use this question as an opportunity to slip in an extra Nugget or two about yourself – '*We didn't really cover the area of XXX*

in the course of the interview. I'd just like to mention my involvement with...' (see page 196, Nuggets).

> **'I do not feel obliged to believe that the same Lord who has endowed us with sense, reason and intellect has intended us to forego their use.'**
> GALILEO

Sitting there like a rabbit trapped in the headlights at the end of the interview does not exactly convey the impression of someone who is in control. This is your last chance to impress upon them your suitability for the role. Don't waste it.

Chapter 4

TYPES OF INTERVIEW...

> *I keep six honest serving-men*
>
> *(They taught me all I knew);*
>
> *Their names are What and Why and When*
>
> *And How and Where and Who.*
>
> **RUDYARD KIPLING IN *JUST SO STORIES***

All sorts of interviewers use all sorts of weird and wonderful questions to find out if you are the perfect candidate. Below, I have outlined the broad and predictable lines of questioning with my detailed thoughts for each one in the following chapter.

THE CLASSICAL 20 QUESTIONS BIOGRAPHICAL INTERVIEW

This style of interview is rarely used in isolation any more – rather it will form part of the modern selection process. Used in isolation, it tells the interviewer relatively little, but it *can* uncover attitudes and motivations quite well and a skilful interviewer will cross-reference your answers to these probes with your responses to other lines of questioning to build a picture of you.

- Tell me about yourself.
- Why do you want to leave your current job/company?
- What attracted you to this job/industry OR this company?
- What are your strengths?
- What are your weaknesses?
- How would you describe yourself? OR Describe yourself with four to six adjectives.
- How would you approach this job?
- Tell me about your hobbies.
- What interests you most in your work? OR What motivates you?
- What aspect of your current job do you most dislike? And why?
- Do you prefer to work in a team or on your own?
- *How* do you work in a team? What style do you adopt?
- Describe how you would typically approach a project or task.
- How would your workmates/colleagues describe you?
- Where do you plan to be in five years' time?
- Describe your ideal boss OR ideal job.
- What do you view as your greatest success to date?
- What has been your worst failure/biggest disappointment to date?
- What particular qualities do you feel you will bring to this job that the other candidates won't?
- I'm sure you must have some questions for me.

OTHER QUESTIONS THAT ARE FREQUENTLY ASKED IN A BIOGRAPHICAL INTERVIEW

- Have you ever had a serious disagreement with your boss or a colleague? Over what? How was it resolved?
- If I asked your current boss for a reference, what would she say about you? OR How did you fare in your last performance appraisal?
- What is your management style? OR How do you get the best out of people?
- In your opinion, what is the biggest problem facing this organisation/ sector? How has it come about and what would you do to resolve it?

- What were your career plans five years ago? OR How have you changed in the last five years?
- You seem a little overqualified for this job.
- You seem a little underqualified for this job.
- You don't seem to have much experience in (*select appropriate deficiency*).
- What other jobs have you applied for recently?
- (Follow-on from '*Where do you plan to be in five years' time?*') How do you plan to get there?

AWKWARD AND NASTY QUESTIONS – STRESS INTERVIEWS

The stress interview has fallen out of favour as a method of hiring as it has been demonstrated over time to simply not work. That being said, this style can occasionally be useful to make a cocksure candidate squirm under the hot lights just to see how he deals with a high-pressure situation – particularly if the job under discussion is of a similarly high-pressure nature. Platform testing (see page 322) has now largely superseded the stress interview as a means of measuring a candidate's ability to perform under adverse conditions.

Interviewers may also use these tougher (sometimes bordering on offensive) questions to test your veracity. If you have been 'flexible' with the truth and they have discerned conflicting signals from your mouth and body, you can expect a few zingers to be flung at you.

The key thing to keep in mind if you find yourself on the back foot and scrabbling for an answer is that *this isn't personal*. The interviewer is merely playing games with you and (unless she's a complete fool) there's a reason for the game-playing. One point of solace here – no interviewer is going to waste their time dressing down a no-hoper. If you are feeling the pressure mounting, it is a strong signal that the other side are taking you seriously.

Don't look at the question head-on. Try and determine why it has been asked. This holds true for almost every question in the interview setting, but it is vital if you feel the interviewer is tightening the screws.

So, slow it down, use your breathing (see page 390), look behind the question and answer with the maximum of aplomb and the minimum of flap.

- (*If the interviewer notices something on your CV that you were hoping to gloss over…*) I see you took longer than usual to gain qualification A – why was that? OR I see that you have a gap of X months between job B and job C – what were you doing in that time? OR Why did you leave job D after such a short time?
- What have you heard about this organisation/me on the grapevine?
- If you caught a colleague cheating on his or her expenses, what would you do?
- How do you feel this interview is going?
- What would you do if you won the lottery and didn't need to work?
- Okay, I don't feel like we're really getting to the heart of the matter here. You're very polished and glib and the clichés are coming out thick and fast, but the mask is still up. Let's start again. Tell me what *really* makes you tick…

COMPETENCY-BASED INTERVIEWS

This procedure-driven approach to interviewing has become increasingly prevalent across the spectrum of organisation types for a number of reasons:

- By focusing on your approach and process, it allows the interviewer to determine if you really did achieve all the successes you claim on your CV and, more importantly, how. Competency-based Interviewing (CBI) is all about identifying transferable skills and attitudes (more so than knowledge) and the processes/methods you apply in order to fulfil your job.
- Structured, competency-based selection techniques have a better track record of identifying the soundest candidate rather than the candidate who merely sounds best. A bad hiring decision nowadays can be immensely expensive for an organisation – cost of the hire,

training costs, severance pay, loss of productivity, impact on morale, cost of re-hiring, etc. (Plus, it can be very difficult and usually quite time-consuming to get rid of an underperforming employee.)

- With an increasing level of litigation, organisations (particularly in the public sector) now need to be able to show irrefutably why they selected one candidate ahead of another. This is a *total* nuisance for the organisation, but if a candidate decides to take an action over whatthey felt was an unjustified disqualification from the hiring process, the hiring organisation needs to have all their ducks in a row. Competency-based interviewing material allows for speedy, accurate note-taking and also includes scoring for each of the key areas examined.

If you are genuinely good at what you do and comfortable talking about how you approach work-related situations and problems, competency-based interviews will present no difficulties for you. But very few people can do that off the cuff.

> **'If you think competence is expensive, try incompetence.'**
> **FROM A TRAINING BROCHURE**

Despite the fact that we talk about our working lives so much of the time, we very rarely have to elucidate our approach or justify the work that we do to knowledgeable outsiders. In preparing, you must focus in on the core skills required in your current position and for the new position. It's not good enough to just be competent at something – you need to be ready to talk about what *makes* you competent.

Questioning will either be *hypothetical* ('how **would** you deal with situation X?') or based on *historical* examples from your current or pre-vious experience ('when such-and-such a situation arose, how **did** you deal with it?'). In either case, the interviewer is interested in (a) your process and (b) the values and mindset that you brought to the process. It goes without saying that they are also *very* interested in how it all worked out – you may have a really excellent, logical and inclusive approach to problem-solving and bring wonderful values to the work-place, but if you can't solve the problem, you are no good to anyone...

STRUCTURED, COMBINATION INTERVIEWS

These intersperse elements from a biographical interview with probes on the most common areas of the competency framework required by employers. The interviewers are supplied with a grid that is structured in such a way as to facilitate note-taking by them (many interviewers using this material would simply tick or circle the positive or negative areas expressed by the candidate) and will typically have a fifth column for scoring.

QUESTIONS	POSITIVES	NEGATIVES	COMMENTS	SCORE
Classification Carefully and very specifically scripted question. Obviates the need for the interviewer to come up with her own questions and also precludes 'leading' or illegal questions.	This column highlights the good stuff that they are hoping to find in you. Typically, this is a little buzzwordy, but that's the world in which we now live...	Too many ticks in this column and they'll be mentally composing a *Dear John* letter to you as the interview progresses.	This column will either be used for note-taking or there may be a sting-in-the-tail drill-down probe suggested for the interviewer to use.	

QUESTION HEADINGS

Here are the major questions, broken out by key heading. As you would expect, a number of the questions appear under multiple headings.

VALUES/MOTIVATION

- Why do you want to move on from your current role? Why do you want to work in (*insert organisation name*) in particular rather than the organisation next door?
- What do you see as being the key functions for the role of an (*insert job title*)?
- What aspect of your current job do you most dislike?
- What interests you most in your career? Why did you choose this kind of work and what aspect of it do you find most satisfying?
- How will you approach this role? What will be your priorities on the job?
- If you could choose your boss, what sort of person would he or she be?
- What has been your greatest success/proudest moment to date?
- Conversely, what do you regard as the greatest failure or disappointment in your career to date? Anything you would change?
- What other positions have you applied for recently?
- I'm sure you must have some questions for me/us.

SELF KNOWLEDGE/STRENGTHS/WEAKNESSES

- Would you rate yourself as average, strong or exceptional in your current/most recent job?
- What makes you so good at what you do?
- What will the aptitude and psychometric testing show as your biggest weakness? What training/development will you be looking for?
- How would you describe yourself? Four to six adjectives?
- How would your colleagues/boss/subordinates describe you?
- We have had a high level of application for this post, and we have a pool of highly experienced, highly qualified candidates to choose from. What do you believe marks you out as the best candidate for this job?

COMPETENCE: COPING/CONFLICT

- How do you cope with the strict, unreasonable or conflicting dead-lines/quality requirements/customer demands that are so much part of the job? Give me a specific example.
- Tell me about a situation where you had to stand by a decision even though it made you very unpopular.
- Give me an example of a time when a colleague/boss/customer really tried your patience and took a 180° opposing view to yours. How did you resolve the impending conflict?

COMPETENCE: DECISION-MAKING

- Tell me about a time when you had to make a quick decision on an important matter/process.
- How did it arise and what was the outcome?
- Tell me about a situation where you had to stand by a decision even though it made you very unpopular.

COMPETENCE: PLANNING/ORGANISING

- Time management has become a necessary factor in personal productivity. Give me an example of any time management skill you have learned and applied at work.
- We are required to document our processes very thoroughly here. Tell me about your experiences with ISO/FOI/Kite marks (*insert appropriate regulation or system*). Do you find it/them useful?
- What is your long-term career plan (a) if you are appointed to this position; (b) if you are not successful?
- How will you approach this role? What will be your priorities on the job?

COMPETENCE: COMMUNICATION

- Tell me about a situation where you had to stand by a decision even though it made you very unpopular.
- This job constantly tests your verbal communication skills. Tell me how you ensure that others understand you fully – particularly in stressful situations.
- This job will also require you to make a considerable number of pre-sentations. Tell me about how you prepare for and deliver your ideas in a presentation setting.
- What has been your experience of giving instruction/training to another person? (Management, training or coaching situations...)
- Would you say that listening is an important part of the/your commu-nication process?
- How would you rate your ability as a listener?
- We are required to document our processes very thoroughly here. Tell me about your experiences with ISO/FOI/Kite marks (*insert appropriate regulation or system*). Do you find it/them useful?

COMPETENCE: INNOVATION/PROBLEM-SOLVING

- Would you describe yourself as an innovative person? Give us an example of something particularly innovative that you have done that made a difference in the workplace.
- In general, what is your approach to problem-solving?
- Give me a specific example of something you did that built enthusi-asm within a team you were working with or managing.
- What would you say is the biggest issue/problem facing (*insert organisation name*), how has it come about and what would you do about it if we hire you/promote you?

COMPETENCE: KNOWLEDGE ACQUISITION

- Your CV seems a bit light in (*insert appropriate shortcoming*) OR
- Is there any aspect of the job in which you feel under-qualified/experienced? How quickly can you get up to speed on this, should the need arise?

COMPETENCE: LEADERSHIP

- What has been your experience of giving instruction/training to another person? (Management, training or coaching situations...)
- What is your approach to mentoring?
- How do you get the best out of your staff?
- Would you say that listening is an important part of the/your communication process?
- What would you say is the biggest issue/problem facing (*insert organisation name*), how has it come about and what would you do about it if we hire you/promote you?
- Give me a specific example of something you did that built enthusiasm within a team you were working with or managing.
- What is your long-term career plan (a) if you are appointed to this position; (b) if you are not successful?
- How will you approach this role? What will be your priorities on the job?

TEAM FIT/SKILLS

- Do you prefer to work in a team or on your own?
- What do you see as the advantages of working in a team?
- *How* do you work in a team? What sort of role do you typically like to adopt?
- Do you have a back-up style?
- Give me a specific example of something you did that built enthusiasm within a team you were working with or managing.
- How would your colleagues/boss/subordinates describe you?

FINANCE

- What has been your experience to date of managing a budget? **If none:** What will be your approach to setting and managing your budget here?

Chapter 5

THE NIGHTMARE INTERVIEW FROM HELL

Inquisition, **n**. Protracted period of intensive questioning or investigation, official inquiry. Tribunal for the suppression of heresy.
Inquisitor, **n**. A person making an inquiry or conducting an inquisition, particularly when regarded as harsh or especially searching. A person in a very good suit relentlessly probing you about your weaknesses and your five-year career plans.
(*Okay, I made that last bit up, but the rest of it sounds familiar, doesn't it?*)

ANSWERING QUESTIONS – MONOLOGUE OR DIALOGUE?

A skilled interviewer will engage in a cut-and-thrust with you as the interview progresses. A good balance of talking time for a middle-ranking role is one third them and two thirds you; so if your answering style is dependent on you 'ploughing through' each answer from beginning to end with no interruptions, you are not going to thrive in a modern interview.

What about the shy/too quiet interviewer? You should encourage a reticent interviewer to keep talking (a) verbally with questions and dialogue and (b) non-verbally with open, inviting signals (see page 288, Body Talk). The more they talk, the more ammunition you garner, which enables you to tighten your approach. That being said, you *are* the person under the spotlight, so it is appropriate that you be ready to talk fluently and comfortably about your history, your motivations, your accomplishments and your approach in the workplace.

Other end of the scale – the interviewer who just won't shut up. They keep on talking about what a wonderful place this is to work and don't really let you get a word in edgeways to sell yourself. This truly is an *awful* situation, usually stemming from an uninterested, nervous or badly trained interviewer. Your approach:

1 Demonstrate interest and patience. Don't let your body language signal your irritation.
2 You will need to break the cardinal rule of interviews and interrupt the interviewer. Don't do this with a sales point, rather do it with a question that allows you to gently move into the driver's seat.
3 If you are being hit with closed questions (the kind of questions that demand 'yes' or 'no' answers) make sure you *immediately* follow your monosyllabic answer with an explanation as to **why** this is your approach, **how** it has worked for you in the past and **why** this makes you different/special/wonderful.
4 Keep asking questions as the interview progresses and start moving the process into dialogue, where you and the interviewer are sharing experiences and discussing the optimal approach to specific problems or issues.

HOW LONG IS LONG ENOUGH?

How long should you talk on any one question? The biggest sin that most candidates commit is talking too little (closely followed by the sin of verbal diarrhoea). Read any of the big questions, starting on page 241, look at the positives that they are hoping to find and then read my comments below them. You simply *can't* compress an answer on, say, the key issue facing an organisation or your approach to managing your subordinates, into 30 seconds. You are immediately inviting a follow-on question and, after a few repetitions of this, the interviewer is going to feel like he is kneeling on your chest pulling teeth rather than conducting a selection interview. An interested, competent and sympathetic inter-viewer will draw a taciturn candidate out – for a while. Poorly trained interviewers, or those who are near the end of the process and believe they have already found the ideal candidate, will not engage you at all. They will write down your too-short answer and move on, and the longer the interview lasts, the less chance you have of impressing them. So how long is long enough? As a broad guideline:

- **List-type answers** (*'What are your strengths?' 'How would you describe yourself?' 'How would your boss characterise you?'*) require 20–40 seconds to answer.
- **Opinion answers** (*'What has been the biggest change in this sector in the last five years?' 'Do you think that X approach or Y approach is better in handling industrial relations issues?'*) require a very short, considered answer, followed by a longer justification/rationalisation – maybe 2 minutes in all.
- **Reassurance questions** (the questions that probe your reasons for doing the things you have or that are merely 'check-list' items) need satisfactory answers and the challenge for you is to compress every-thing that they need to hear into the minimum timeframe. Try not to spend more than 90 seconds to 2 minutes on these. Kill the subject off and move on.
- **BIG questions** demand long, essay-type answers – up to 4 minutes for entry and mid-level positions; as long as it takes for senior posts.

The name of the game is providing complete answers in the tightest timeframe possible. Brevity will always be appreciated; paucity will not. The interview map (see page 193) is your most important tool here – it will ensure that you are not deviating from the message and that there is consistency in your approach.

Put yourself under the spotlight and get used to this kind of scrutiny; you will be facing it *many* times in your career, so you might as well get comfortable with the process.

BUILDING AN ANSWER – AN EXAMPLE

An example, to illustrate: you are asked a competency question about your approach to resolving conflicts. No doubt you have had many conflictual situations in your working life, but which one is best to use in answering this question? If you were hit with this question on the fly in an interview, you *might* come up with an example that showed your skills off to best advantage, but you could just as easily blow it.

Far better to have done the work in advance. Sit and think it out. Unless you are the reincarnated spirit of Mahatma Gandhi, it is unlikely that your early efforts at conflict resolution were entirely successful; so pick recent and pertinent examples to consider – say six to eight situations. Rank them in order of the ones that you solved best. Then rank them on a separate piece of paper in terms of the ones that mattered most to your employer or the organisation as a whole. Hopefully, there is some correlation here and you can talk about a meaty conflict that impacted on a whole division, department or project and which you had a large part in bringing to resolution. Now think again about all of your examples – *how* did you go about bringing the parties (including yourself) together? Was your process consistent across all the examples or did it vary? Did you:

- Remain solution-focused throughout the process?
- Maintain emotional control, setting aside your personal feelings (no matter how strong), and get on with solving the problem?
- Look for points of agreement between the parties?
- Listen really carefully and closely monitor the non-verbal cues, checking to see reaction to moves on both sides?
- Suggest minor (or major) concessions from one or both parties?
- Seek reciprocity from the other party following a concession?
- Attempt to gain substantial satisfaction for all concerned?
- Enable comfortable working relationships to continue after the issue was resolved?

Once that work is done, you can look at how the conflicts arose in the first place – is there anything you can learn here or do better the next time? Now you are in a position to pick and hone your answer according to the SPOUT Model.

THE SPOUT MODEL

A beginning/middle/end structure to your answers is essential – **S**ituation, **P**rocess, **O**utcome (SPOUT) – and delivering these answers well requires a great deal of meticulous preparation. An excellent way to prepare and practise for competency-based interview questioning is to write your answers out, using the SPOUT Model (see page 402, Appendix 1), and reverse engineer your approach – start from the most positive outcomes, pick your examples accordingly and use these as the basis for your answers. When you have each answer roughed out in long form, distil it down to a 3x5-inch card – if you can't make it fit, you probably need to do more trimming (see page 65, the 'So What?' rule).

THE WHOLE ENCHILADA

Here is the whole hellish interview, laid out as the interviewer would have it, with my thoughts or comments following each question. I have deliberately not provided 'pat' juicy phrases or pre-scripted answers as you will merely sound like every other person who has read this book and will disqualify yourself from consideration with this sort of copycat approach.

Do the work, take the time and build answers that are (a) true, (b) cogent and (c) sell your most desirable attributes. You *must* take the time and trouble to map yourself and your abilities out against the jobs you are applying for in this way. A parroted recitation of a scripted set of answers will be quickly discerned as such by any skilled interviewer. If you really want their job, be prepared for the work that is involved in getting it...

QUESTIONS	POSITIVES	NEGATIVES	COMMENTS
Opener We've got a flavour for you from your CV; but maybe you could give us a quick précis of your career to date.	Logical delivery. Concise. Articulate.	Irrelevancies/ waffling. Passive terms. Unprepared.	

The reliable old opener – see page 209, Introducing Yourself Well. Remember, this is a moment of truth, you will be asked to do this more often than not and you'd *better* get off to a good start. Make sure your answer is structured, brief and relevant. During the Gold Rush, land-owners used to 'salt the mine' by putting small amounts of gold dust at the entrance to a mine they were trying to sell. You should also salt the mine by including a couple of Nuggets as you go, to prompt questions on the good stuff that *you* want to talk about later.

QUESTIONS	POSITIVES	NEGATIVES	COMMENTS
Motivation Why do you want to move on from your current role? Why do you want to work in (*insert organisation name*) in particular rather than the organisation next door?	Better job. Better organisation. Professional approach – research. Realistic expectations. Balance of needs.	Lack of security. Fired. Personality clash. '*Big, brave and strong.*' '*Gizzajob, I can do dat…*'	Redundancy. Temporary/ contract. Location.

Unless you are being headhunted, they will *always* ask this question, in some shape or form. It's a reassurance question, but many people just don't take the opportunity to answer it well. Alan Bleasdale's '*Gizzajob, go on gizzit!*' is not really what they're looking for, nor is '*Well you advertised, didn't you?*'

For younger candidates graduating from formal education, this question quickly elicits the level of knowledge that you have gained about the organisation. The '*Oooh, your organisation is so big and brave and strong*' approach will win you very few points. Talk about the research you have conducted, the kinds of people you have spoken to, and the opinions you have formed as a result.

Your answer as to why you want to move on should address what is lacking in your current employment (if it was perfect you wouldn't be attending this interview) and what you expect to find in this new organisation. They shouldn't have to ask you this – you know that it is coming, so round off your previous answer(s) with your reasons for wanting to leave your current organisation. You will need to have completed some choice research to answer this one well. It's an early opportunity to mark yourself out from the crowd; don't waste it (see page 209, Introducing Yourself Well).

QUESTIONS	POSITIVES	NEGATIVES	COMMENTS
Strengths/Self Knowledge Would you rate yourself as average, strong or exceptional in your current/most recent job? What makes you so good at what you do?	Concise? Relevant?	Irrelevant? Obvious weaknesses?	What does the *candidate* think are his/her important qualities?

Keep this very short and punchy – bullet point your answer – as they are not looking for evidence of each strength at this stage. List 'em off, unless you are interrupted with a *'Can you expand on that?'* question.

And *please*, keep it relevant to the job under discussion – yammering on about how kind you are to children and animals is fine, as long as you're going for a job as a Paediatrician or a Vet. Sorry to state the obvious here, but *stick to the point!* We all have *general* strengths, many of which are of zero interest to the prospective employer, so do a bit of thinking and stick to those points of brilliance that pertain to the new job.

QUESTIONS	POSITIVES	NEGATIVES	COMMENTS
Values/ Motivation What do you see as being the key functions for the role of an (*insert job title*)?	Quality of research. Depth of knowledge on the organisation. Depth of knowledge on the role. Match of strengths/experience to job requirements.	Reiteration of the advertisement?	

Subtext: *'Do you really know what this job entails?'* If you sincerely think you deserve the job, you will have an answer for this question. Don't just recite the recruitment advertisement back at them (or the job description) – do your digging, then sit and swivel on your chair thinking about what it would be like on the job and what you would be doing on a day-to-day basis.

For an excellent answer, take it a step further and think about what you would like to *achieve*. Structure your approach (IDI – **I**nquire, **D**ecide, **I**mplement) and, if you can, timeframe it (*'In my first 100 days...'*). Poorly prepared candidates or those who are merely chancing their arm tend to die a death when you ask them this question – they haven't envisaged themselves succeeding and it shows straight away.

QUESTIONS	POSITIVES	NEGATIVES	COMMENTS
Weakness What will the aptitude and psychometric testing show as your biggest weakness? What training/development will you be looking for?	Self knowledge? Confident to discuss? Remedial action?	Cliché. Evasive or irrelevant answer.	**Probe** And how does that affect your performance on the job?

Such a lame question and yet it still trips up so many candidates. Unless you are *completely* clueless, it won't be the answer you give that trips you up – it will be the drill-down.

Clichéd answer: '*Well, I'm a bit of a perfectionist and that sometimes irritates my colleagues.*'
Their drill-down: '*Really? And how exactly is that a weakness? Does it make you late for deadlines or impossible to work with?*'
Your (slightly panic-stricken) response: '*Oh no! Nothing like that.*'
Their smug follow-up: '*Well then it isn't really a weakness is it? See if you can think of something else…*'

Don't try to duck this question by talking about knowledge or technical gaps and avoid the clichés – talk about your awareness and self-development efforts. If you are coy in response to this line of questioning, they will either come after you with all guns blazing or write you off then and there (see page 215, Talking About Weaknesses).

QUESTIONS	POSITIVES	NEGATIVES	COMMENTS
Coping/Patience How do you cope with the strict, unreasonable or conflicting deadlines/quality requirements/ customer demands that are so much part of the job? Give me a specific example.	Good coping – positive, reasoned approach? Time management skills? Ability to distinguish priorities? Problem-solving skills?	Negative expression or language in talking about the pressure?	Results?
Decision-making/ Prioritising Tell me about a time when you had to make a quick decision on an important matter/process. How did it arise and what was the outcome?	Timely, effective and good outcome? What process/guidelines did the candidate use/follow?	Inaction, panic, bad decision? Ignoring procedure?	Outcome?

Two classical CBI questions (see page 228, Competency-based Interviews). The SPOUT model makes this kind of question much easier to field. The operative word in the second question is 'important'. Have a gander at the buzzwords in the 'positives' column – do you apply this kind of approach to the issues under discussion? Spend 10–20 per cent of your answer time on the Situation, 66–75 per cent on the Process and the remainder on the Outcome.

QUESTIONS	POSITIVES	NEGATIVES	COMMENTS
Planning/ Organising Time management has become a necessary factor in personal productivity. Give me an example of any time management skill you have learned and applied at work.	Sought training? Applied it? Conscious of the importance of deadlines/ prioritising? Strategic approach to time management across a variety of situations?	Repeated crises? Socialising/pleasant activities in work time? Little emphasis on productivity?	**Probe** What resulted from use of the skill?

Time management is a skill that very few people truly have. If this subject is a mystery to you, you should, at the very least, do some quick reading about it on the web. Psychologists consistently demonstrate that women are *far* better at multi-tasking than men. It all comes down to determining what is really important and being able to reduce a series of large projects or tasks to bite-size chunks and intermingle them with the day-to-day demands on your time. If you have that ability naturally, you will never starve – you can always get work as a plate-spinner in the circus. If you have had training or have done some reading on the subject, this question will pose no horrors for you.

But if your time management is not up to scratch, despite reading and training, and if your preference is for immersing yourself in one task at a time, you need to be *very* careful what sort of jobs you apply for…

QUESTIONS	POSITIVES	NEGATIVES	COMMENTS
Coping/Patience Give me an example of a time when a colleague/ boss/customer really tried your patience and took a 180° opposing view to yours. How did you resolve the impending conflict?	Mature approach? Ability to set aside personal difficulties and get a solution? Emotional control? Good understanding and ability to distance self from the conflict?	Repeated instances? Not learning from mistakes? Surrender? Withdrawal? Attacking? Unaware of impact of self on others?	Result?

The ability to resolve a conflict is prized by most employers. Even if the job you are applying for does not immediately or obviously require this skill, you may still be asked about it. As always, take a hard look at yourself – are you actually any good at doing this? I ask this because *veeeery* few of us really are. It requires vast reserves of patience, a great deal of maturity and the ability to climb into someone else's headspace.

Conflict resolution is all about being **solution-focused**. The big mistake that I see when inexperienced candidates answer this one is that they talk about *winning*. Conflict resolution is not about winning; crushing the other guy is about winning, but resolving conflictual situations is not. In an ideal world, we are looking for an outcome where both parties walk away not frowning (they may not be smiling, but they *definitely* should not be frowning). So, how do *you* accomplish this?

Attacking the other party, withdrawal from the process and sulking are not valid approaches and are noisy indicators of your lack of ability in this arena. Young children use an approach called 'tactical anger' to try and get their own way – otherwise known as a tantrum. They're not really angry at all, they have just learnt that screaming, biting and lying down pounding the floor with their hands and feet (preferably in a public place) gets them the ice-cream/sweetie/Barbie®/box of crayons/hamburger or whatever. This is generally not a recipe for success in adult conflicts, although I frequently encounter bullies in the corporate setting who are very much in touch with their inner child.

Maintaining a cool, calm and collected demeanour; striving for a solution and keeping your eye fixed on that target are a good start. Looking for points of commonality/agreement is another key element in the mix. Concessions and reciprocation plus being able to understand and iterate the opposing side's argument(s) are useful too. But the bottom line is compromise – you have to be prepared to walk away with a 'win' rather than a 'WIN!' which could prejudice further discussions and your future working relationship with the other party.

QUESTIONS	POSITIVES	NEGATIVES	COMMENTS
Decision-making/ Communication Tell me about a situation where you had to stand by a decision even though it made you very unpopular.	Stuck to principle/ procedure? Considered impact of the decision and how best to break the news?	Impulsive? Poor judgement in the first place? Pride? Rushed?	On what was this important decision based?

This is actually something of a trick question. It looks more to your skills in management and communication than in decision-making *per se*. We all have to deliver unpopular news at some point in our careers, but if it comes as a nasty surprise, if you have not sought consensus or buy-in, if you have not considered the ramifications of conveying this unpopular decision on organisational morale, then you're not a very good communicator or leader now, are you?

QUESTIONS	POSITIVES	NEGATIVES	COMMENTS
Verbal communication This job constantly tests your verbal communication skills. Tell me how you ensure that others understand you fully – particularly in stressful situations.	**Key terms** Empathy. Listening. Appropriate language – adapting if necessary. Inquiry to check understanding. Persuading or advocating opinion effectively. Double checking.	*'Others not listening.'* *'Not understanding what I meant.'* Candidate who loves the sound of their own voice. *'Me... I... me'* talk.	Results due to verbal skills?

We're moving just a *leetle* bit beyond '*I'm good with people*' here... I'm sure you are a splendid communicator, but is that by accident or by design? If you understand how you do it, well then maybe you can pass those skills on to others and *that* makes you a useful hire. When faced with two candidates with broadly similar educational and experiential backgrounds, every interviewer is going to pick the candidate who displays the greater self knowledge.

Look very carefully at the positive elements above – is your approach genuinely built around these things? Do people ever misinterpret what you are saying? What kind of people and in what kind of situations? If you have discovered an instance of this in the past (even if it wasn't your fault), have you allowed for it in the way you address people since? There is a very fine line here – overdo it and you become dogmatic and patronising; assume that everyone understands you and you are demonstrating lack of concern for both your audience and the outcome of the discussion.

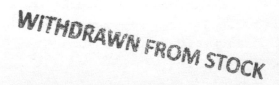

QUESTIONS	POSITIVES	NEGATIVES	COMMENTS
Verbal communication This job will also require you to make a considerable number of presentations. Tell me about how you prepare for and deliver your ideas in a presentation setting.	Audience centred. Style/substance balance. Strong ratio of prep to delivery time. Rehearsal. Adaptive style.	'Seat of the pants' approach. Loves the spotlight. Lack of concern for outcomes.	

Moving on to the larger audience. See page 326, Public Speaking at Interviews, for ideas on this topic.

QUESTIONS	POSITIVES	NEGATIVES	COMMENTS
Team fit How would you describe yourself? Can you give me four to six adjectives which encapsulate who you are?	Talks freely about self? Concise? Well-rounded (mix of social and professional skills)? Confident?	Waffles. Irrelevancies. 2nd or 3rd person. Qualifiers: *'I think I'm…'* *'I would say that I'm…'*	Does the candidate back up answer with feedback from others?

The unspoken and operative word in the question is *relevant*. Don't just re-state your strengths: round yourself off by giving a sense of how you interact with your fellow man. So, if 'Interpersonal Skills' was one of your strengths, you might talk about how 'approachable' or 'empathetic' you are. The other interesting thing here is to see how a candidate who is talking off the cuff deals with this one:

'Well, I'm analytical, thorough, focused, strategic and very intelligent.'
'Let's see, five adjectives... I would say that I'm articulate, persuasive, sensitive, a good team player and I have a rich sense of humour.'

The first person sounds just a little cold, don't you think? And the second one may be the life and soul of the party, but can he get the job done? So start writing and pick a balanced but, above all, *relevant* (to the new job) mix of descriptive terms.

QUESTIONS	POSITIVES	NEGATIVES	COMMENTS
Innovation Would you describe yourself as an innovative person? Give us an example of something particularly innovative that you have done that made a difference in the workplace.	Logical/lateral. Persistent. Harnessing the energy of others. Always looking for a better way... Questioning.	Rocking the boat. Resistance to established best practice. No follow-through.	

Contribution, contribution, contribution. Do you have a history of it? Is it your normal practice to look for better ways of doing things? Do you bring a fresh viewpoint to everything you do? A semantic point here – *innovation* is amending existing things, *creativity* is dreaming stuff up from scratch. If you have developed your CV to reflect your history of achievement and contribution, this question will not pose any difficulties.

More than anything, the question probes whether you have a 'can-do' attitude or not. Do you care enough to try something new? If you meet resistance to change, what is your approach? Employers used to hire staff for knowledge and then train them in the appropriate attitudes – a *ludicrous* concept when you see it written down baldly like that.

Changing people's attitudes? How many marriages have failed because one partner tried to change the other? The rise of structured interviews reflects the new approach. Employers start and finish with attitude – if that is right in the employee, everything else can be grafted on.

QUESTIONS	POSITIVES	NEGATIVES	COMMENTS
Team skills Do you prefer to work in a team or on your own? What do you see as the advantages of working in a team?	Clear, mature understanding of benefits of teamwork? Enthusiasm for teams – positive examples. Buys in.	'*I… me… I.*' Arrogance, assuming authority. Grudging acceptance of the need for teams. Negative experiences – reasons? Solo flier.	**Probe** And the disadvantages?

Operative word in the question: *prefer.* The ability to motivate yourself and be a self starter is usually valued by employers, but they also want you to be able to get on with and work alongside fellow employees. If your preference is very definitely for solo work, the crude and simple answer is to make sure that you are not applying for team-based roles. If that is not possible in your sphere and you must apply for a team job, find out in advance just how closely together the team works and what systems they use. Negative experiences working with others are very common and it can be extremely frustrating to work with people who don't share your standards/values or who consistently fail to meet your expectations.

Some self questioning may be in order here – do these people have a hard time working with everybody, or just you? Are the standards that you set and the expectations that you have (a) reasonable and (b) germane in this work setting? How have you dealt with friction with others in the past? Teamwork is prevalent in the workplace because, when it works, the resultant synergy makes for *tremendous* productivity. Not all projects or tasks require a group approach, but organisations would not invest as heavily as they do in team-building and training if they weren't getting a return. The interviewers will be looking for a whole-hearted buy-in to teamwork and if your answer indicates an, at-best, grudging acceptance of the need for teams, they are not going to like it…

QUESTIONS	POSITIVES	NEGATIVES	COMMENTS
Team skills *How* do you work on a team? What sort of role do you typically like to adopt? Do you have a back-up style?	Innovator/Explorer/ Initiator. Facilitator/ Mediator. Leader/Lieutenant. Worker bee. Analyst. Devil's Advocate. Policeman.	No insight into personal style. Non-adaptive. Drives own agenda.	

Much bigger question and one that explores your motivations and likely fit into the organisational culture. The interviewer knows the make-up and disposition of the existing players in the company/division/department/project/team. You do not. Second-guessing is a waste of everyone's time, so don't go down that road. Think back – are you as constant as the sun or does your style and mode of contribution vary according to the people that you work with? How do you like to behave and contribute in team settings? Which projects worked best in your past and how were you participating in them?

Were you the Innovator/Explorer? Maybe you were simply the Leader or took on a Lieutenant's role, supporting the Leader. Did you smooth things over and keep things on the boil? (Mediator/Facilitator.) Did you question the team's approach and suggest that they consider other angles? (Devil's Advocate.) Maybe you kept the team on track and ensured that they worked in a structured way, never losing sight of the overall objective(s) – in short, were you the team's Policeman?

You need to know this stuff about yourself – not just for interviews, but also to facilitate your progress from cubicle to corner office. Feedback and appraisals over the years should have given you some perspective into your operating style, how and when you are effective and, most importantly, how you are perceived. If you don't have an accurate picture on this topic, it's time to build one. Conducting the 360° (see page 80) on yourself should give you valuable material to use in discussing your operating style and how you are perceived in team settings.

QUESTIONS	POSITIVES	NEGATIVES	COMMENTS
Leadership/ Verbal communication What has been your experience of giving instruction/ training to another person? Management, training or coaching situations… What is your approach to mentoring?	Helpful? Clear? Confident? Result-oriented while being mindful of others' feelings?	Inadequate preparation? Anxiety in advance of the situation? Expressions of negative interaction (attack, withdrawal)?	Good outcome? (*Probe on the result.*)

See below…

QUESTIONS	POSITIVES	NEGATIVES	COMMENTS
Leadership How do you get the best out of your staff?	Adaptive style? Clear understanding of effective management principles? Clear communicator? Comfortable with role? Result-oriented while being mindful of others' feelings? Motivational techniques used?	'One-size-fits-all' approach. Too productivity-driven. Too concerned with people – no balance. Inconsistent. Vacillates.	Good outcomes in the past? (*Probe on results.*)

What is your management philosophy? Do you have one? If no, why not? If yes, is it in keeping with best practice? Are you schooled in the techniques of managing people? Have you done any reading on this most crucial of subjects? Questions of this nature are most difficult to deal with when you are making your first foray into the world of managing staff. There you are, a skilled operator in whatever it is you do; your name has appeared on the radar scope and now you are being considered for your first role on the management ladder. You have never had occasion to marshal the troops before and here is this lousy interviewer asking you about the specifics of how you are going to handle this...

Do the spadework! There are a million and one tomes on the subject of good management practice – read a few of the ones that have sold well in your vicinity. Take notes and think about how you would apply some of the principles and tactics detailed. What about extra-curricular activities? Have you ever had occasion to co-ordinate anything – a team, an event, a big party, a one-off project, whatever? How did you fare? Who came onside and why? Who resisted your suggestions and why? Who disengaged from the process altogether and left you high and dry – and *w-h-y*?

There is a line of reasoning that you should consider here – leaders are born, managers are trained. At some point in their careers, every household name in the management arena was given his or her chance. Someone spotted potential and took a risk (calculated or otherwise) to put that person in charge of other human beings. Jack Welch did not arrive on this planet with 50,000 employees at his beck and call. The fact that you are reading a book of this nature tells me that it is likely that you want to climb the ladder. Think about what that is going to involve. Watch your supervisors and managers closely – how much time do they spend face-to-face with their subordinates? Are they permanently behind the desk or do they go a-visiting? Which is better? Why?

Once again, we are not talking about rocket science here – most of what you learn at management seminars is an accumulation of good sense. Likewise, we are not talking about re-inventing the wheel – there are blueprints for a perfectly good wheel lined up in the 'Management' section of your local bookshop. My broad-strokes thoughts for dealing with questions on this topic:

STRIKING A BALANCE

Balancing concern for people with concern for productivity is the biggest management headache of them all. Consistency is the key – if you turn into a slave-driving, whip-wielding megalomaniac at the end of every reporting period and you are Mr Sweetness-and-light the rest of the time, your staff will not trust you to stand by them should the need arise.

TALK THE TALK

Real, honest-to-goodness, open communication is the other key to developing a consistent management style that engenders trust and respect from your subordinates. The ratio of preaching to practice on this ideal is so disproportionate, it is not even funny – the sheer volume of lip-service paid to the concept of open communication defies description. This 'Do as I say, not as I do' approach is the root cause of staff retention issues; and yet the quandary seems to be self-perpetuating – each new generation of young managers makes the same boring, predictable, brainless errors as its predecessors. But, of course, you won't do that, will you?

BEING ALL THINGS TO ALL PEOPLE

Adaptive management is a buzzphrase that hails from the early 1970s and can mean two things:

1 Management constantly learns and adapts its approach in a continual improvement (*kaizen*) strategy to maximise efficiency and outdo the competition.

2 The individual manager adopts differing approaches with individual staff members, depending on their level of readiness, motivation and experience. If you have a team ranging from greenhorns with a few months of experience to 'lifers' who want to stay at this level for the

foreseeable future, you clearly cannot adopt a one-size-fits-all approach to assigning tasks. The lifer needs unequivocal direction and the knowledge that you are there as needed; close supervision is not likely to be needed or appreciated. The greenhorn, on the other hand, needs crystal-clear instruction, the task to be broken down into bite-sized chunks and a checking mechanism ('*drop in to me at 4.00pm*') as it progresses. Once you are both satisfied as to the greenhorn's capability, you can pull gently back and start looking for inputs and initiative from said greenhorn.

WELL DONE

Praise as part of the management toolkit probably goes back to the caves ('*Nice job spearing that mammoth, Thag*') but has been discussed slightly more recently, and most pithily, in the marvellous *One Minute Manager*. It is fair to say that most staff get nervous when they are summoned to the boss's office – you usually don't get called in unless you are about to be chewed out. Children love praise and it has been shown time and again to have beneficial effects in the classroom, on both learning capacity and motivation.

Well, *sur-priiiiise!* It works on adults too! *Everyone* loves to be praised, but just as the bullied kid grows up to be a bully and the abused child is much more likely to abuse as an adult, the manager who doesn't receive any praise from above is very unlikely to pass any on to his staff.

The two excuses I constantly hear on this are: '*If I praise them, they'll be expecting a big pay rise at review time.*' And argument number two is the ever-popular: '*But that's what they're paid for...*' If you have ever said either of those two things, read *The One Minute Manager* right now and learn about the power of appropriate praise in the workplace.

STUCK IN THE MIDDLE

Sandwiching is the logical follow-on to appropriate praising. It enables the manager to highlight an issue or inappropriate behaviour in the midst of a discussion of the subordinate's overall performance – '*John, I just wanted to raise something with you. You know how strongly I value your* (positive attribute, positive contribution, positive result), *which makes it all the more surprising that* (negative behaviour) *has been raised by one of your customers. This doesn't seem like you – was there a context I should know about or is there anything I can do to help?*' Discussion ensues, culminating with the manager escorting John out of the office saying: '*Great! Let's iron this little wrinkle out together and...*' Positive, negative, positive – ooh, complicated!

QUESTIONS	POSITIVES	NEGATIVES	COMMENTS
Finance/ Budgeting What has been your experience to date of managing a budget? *If none:* What will be your approach to setting and managing your budget here?	Forecasting. Accurate historical records. Fixed, variable and contingencies. Monitoring techniques. Return on the spend – long-term and short-term.	Trial and error approach. Inadequate controls. Not concerned with value for spend.	

Remember, you're going to be spending *their* money. In a privately owned organisation, the cash may actually belong to someone across the table and you can be damn sure they want to be able to measure the return on investment ('bang for the buck'). So you'd better (a) be able to, and (b) want to, as well.

Look at the buzzwords – if any of these terms are a mystery to you, head out to your library straight away.

QUESTIONS	POSITIVES	NEGATIVES	COMMENTS
Verbal communication Would you say that listening is an important part of the/your communication process? How would you rate your ability as a listener?	Empathy? Inquiry? Re-statement to gain clarification? Taking time to reflect? Encouraging others to open up?	Interruptive? Jumping to conclusions? Missing details? Bias? Pre-conceived ideas? Not paying attention?	**Probe** Pin the candidate down on a concrete example of when his or her listening skills really paid off.

HUGE question. Any role that requires effective, active listening will include this line of questioning and the interviewers will also be measuring your listening skills as the interview progresses.

Everyone thinks that they are a good listener but how many people do you know who actually are? You not only have to be good at it – in an interview you have to be able to *show* that you're good at it and you have to be able to clearly articulate how you approach listening to your fellow man.

Look for feedback on this vital skill as part of your 360°. If you are guilty of any of the common failings in the 'negatives' column, think long and hard about how you are going to redress them.

QUESTIONS	POSITIVES	NEGATIVES	COMMENTS
Team skills Give me a specific example of something you did that built enthusiasm within a team you were working with or managing.	Awareness of mood of team? What techniques used? Drawing out the quieter members of the team? Personal energy influencing others?	'Me, me, me', 'they, they, they' instead of 'us, us, us'?	Simple, inexpensive ideas?

Another key question for leadership roles. This is all about knowing the mood of your team and getting the maximum productivity out of them without breaking the bank. Sure, we're all paid a wage to show up and perform; but what do you do when it's *not* business as usual? When everyone has to cancel their evening or weekend plans to get something done?

Having a sense of everyone's humour, tiredness and blood-sugar levels is what good management in these situations is all about. Knowing when to order a tools-down coffee break (and you supply the doughnuts) or when to phone for Chinese food. Be the person who thinks to buy ice-cream on a hot summer's day as you come back from your lunch break to what you know is going to be a tough afternoon's work for the whole team...

QUESTIONS	POSITIVES	NEGATIVES	COMMENTS
Self knowledge/ Team fit How would your colleagues/boss/ subordinates describe you?	Cross-reference to descriptions of self?	Negatives leaking into the answer?	

Clearly, this back-references to the question on describing yourself with a handful of adjectives, so there needs to be a good deal of correlation with that answer. The other reason for asking it this way is that people are frequently more comfortable talking about themselves outside of the First Person ('*Well, they would say that I am...*').

If the interviewers use this indirect line of questioning, you can drop in a Nugget about yourself that might sound self-aggrandising if you mentioned it in response to a direct question – '*Well, my boss would say that Manahan has the Midas touch and that every project he is involved in goes really well*.' (NB: You might want to invest in a good thesaurus to make sure you're not using the same language over and over about yourself through the course of the interview.)

QUESTIONS	POSITIVES	NEGATIVES	COMMENTS
Written communication We are required to document our processes very thoroughly here. Tell me about your experiences with ISO/Kite marks/ FOI/(*insert appropriate regulation or system*). Do you find it/them useful when you are working on a project?	Does the candidate understand and emphasise the importance of accuracy and records? Logical, organised approach?	Committed to the process or grudging acceptance/ avoidance?	

Subtext: If you stepped under a bus tomorrow, would the project die with you? Do you document everything or is it all in your head? Are you process-driven? Do you timeframe your work? Are you results focused? In a word, are you *professional?* This is basically a re-hash of the earlier question on how you will approach the job. The big elements for consideration on a project-based question are:

- Clear objective, clear budget, clear timeframe.
- Inclusive/collaborative approach.
- Structured and agreed process.
- Milestones and monitoring techniques.
- Make it happen.
- Happy ending.

QUESTIONS	POSITIVES	NEGATIVES	COMMENTS
Problem-solving In general, what is your approach to problem-solving?	Anticipation. Preparation. Identify/name it. Consultation, inquiry. Logic, review alternatives. Decide optimal approach. Milestones, monitoring. Ensure problem doesn't arise again. Lateral approach. Intuition, gut-feeling.	Superficial answers. Trial and error. Undocumented, oversimplification. No alternatives explored. Result inadequately checked. Over-reliance on gut.	Very open question – assesses the candidate's ability to present a logical, structured overview answer on a broad topic.

MASSIVE question, and very difficult to answer succinctly. Almost all jobs are fundamentally about problem-solving, so just how do you do it? How often do you get it right? Do you learn from your mistakes and also from your successes? For senior roles, this question is at least as much about your ability to talk coherently and fluently as it is about your approach to solving dilemmas.

QUESTIONS	POSITIVES	NEGATIVES	COMMENTS
Values/ Motivation What aspect of your current job do you most dislike?	Confident to admit a dislike? Ability to overcome it or make it a strength?	Talks to a core function of the role?	Cross-reference to stated motivations and reason for moving.

Slightly tricky question, cross-referenced to '*Why do you want to leave your current job?*' If you are fudging on your answers, this cross-checking approach will usually pull out an inconsistency. I repeat my contention that it is not a good idea for either side to hire under false pretences/impressions.

Sure, there is seduction going on during the recruitment process, on both sides of the table; but just as there is no point in lying to someone you want to have a serious relationship with, there is *absolutely* no point in not being yourself at interview. If they don't like you, fine – take the Dear John, get your feedback and move on; but if they like what you are *pretending* to be, you are inviting a lot of stress and strain into your life as you try and live up to that pretence.

So, what genuinely ticks you off in your current role? Are you sufficiently confident to admit an issue or to talk about how you overcame it? You may not be able to mention it ('*My boss is a psychopath with a Napoleonic complex*'), but you should crystallise what is lacking/wrong with your current situation and use that germ of truth to build your answers to this line of questioning. And don't try to dodge this one; remember the subtext: '*We know that your current job is not perfect, otherwise you wouldn't be sitting in that chair looking for a job here – so what's the story, pal?*'

QUESTIONS	POSITIVES	NEGATIVES	COMMENTS
Three-parter What would you say is the biggest issue/problem facing (*insert organisation name*)/this sector, how has it come about and what would you do about it if we hire you/promote you?	Depth of industry/ sectoral knowledge and preparation. Listening skills. Overall intelligence. Articulation/ Fluency.	Answers only 1 or 2 parts of the question. Bluffing on the core issue.	1. 2. 3. (Tick here as candidate answers each of the questions.)

This is a frequently used, and very important, question. The interviewer is measuring a number of things here: (1) Your **listening skills** – very few people hear and answer all three of the questions. (2) Your **intelligence** – are you capable of holding three concepts in your head and bridging smoothly from one to the next? (3) The quality and depth of your **research** – do you really know (or care) what is going on in this organisation/sector?

There is a misconception that this line of questioning is only used at senior executive level interviews. Wrong! You can be asked this on a milk round 'chat' coming straight out of college. Why? Primarily because the bar has been raised and there are young candidates out there now who are capable of dealing at this level (see page 38, The Bogeyman).

Bluffing here is absolutely pointless (see page 284, Clangers); you either know your stuff or you don't. This is the difference between job-hunting and career management. If you are just looking for a pay-the-bills job to give you a bit more drinking money for the next few weeks/months/years, why would you bother to find this kind of heavy stuff out? But employers are funny fish and for some unaccountable reason they don't seem to like hiring that kind of short-term-thinking, self-serving person. So even if you are just blagging it, you should probably expend a bit of shoe leather and come up with a good answer to this question.

If you notice the interviewers using multi-part questions, there are two simple mnemonics you can use: (1) repeat and enumerate the question back to them as you consider your answer; (2) dig the requisite number of fingers into your leg and lift a finger as you answer each part of the question. If you've still got a finger on your leg, you've missed something! If you don't know what the big issue facing a business or sector is, you haven't done the spadework (see page 162, Research).

QUESTIONS	POSITIVES	NEGATIVES	COMMENTS
Team fit/ Motivation What interests you most in your career? Why did you choose this kind of work and what aspect of it do you find most satisfying?	Motivation – committed to this work or using it as a stepping-stone? Work ethic? Attention to detail? Big picture/little picture?	Passive terms. Fell into this sort of work. Forced down this path.	Cross-reference to dislikes and reason for moving/joining.

Subtext: '*Other than money!*' I had one candidate answer like this – '*Well, let me put it this way. If I had a rich, dying grandmother, I wouldn't be here right now; I'd be at her bedside patting her wrist.*' He got a huge laugh and then went on to talk about what else got him out of bed on a Monday morning. If you are being interviewed by a Fanatic (see page 41) or a Silverback (see page 40), this is a pivotal question. She will be probing and following up and may be looking for a mirror image of her own motivations, so this is a toughie.

This question is all about answering the big underlying and very hard to measure concern '*Will you do this job well?*' Unless you have lied through your teeth all over your CV, your basic capacity to do the job is not really the core concern. Anyone who gets to the interview stage has, in theory, the capability to do the job. The big question then is not '*Can you do this job?'* but rather *'Will you do it well?'* and *'Will you fit in here?'*

So it is imperative that you don't lie at this point. If they think that you are a driven, high-energy, self-starting stress puppy because of what you imply (or directly tell them) in the interview, they are going to be *seriously* miffed if they discover that you are, in fact, a needy slug. Now, I accept that there aren't too many recruitment advertisements out there that start out with 'CALLING ALL NEEDY SLUGS!' but unless your sloth-fulness is massively out of kilter with societal norms, I am making the generous assumption that it shouldn't be impeding your career. If it is, that's another day's work and a very different discussion.

> **'It is fitting that a liar should be a man of good memory.'**
> MARCUS FABIUS QUINTILIAN

QUESTIONS	POSITIVES	NEGATIVES	COMMENTS
Planning What were your career plans five years ago/ten years ago?	Had a plan? Consistent with progress? Set and achieved goals?	Passive terms. Path of least resistance.	

This is a variation on the *'Where do you plan to be in five years' time?'* question. It is a cross-check on your opener and also examines if you are working to a plan or merely following the current downstream. Is this move, that we are sitting discussing here today, part of a plan? Were you using previous jobs as stepping stones and, by extension, are you doing the same thing here? Even an unschooled interviewer will be capable of exposing a drifting, directionless candidate with simple questions like this.

Quite apart from being capable of answering this question well, it is interesting to look back at yourself and see how you *have* changed. A simple exercise to help you: draw a line down the middle of a page. Write today's date in the right-hand column and the same date five years ago in the left. Now fill the left-hand column. What was your age, marital status, number of children, most recent qualification, most recent training course/effort, income, mode of transport, accommodation, job title, company name and boss's title? For your job, what were your key responsibilities the day you started the job (even if that doesn't coincide with the date above)? Did you have staff? Did you control a budget? What were the minimum entry requirements/skills you needed in order to fulfil the job? How was your performance measured? Maybe you can dig out an old job description or review from this time to help you here (see page 404, Appendix 2).

Now, fill in the today column with all of the same information. How has your education and training progressed? Who paid for it? Who suggested that you needed it? Was it beneficial? Have you been promoted? Has your remit expanded within the job? Bigger budget? Tougher projects? More staff? What have been your most significant accomplishments on and off the job? How have you *changed*? Have these changes been to your benefit? Have the changes been self-directed or forced on to you?

QUESTIONS	POSITIVES	NEGATIVES	COMMENTS
Planning What is your long-term career plan (a) if you are appointed to this position; (b) if you are not successful?	3 percenter? 7 percenter? Strategic thinker? Mapping? Plan B?	90 percenter? No structured thought. No plan B. Contradicts previous answers on motivations.	Ivy League model.

This question makes even the best-prepared candidates wince. Chances are, you're not one of those 3 per cent who slavishly map out their lives and follow a written plan for everything. But if you are, or if you are one of the 7 per cent who have a pretty clear picture of where they are going, then part (a) is going to be a no-brainer for you.

Why do they ask it? The career-plan question is a very common old chestnut and is used in different ways for interviews at all levels. Many interviewers don't have a clear reason for asking this one (I had a senior manager recently tell me that he asked this question *because it's on the list*) but you will still encounter it, in some form, more often than not. In brief:

- They are assessing your commitment to the organisation (do you really want *this* job or will any old job do?).
- They are assessing the quality of your preparation for the interview. Do you have a strong, well thought-out answer for this obvious question?
- If the organisation that you are planning to join uses Succession Planning, then your answer to this question will assume even greater importance. Under this model, you are not just being interviewed for the job you applied for, you are also being evaluated for your potential to ascend to the next level and above.
- Most importantly, they are assessing your ability to map out your career and your life (and, by extension, the likely return they will get if they decide to invest in you).

Studies consistently show that those who work to a plan for their lives/careers tend to get ahead in this world and employers are always on the look-out for these rare candidates (about 3 per cent of the population). The five-year-plan question is useful in identifying these players and in eliminating short-term-thinking, stepping-stone candidates.

Interviewers can also use this question to skate around the edges of employment equality legislation. They may glean information about you that you otherwise wouldn't volunteer and that they cannot, under law, directly ask you. A tricky question, which you should be ready for, and please, PLEASE, do not say, '*I plan to be sitting in your chair in five years' time*'.

Part (b) is the killer question for everyone. Have you planned for failure? What is your contingency? Does it coincide with your stated intentions from earlier in the interview? You should, *at the very least*, talk to getting concrete feedback (see page 307, After the Interview) and using this as a valuable learning experience.

QUESTIONS	POSITIVES	NEGATIVES	COMMENTS
Learning curve Your CV seems a bit light in (*insert appropriate shortcoming*) **OR** Is there any aspect of the job in which you feel under-qualified/experi-enced? How quickly can you get up to speed on this, should the need arise?	Self reliant. Ability to research, home study. Work closely with others who already use the skill/knowledge. Achieved results in the past using recently acquired knowledge.	Candidate is looking for lots of training. Wants to beef up CV. Inflexibility. Lack of enthusiasm for learning.	**Probe** Can you give me an exam-ple of when you had to learn something new, and quickly apply it in the workplace?

Your immediate inclination when being told that you are not up to scratch is to yell, 'Well then, why am I at this interview, matey?' Is the deficiency a core function of the job or a nice-to-have? If it's a core function, they shouldn't be interviewing you, full stop. If it is something that you *should* have or if it would be a distinct advantage in your new role, then you need to reassure them that (a) you are capable and willing to quickly acquire this ability or (b) you have other sterling qualities which *more* than make up for the shortfall in this area.

This is an awkward question if it catches you on the hop, so ensure that your research has given you a full and real picture of the day-to-day operation of the job. Then you can speak with some authority when you reassure them on this one. Sometimes interviewers use this line of ques-tioning merely to put you on the defensive – don't let that happen. Politely, but firmly, kill this off.

QUESTIONS	POSITIVES	NEGATIVES	COMMENTS
Work style How will you approach this role? What will be your priorities on the job?	Timeframed? Structured/logical? Awareness of the realities? Awareness of core responsibilities?	Generalisms. Hasn't really given it any structured thought. Ill-researched or ill-prepared.	

An absolute **monster** of a question, typically asked towards the end of the interview, when you are flagging. Olympic-level athletes now spend a lot of time lying down using NLP and visualisation techniques to improve their performance in races. You should do the same. The major subtext to this question is: '*Do you believe that you really deserve this job?*' If you really think (and believe) that you are going to succeed, you will have given it some serious thought...

All right, so they appoint you – what are you going to do in the time before you take up the new job? Are you going to do some more reading and research? Meet with your new boss (or the outgoing incumbent, or both) a couple of times to talk through the big issues? Familiarise yourself with your new staff by reading their personnel records?

What about your first week in the office? How are you going to be introduced to everyone? Who will introduce you? How will you remember everybody's name? Will you meet your staff in a group or one by one – or both? What message and impression do you want them to take away from that first meeting? What will you do on your first Friday? Go out for a drink with the team? Buy lunch?

On the macro level – what are the issues facing the business that come under your remit? How are you going to identify them and prioritise your responses? How will you arrive at the big decisions that will impact on your first year with the organisation? How will you implement and monitor your responses?

QUESTIONS	POSITIVES	NEGATIVES	COMMENTS
Team fit If you could choose your boss, what sort of person would he or she be?	**Look for** The candidate who knows their own strengths/weaknesses, who wants direction, but who shows initiative and flexibility. Comfortable working with different styles.	**Avoid**: Me, me, me candidate who needs constant reassurance/direction/monitoring. Candidate who can only work well with one type of person.	

This is what I call an *Eliminator Question* – the ideal boss question is very tricky and I have seen numerous candidates inadvertently disqualify themselves with their response to this one. The catch is this – the interviewer is either going to be your direct boss or knows your direct boss's style very well. Let's say your answer is something along the lines of '*Well, I'd like to work for someone who gives clear direction, but allows me to demonstrate my initiative and has an open door policy to enable me to quickly run ideas and issues past her.*' Sounds fairly reasonable and safe, doesn't it?

The only problem is that the interviewer knows that the guy down the hall who will be managing you is an appalling communicator, constantly changes the brief (and expects you to pick this up by telepathy) and either snarls at anyone who has the temerity to knock on his (very firmly) closed door or proceeds to micro-manage every detail of the task. So your seemingly safe answer has just disqualified you from consideration.

The boss question is all about you and your needs. *Everything* that you say in answer to this question betrays those needs, so you must think back over the spectrum of people you have worked for and look at what was good and bad. The key point for you is this: were you *effective* working under all of those different styles? (*Effective* mind you, not necessarily *happy*.) If so, your answer is a snip, built around this model: '*(a) I can work effectively for anyone – just look at my track record, and (b) in this world you don't get to choose your boss or your family – you just do the best you can with what you have been given. Next question please.*' Dangerous, dangerous question – think very carefully.

QUESTIONS	POSITIVES	NEGATIVES	COMMENTS
Motivation/ Values What has been your greatest success/proudest moment to date?	Recent? Relevant? Still highly motivated?	Harking back to happier times...	

Your answer here needs to be something that (a) is recent, (b) is pertinent to the job at hand and (c) demonstrates that you are still very enthused about the work you do. If you are in your 40s and start droning on about winning some cup in secondary school or getting a first for your thesis, the interviewer will draw a line through your name on the spot. The question also looks to your values – what is important to you, what do you regard as a success? It goes without saying (but I'm going to say it anyway), if the interviewer regards your great moment as something trivial or insubstantial, you are in trouble.

A safe guideline is, who did it matter to – you or the organisation? If it is important to the organisation, you won't go far wrong (see page 82, Accomplishments under the 360°). Thoughts:

- Bringing a key project in under budget or above specification.
- A very successful product launch/achieving market leadership with a product.
- Moving over to a new system (IT or otherwise) while maintaining continuity of service.
- Re-drafting a significant policy or procedure.
- A big cost-saving idea.

- Staving off a disaster – spotting a compliance issue, a breach of contract, or similar…
- Co-ordinating some big event/project – personal or professional.
- Personal stuff – getting married, some *huge* sporting achievement, getting through a crisis…

QUESTIONS	POSITIVES	NEGATIVES	COMMENTS
Values Conversely, what do you regard as the greatest failure or disappointment in your career to date? Anything you would change?	Confident to discuss? How did it happen? Learnt from mistake?	Too hard on self. Smugness/complacency. Blaming others? Clichéd answer?	What does the *candidate* regard as a mistake or failure?

Ah yes, the other side of the coin. Still a big values question here, but this one goes a little deeper. Are you sufficiently self-assured to discuss a failure? Do you take ownership for it? Is the failure or disappointment something relatable to the job you are being interviewed for? Did you learn anything from the mistake?

There's another factor here, which relates to your confidence level and your conscientiousness – are you being too hard on yourself over this relatively trivial error, or are you complacent about it, not really accepting that the fault was yours? In short, what do *you* think constitutes a failure?

You can go the flat denial route (depending on how the question is phrased) – '*Sure, I've made mistakes, haven't we all? But there's nothing I would go back and do differently. I don't think that sailing blithely through life is necessarily a good thing – I have been tested by my failures and mistakes and not been found wanting.*' Risky approach that borders on arrogance, but it can work for some people.

Another way is to look at something that you just weren't happy with, even though others were – '*When we launched Product X, I analysed the market and saw an opportunity to really come thundering in ahead of the competition. I built my case and presented it to management, but they said that I was shooting too high and that they would be happy with a lower spend and half the market share that I was aiming for. So we launched and comfortably achieved those lower targets and the management team were very happy, even though I wasn't. But a competitor came in a year later, utilised the strategy that I had been proposing and they beat everyone in the market (including us) hands-down. I was right in my initial assessment and I should have fought harder for my beliefs…*'

QUESTIONS	POSITIVES	NEGATIVES	COMMENTS
Team fit What other positions have you applied for recently?	Check against motivation and answers to HR about why the candidate wants to work for the organisation.		

(a) None of their damn business and (b) do they seriously expect you to answer honestly? This tack will usually not be taken directly. It may be a talkative and sympathetic receptionist who idly (ha!) chats with you about how tough it is doing lots of interviews back to back. Or it may come up in a social element of the selection process.

If you have admitted that you are talking to other potential employers during the course of the interview, well and good. If you have gone the '*I want to work for you and no one else, I'll **die** if I don't get this job*' route, then you might need to be just a tad more circumspect in dealing with this probe.

QUESTIONS	POSITIVES	NEGATIVES	COMMENTS
Strengths/Self knowledge We have had a high level of application for this post, and we have a pool of highly experienced, highly qualified candidates to choose from. What do you believe marks you out as the best candidate for this job?	Listened to the question. Self knowledge. Self acceptance. Analysis of peers. Staying power. Confidence. Conviction. Clear understanding of what the job entails.	Simple reiteration of strengths. Self deprecation. Arrogance. Stumped.	**Probe if poor answer** Yes, but all of the candidates could say that – what makes you the *best* candidate?

The clincher – most candidates blanch when they hear this one for the first time. The nub of the question is this: if *you* don't know why you're the best person for the job, how can you expect *them* to? Another way of phrasing it: '*What makes you so damn special? And please keep your answer pertinent to the job at hand.*'

Most candidates simply recap their strengths at this point and wait for the interview to end. I suggest you go further – in building your picture of yourself for the job-hunt (see page 80, 360°) ask what is the most distinctive thing about you and your style on the job. What *really* marks you out from the crowd? The answer(s) may surprise you. The answer(s) may also seem somewhat trite to you, but work on this, because it is the core of your self knowledge – what makes you memorable, special, remarkable, effective?

Then you can answer by reciting your strengths, then pause and say something along the lines of, '*But we've covered all of that already and I'm sure that most, if not all, of the candidates could say the same things. In preparing for this interview, I went back over old appraisals, talked to past colleagues and bosses, friends and family and really tried to build a coherent picture of how I operate and how I am perceived, and the one consistent piece of feedback I got from them all was...'*

In organisations that use structured recruitment techniques, the interviewers will have to write a brief statement recommending why each candidate gets through each round of the hiring process. Write it for them. Give them 50–100 words on why you are the *perfect* person for the job. The headings under the Positives column above should give you plenty of food for thought and your 360° will give you the insights necessary to build this answer.

QUESTIONS	POSITIVES	NEGATIVES	COMMENTS
Motivation I'm sure you must have some questions for me/us?	Quality of preparation. Strategic or tactical thinker.	Self-serving. Needy. Clichés.	Listening to responses or just asking *pro forma?*

Subtext: *'Are you a player and just how well have you researched us?'* (see page 219, Asking Them Questions).

OTHER QUESTIONS THAT ARE FREQUENTLY ASKED

Q: If I asked your current boss for a reference, what would she say about you? OR How did you fare in your last performance appraisal?
A: More *'How would others describe you?'* stuff here. It is likely that, at some point, your new employer is going to talk with your old boss (see page 177, Managing Your References), so lying in response to this line of questioning is a *baaad* idea. If you work for an organisation that uses a formal, written review process, the interviewer(s) may even ask to see your most recent appraisals at some stage in the selection process. You need to be ready for this line of questioning and your answer needs to tie in with your responses on what others think of you and why you want to move.

If you have been having screaming toe-to-toe rows with your current boss, think about why they have been happening. Is it because she is a useless fossil and her approach is going to bring the organisation to ruin or is it because your approach is rankling and you have not convinced your boss that this way is going to make her life easier in the long run? By the time you are being asked this question it is *way* too late to mend fences, but you should be sufficiently on top of managing your career that this sort of question holds no fear for you. If not, be ready for some tough follow-up questions.

Q: You seem a little overqualified for this job.
A: Situations where this line of questioning could arise include a candidate who is making a career transition and is taking a step back in order to do so, a candidate who has been downsized and has to take the lower level job to survive or the candidate who has been promoted beyond her or his level of competence and just wants to go back to a simpler life...

The interviewer basically wants reassurance. **Subtext:** *'You're not going to walk out to a better job after three months are you?'* OR *'So why will no one hire you at your expected level?'* OR *'Are you going to be looking for my job and become a threat to me?'* You'd better be unambiguous as to your reasons on this one, because if you are in any way hesitant in your answer, you will be immediately disqualified from contention.

But for the purposes of this discussion, why *are* you swimming downstream? No one has ever been accused of trying to sleep their way to the bottom, so why are you pitching yourself downwards like this? If you have been asked this question more than once, it's likely that there is something off-beam with your career plan.

Q: You seem a little underqualified for this job.
A: The smart-ass answer to this one is: *'So how come you invited me to interview then?'* And therein lies the kernel of your answer. *Someone* on the other side of the table reckons you can do this job, otherwise you wouldn't be sitting there in your best suit and shiniest shoes. The person asking the question may have already decided who is going to get the job (obviously not you!) or may be resentful of his lack of input into compiling the shortlist.

If the job is a step up for you, with new responsibilities, you need to provide reassurance as to your readiness level and as to the steepness of your learning curve. Obviously, it would be nice if you were able to point to a similar circumstance from your recent past – '*Well, in my current role, at the time I was promoted I was the youngest member of the divisional team at my level, and I had only three of the five minimum entry requirements for the role. However, I was a known quantity, I had demonstrated my commitment, my effectiveness and my learning curve, so they decided to take a chance on me. As you can see from my CV, that risk more than paid off. I view the role that we're talking about here as a step up, but it's a far less risky proposition than my previous one, so while I may not be hitting the ground sprinting, my track record demonstrates my ability to play catch-up very quickly.*'

The other line of reasoning you can draw on is that you will be *thrilled skinny* to get this job, because it is a step up for you, whereas someone who is already operating at, or near, this level may be somewhat jaded and will attach less importance to this 'sideways step' than you will.

Q: Tell me about your hobbies.
A: People do asinine things on their CVs, like claiming an interest in something that looks impressive but that they aren't really involved in and know nothing about. Don't talk yourself up here – if you are caught out, it immediately and irrevocably blows your credibility. Who are we kidding here? Most of us are couch potatoes – so think very carefully before you write down something that you can't back up (see page 133, Little Boxes – Application Forms).

Q: (Follow-on from '*Where do you plan to be in five years' time?*') **How do you plan to get there?**
A: This is the drill-down that the interviewer will use if he suspects that your answer to the first question was a clockwork parrot job. For someone managing their career, who is working to a plan and has identified the key steps along the way, this question is a doddle. The only problem may be that you will scare the hell out of the interviewer if you reveal all of your intentions. Be ready to talk about further qualifications you intend to gain, self-development exercises and formal training you want

to complete, experience you need to gain, and then, as the kicker, map that against what you expect the organisation and the sector to be doing in the same timeframe. I would also avoid discussing specific job titles and thus leave your options open – '*Well at the moment, I want to advance in the Logistics division by doing X, Y and Z, but I'm certainly not going to be closed-minded about opportunities that may arise in other departments along the way.*'

AWKWARD AND NASTY QUESTIONS – THE STRESS INTERVIEW

Q: (*If the interviewer notices something on your CV that you were hoping to gloss over...*) **I see you took longer than usual to gain qualification A – why was that? OR I see that you have a gap of X months between job B and job C – what were you doing in that time? OR Why did you leave job D after such a short time?**
A: If such incidences exist in your past, assume that someone will know about them, spot them or hear about them through a reference check, and be prepared to address them in a positive light (see page 196, Questions I Hope They Don't Ask..., in the chapter on Interview Mapping).

ACADEMIC PROBLEMS

'*I was an immature dolt, but I got a real wake-up call from that failure and I went on to...*' Unless you had a grievous illness or a death in the family, it's pretty hard to sound convincing about any academic failure. Better to be disarmingly honest and move on. If this was a recent failure, I hope that you are able to show the interviewer the scar, or point to a missing limb...

GAPS

What is the interviewer thinking? *'Making licence plates in prison? Nervous breakdown? Couldn't get hired anywhere because of a bad reputation that I don't know about yet?'* It's reassurance time again, folks! Hopefully, your CV is not peppered with gaps. Were you considering your options? Travelling? – the *'much-needed career break'* approach. Doing contract work to fund a job search for a more fulfilling career? What was the state of the market at that time? If it was buzzing and you couldn't land a job, you are going to have some explaining to do.

QUICK DEPARTURES

These happen and they look just *awful*. **Example**: you were headhunted for a lot more money, but the organisation was like the ninth pit of hell and you ran screaming out of the door after six months. The tack to take on this is that it took immense courage for you to do this and to admit your mistake not just to yourself, but also (through your CV) to the market. And what did you learn from this experience? Well, at the very least, I trust that you have checked out the organisation you are applying to now *with a microscope*, so there are going to be no unpleasant surprises on either side this time.

A note of caution here – do be careful about bad-mouthing a previous employer, no matter how much they deserve it. Any interviewer listening to your vivid descriptions of the lake of fire in the Finance department of Company XXXX will be thinking, *'I wonder what this person will be saying about this company/me in a few years' time?'*

Q: What have you heard about this organisation/me on the grapevine?
A: This is becoming a very common line of questioning and directly examines the level of research that you have undertaken. (It will *always* be raised if there have been quick moves from job to job on your CV.) Why are they so hung up on this? Simply because no sensible person would make a dramatic life change without doing some research.

Furthermore, the effort you put in on your own behalf is a measure of your thoroughness, professionalism and work ethic. And if you are in any way sloppy on your own behalf, then it is not unfair to conclude that you will be *very* sloppy on behalf of your employer.

There are three axes you can talk to here. The X axis is the competitive environment and all the moves and strategic shifts therein. The Y axis is the supplier-to-customer chain with your target company in the middle. The Z axis is the broader environment: regulatory and legislative changes, representative bodies — *It's the economy, stupid!* (see page 162, Research, and page 168, Networking).

Q: Okay, I don't feel like we're really getting to the heart of the matter here. You're very polished and glib and the clichés are coming out thick and fast, but the mask is still up. Let's start again. Tell me what really makes you tick...
A: *Hideous* question. To paraphrase: '*You are a LIAR! Everything you have told me so far in the interview is a big fat LIE! Start again, and don't you dare try any of your carefully chosen phrases on me this time, you little whippersnapper.*'

This very aggressive approach is usually wheeled out by slightly insecure interviewers who find themselves unsettled by an obviously capable, relaxed candidate. They have tried all of the usual probes in their repertoire, but nothing seems to be rattling you. If you think that this is what is behind the question, I would be very careful about accepting a job offer from the type of person who tries on this kind of *crap* — particularly if she is going to be your direct boss.

If you decide to dignify the '*You're a liar*' question with a response, you can go three routes:

1 Cave in completely, although this wouldn't be *my* preferred choice.
2 Start again, but stick to your guns and basically do the interview over, *verbatim*.
3 Say something like this: '*I am articulate, not glib. I'm sorry if you feel we aren't getting to the heart of the matter, but what you see here is what you get. This is a professional interview. If it goes well, we will probably have one or more further meetings, including a negotiation on salary, at*

which point you may decide to offer me the position. And if I accept, we STILL WON'T BE MARRIED! Shall we continue?'

The other reason for including this kind of insulting nonsense in an interview is to see how easily led you are. Would you tolerate that sort of behaviour from a supplier or a customer? How about if it was being done by the CEO of your customer's firm? In this instance, the person who has done this to you is the person who has the power of hire-or-not over you and they are just licking their lips to see if you wilt. If you think that this is the sort of game-playing behind the question, I recommend keeping your cool while volleying this one back between their eyes.

Q: If you caught a colleague cheating on his or her expenses, what would you do?

A: Another integrity question which trips up a lot of candidates – probably because of the 'squealer' connotations, which run contrary to everything we learnt in primary school. There is only one acceptable answer here: *'I would report them on the spot.'* You can add a tiny qualifier to open the discussion up if they want: *'I cannot conceive of a situation in which I wouldn't report them on the spot.'* **Subtext**: *Who is being cheated here and whose side are you on?*

Q: How do you feel this interview is going?

A: Weird, perplexing question; again typically asked by insecure interviewers. Unless your questioners are lousy card players, it is unlikely that you will be picking up much from them as the interview progresses. You may be able to qualify an answer as a result of a frown, but you are very rarely going to get a sense of how you are doing overall – unless you are doing *very* badly or *very, very* well.

Talk about the professionalism of the organisation (and therefore of the interviewer) and how you are immersed in the process and don't really have an overview yet. *'I like the way you are running things, I like the meaty questions and issues that we are getting into, but I don't really have a strong sense of how it's all going – you are too good a poker player for that. Ask me that question again tomorrow when I've had a chance to mull everything over and I'll probably give you a better response.'*

Q: What would you do if you won the lottery and didn't need to work?

If you won the lottery, would you pack in your job?
64% YES, BUT I'D FIND SOMETHING WORTHWHILE TO OCCUPY ME.
21% DEFINITELY – HOLIDAYS HERE I COME.
13% NO.
Source: http://forums.monster.co.uk/poll.asp?pollid=876

A: Hmmmmm. Of course, if you have completed the three Roads exercise (see page 351), you know exactly what you would be doing, but unless that closely coincides with the job that you are being interviewed for, I very much doubt that honesty is going to be your best policy here. You could try a little finesse to get you out of this by saying, '*Actually, I don't play the lottery, so I don't think that really applies to me*' but the interviewer is likely to continue probing. Careful thinking needed for this one – you may want to develop a few answers in advance and decide which one to use on the day, having got a flavour of the interviewer.

> '**Always be sincere, even if you don't mean it.**'
> HARRY S. TRUMAN

> '**Always be sincere, *especially* when you don't mean it.**'
> GROUCHO MARX

Chapter 6

CLANGERS

Author of the Declaration of American Independence and of the Statute of Virginia for Religious Freedom, and Father of the University of Virginia.

THOMAS JEFFERSON'S EPITAPH

TERMINOLOGY AND CLICHÉS TO AVOID

- *'I believe that I'm...' 'I think...' 'I feel...' 'I would say...' 'I suppose...'* Banish passive, equivocal responses that begin this way from your delivery. Qualifying what you are going to say (particularly about yourself) devalues everything that follows. Be concrete and specific. Give third-party evidence of your abilities in answer to open questions – how you solved a difficult problem, or feedback that a superior gave you. Don't use these qualifiers in your answers – practise using crisp, unequivocal language that doesn't creep into arrogance.

- *'I only have...' 'I'm afraid that I only have...' 'I don't have much...'* No apologetic language either! They think you can do this job. *You* think you can do this job, otherwise you would not have applied. Don't apologise. An interviewer who is trying to advocate another candidate may introduce leading questions to make you use this sort of tone. Don't.

- The word '*challenge*' – it has been used to death. What do you really enjoy in your work? Is it getting your teeth into something meaty? The intellectual tickle? Winning? Finding an elegant solution to a problem? Pulling disparate personalities together into a cohesive team? Let your competition use extinct terms like '*challenge*' – show them up by being focused and unambiguous.

- The phrase '*I'm good with people*' – it is meaningless and you sound like a contestant in a beauty contest when you say it. Be specific about your interpersonal skills. Key terms: your ability to Empathise, your ability to Listen and your ability to Articulate a point plainly and clearly (acronym ELA).

- Admitting to '*perfectionism*', '*overworking*' or not '*suffering fools gladly*' as a weakness. A trained interviewer will draw a line through your name on the spot if you try this sort of nonsense (see page 215, Talking About Weaknesses).

- Little jokes about sitting in the interviewer's chair in five years' time – yawn (see page 236, The Nightmare Interview from Hell). There are a lot of reasons for asking the '*Where do you plan to be in five years' time?*' question; but the smart-alec answer will satisfy none of them.

- Name-dropping – unless you are *100 per cent* certain it will get you the job. Name-dropping just makes the interviewer feel unimportant and excluded from the decision-making process. Not a good idea. Name-dropping to lend weight to your opinions or research is okay, as long as you don't overdo it.

- Any negative reference to a current or previous employer. This is often quite difficult to avoid, but showing up on a first date and spending the evening bitching about your previous boy/girlfriend wouldn't exactly endear you to the person on the other side of the dinner table, would it?

STUMPED?

It happens sometimes – they hit you with a question that, despite all your hard work, you just don't know the answer to. Maybe you should know it. Now that you hear it, it seems so *obvious*. How could you have overlooked that in your research? And all the while the interviewer is looking over at you expectantly, pen poised. What are you going to do?

You can (a) admit ignorance, (b) bluff or (c) try to divert the question off into something that you *do* know. I don't recommend (b) or (c) – for obvious reasons. There is also a less obvious reason: the Machiavellian interviewer who deliberately asks a Stumper just to see how you will respond. They *know* that you couldn't possibly know the answer, but how will you deal with it...?

How about this? '*Well Mr Interviewer, ya stumped me. Maybe I should know the answer to that one, but I haven't come across it in all of the digging and prep that I did for this interview. So let me answer as I would if I were on the job. If you walked into my office and hit me with that, I wouldn't try to bluff you on it, I'd go and find out the full and correct answer and I'd get back to you as soon as I had it. So, that's what I'm going to do here – can I have your fax number/e-mail address and I'll send you through a response on that one later today?*'

Interviews are all about trying to identify patterns of behaviour in the candidate that will carry through from the selection process to their working life. How do you think an answer like the above would bode for you? Slightly better than a transparently obvious bluff maybe?

CLANGERS

IT people have a thing they call an '*ohno second*' – it is that minuscule amount of time in which you realise that you've just made a HUGE mistake that the undo button won't remedy.

There you are, with your mind reeling. You have just dropped the clanger of all time in the middle of the final interview and it is sitting there like a steaming pile of rhinoceros dung on the table. The interviewer looks a little startled for a moment, but then solemnly writes down what you have just said. Aaaaaaah! He not only noticed it, he's probably going to submit it to the funnies and bloopers column in the *Financial Times* or *Fortune* magazine. What can you do?

The short answer is – nothing. You have screwed up royally and probably cost yourself the opportunity for a really excellent position. *Any* attempt at retrieval ('*I can't believe I just said that*') is a case of too little too late. So practise. Come down off your high '*Oh I'm better when I'm not over-rehearsed*' horse and *practise*. Think about what they are likely to ask you. Think about why they are asking it. Think about your most positive attributes, experiences and achievements and build a picture that you can sell in the interview. Then start saying it out loud over and over again in advance of the interview. Actors do it. Singers do it. TV presenters do it. Children do it in advance of a recital. What makes you so damn special that you can get away without having to rehearse? Are you really that fluent? Articulate? Forceful? Credible? Memorable?

If you do drop a noisy clanger, the only thing you can do is plough on regardless. The one saving grace you have is that there is an issue of perception here – what seems catastrophic to you might be deemed to be a '*somewhat regrettable slip in the midst of an otherwise very strong performance*' by the interviewer. So if you fall apart at this point, you really are dead. This is a test of your *chutzpah/savoir-faire* (why isn't there a good phrase for this in English? Intestinal fortitude maybe?) – so get back to the agenda and start selling again.

Interviews are highly predictable and you can do a great deal of advance work that minimises your chances of elimination. But they can also be tricky, unpredictable beasts and if you find yourself straying out of your comfort zone, it is almost certainly going to be because you didn't do the groundwork. If this happens to you, it's pretty hard to kick your own backside afterwards, but if you would care to drop in and visit me, I'd be *more* than happy to do it for you…

Chapter 7

BODY TALK

You can fool all of the people some of the time; you can fool some of the people all of the time; but you can't fool all of the people all of the time.
ABRAHAM LINCOLN

Psychologists across the world argue as to just how much information we communicate with our bodies; but put a group of them in a room together and they will all agree that we receive very little information merely from what people say.

UGLY FACT NO. 9

JUST 10–30 PER CENT OF ALL THE INFORMATION THE INTERVIEWER TAKES ON BOARD WILL BE AS A RESULT OF WHAT YOU SAY.

So make sure that your body is not disputing what your mouth is saying. The easiest way to do this is by telling the truth. This will also ensure that no one is hiring you under false pretences and you are likely to be happier (and survive longer) on the job. Once again, Manahan's mantra: *If you have to lie to get your foot in the door, this probably isn't the job for you.*

NON-VERBAL CUES

Rules of thumb for the interview:

- The over-riding rule of body language in interviews for both men and women is that **Stillness Projects Strength**. You rarely see a news-reader gesturing to camera. You don't have to sit like a statue, but make sure you get yourself comfortable in the chair – with the base of your spine well against the seat-back – and keep your non-verbal cues relaxed and open.
- Keeping your body language open and relaxed demonstrates self assurance. You don't have to perch nervously on the edge of your seat to display attentiveness, but slouching back and placing your hands behind your neck won't exactly endear you to the interviewer either. In most settings, your legs will be hidden below the table, so you can cross and un-cross your legs at will. If your legs *are* visible, an ankle cross is generally deemed acceptable, the typical alpha-male ankle-to-knee cross is not.

FAQ
'What do I do with my hands?'

- Crossing your arms is definitely a no-no. You can rest your hands in your lap. Rest one on your leg and the other on the armrest of your chair (don't grip too tightly!). Interlacing your fingers briefly or rubbing your palms slowly together are usually signs of deep thought; scratching your head or playing with your hair is less acceptable. If you have a notebook with you, put it on the table/desk. You can hold your pen, but don't 'fiddle' with it.

FIRST IMPRESSIONS

- First impressions – the smile, the posture, the handshake. Meaningless trivial pleasantries or life-and-death moments? Try doing these badly and see what happens…
- The handshake: to crush or not to crush? Hold the handshake for two or three beats and try and match the other person's pressure – unless they are obviously trying to crush your hand, in which case trying to out-Silverback a Silverback is probably not the smart move. Maintain eye contact for the handshake until you are aware of the colour of the other person's eyes.

EYE CONTACT

- Eye contact as you speak is very important too. This is more difficult to maintain in a panel interview setting where you have to sweep back and forth. Don't stare the interviewers down, but you should look at them for 66–75 per cent of the time while you are answering.
- There are all sorts of theories about what is going on when you break eye contact while you are speaking. As a general rule, a trained interviewer will not be impressed if they have asked you a fact-based question and you look to your left. (The inference is that you are drawing on the right, or creative, side of your brain by doing this – i.e. you are making your answer up as you go along.) Most people seem to look to the right when they are drawing information out of their memory.
- A good time to maintain *very* close eye contact is when they are asking the question – to ensure that you have picked it up fully and correctly.
- You can non-verbally demonstrate that you are listening as well – head inclined to the side, a little smile or nod. Be obviously alert and interested while they are talking. You can back this up verbally with little '*uh-uh*' and '*mmmm*' noises. Further reinforce their impression of your alertness and intelligence by echoing their language or specific terminology back at them as the interview progresses. This is particularly

effective when you are asking questions at the end of the interview (see page 219, Asking Them Questions).

IRRITATORS

FAQ
'Should I use humour or tell jokes in an interview?'

- Using humour or not depends on the nature of the role (are you being interviewed for a sales or an undertaker's job?), the interviewer's style and you. Many candidates use humour out of nervousness, thinking that it will mask their discomfort. For an entry-level position, you risk coming across as a smart-alec or as not taking the process sufficiently seriously. For a more senior position, you may be perceived as not having sufficient *gravitas*. So, humour can be a very risky approach to take. However, if the interviewer is adopting a breezy style and injecting some humour, it may be appropriate for you to respond in kind. But it will only be a useful tool if you have the ability to use your wit to make your points more memorable *and* the ability to closely gauge the interviewer's reaction so you can modify your approach as needed. You should look for a meaningful benefit to any approach that you decide to take at interview and humour is no exception.
- Gesticulation (that 'dink-dink' quotes gesture that people make with their fingers? AAAHHHhhhhhhhhhhhh!) rarely accomplishes what you intend. Be aware of your usual pattern and practise to get it down to an effective minimum. When we are agitated, we also tend to use quick, jerky motions with our hands. **Occasional**, **strong** and **slow** are your watchwords for gesturing.
- Repetitive phrases used for emphasis, or to buy time, quickly become irritating to the interviewer. '*You know*' '*Sort of*' '*Kind of*' '*Like*' '*Buuuuut*' '*Thaaaat*' '*Weeeelllll*'. Silence has a place in interview. You don't have to, nor should you, jump in straight away with a response to their

question. The tenth time you say 'You know' (to buy time or out of nervousness) in the interview is the moment at which the highly irritated interviewer wants to scream, 'NO! I don't know! That's why I'm asking you, you dolt!'

- Your voice is a vital asset at interview. It is critical that you use the appropriate words, but most listeners will take more from how you say it rather than the micro-specifics of what you say. Exercise your voice. Practise with different emphases, pauses and pacing. A little work here can make a huge difference. Pay particular attention to pace – most candidates speak far too rapidly at interview (see page 326, Public Speaking at Interviews).

- Licking lips, stamping feet, playing with jewellery or hair, touching your nose, leaning suddenly forward to make your point. Most of us have at least one physical 'tic'. Find 'em and kill them off.

- Sighing or blowing air out through your pursed lips are indicators of a problem question that is giving you real pause for thought. You may want to deliberately give that impression once or twice, but no more than that.

ESTABLISHING A PRESENCE

I think it's fair to say that very few people relish the idea of a job interview. We all experience nervousness and we all manifest it in different ways. Remember Tigger, the bouncy, flouncy, pouncy, trouncy tiger from Winnie the Pooh? Now don't get me wrong, I love Tigger as much as the next man. But I don't particularly want to meet him when I'm interviewing on behalf of a client company. It has happened so often: I read the CV and I like what I'm seeing; I meet the candidate and they are confident and beautifully turned out; they sit down and the opening of the interview goes very well; but then I get into some below-the-surface probes and, suddenly, Tigger is bouncing around the room! Even a well-trained interviewer will find it hard to focus on what you are saying if your body language is pinging all over the place.

BODY LANGUAGE RULE
STILLNESS PROJECTS STRENGTH.

BODY LANGUAGE COROLLARY
IF THE NON-VERBAL CUE DOES NOT REINFORCE
THE VERBAL MESSAGE, KILL IT OFF.

BECOMING AWARE OF YOUR PHYSICAL SELF

The majority of us are blissfully unaware of our physical presence and its impact – just look at how people react when they hear themselves on tape or see themselves on camera for the first time: *'Do I really sound like that?' 'I don't have that many chins, do I?'*

Grab a tolerant friend and a video camera and tape yourselves having a conversation over the course of an evening. Watch the playback and note body language or phrases that might irritate. Then do the same for an interview dry-run. Play the tape back at high speed and it will reveal any bad physical habits. You will have to listen very carefully to spot the verbal ones (see page 406, Appendix 3 for the Annoyance Check-list). Video cameras used to be a rarity and they were so expensive, borrowing one was the equivalent of taking ownership of the Crown Jewels for a night. As such, people rarely had occasion to see themselves on screen and gain an insight into how they looked and sounded. There is no such excuse now. Almost anyone can get hold of a video camera, and if you are not prepared to do this and view yourself in the cold light of day, it says a lot to me about your level of commitment.

MOCK INTERVIEWS

FAQ
'Is there any advantage in going for a mock interview session?'

The advantages of a practice interview with a stranger are that it will (1) provide you with objective feedback and (2) desensitise you to at least some of the unpleasantries of the interview process. A tailored session will allow you to voice your concerns and gain insight into the most positive methods of self presentation. If you can't afford or access a fully fledged mock interview, use the questions from this book or download some more questions from the internet and get a friend to take you through them and tape or film you as you answer them. You will probably be amazed by how you look and/or sound, but the experience is invaluable.

A *caveat* on professional mock interviews here. Many companies offer these services and some of them are very good. But many of them are not. Watch out for these warning signs of a poor service:

- The session will be of a fixed duration (usually 1.5–2.5 hours). What if you just want to fine-tune your approach on one or two areas of questioning? What if you collapse in a puddle of tears and require two or three sessions? Does the organisation have that sort of flexibility? There is nothing more frustrating than feeling that you are being 'shoe-horned' through a process. You are just getting to grips with a novel approach to the weakness question and the mock interviewer glances at his watch and says, '*I'm afraid we'll have to move on now…*' Worse than useless. The session will take as long (or short) as the session needs – any company that can't accommodate that is not worth your time or money.
- The company doesn't ask you about the job you are going for or doesn't ask to see your CV in advance. The first means that you are going to be put through a 'by the numbers' generic interview, with no tailoring to the nature of the role. The second means that the mock interviewer will be spending 10–20 minutes at the beginning of the session familiarising herself with your CV – probably while you fill in a bunch of forms. To make the session worthwhile, they should be asking for your CV, cover letter and any other written materials from your side, *plus* a full spec on the job – the advertisement, the job description and anything you have been able to dig up on it. They should also be sending *you* pre-work materials to get you focused and ready for the session.

- The company insists on videotaping the session and trumps this as some sort of BIG DEAL. If you have significant concerns about your ability to perform effectively in the interview setting, someone shouting '*Lights, camera, action!*' as you begin a dry run is probably not going to be helpful. Audio- or videotaping has its place, but a perceptive, empathetic adviser who just plain *talks* to you is probably going to be more useful at the outset. If it is a senior role and you are doing multiple sessions preparing for it, then the camera is invaluable. If you get the feeling that the session is built around the camera because '*that's how we do things around here*', look elsewhere.

- The biggest failing that I constantly hear about in mock interview sessions is a weak counsellor. If the person conducting the session has no commercial or industrial experience and that is the nature of your upcoming interview, ask yourself just how useful they are likely to be. If the individual is a highly qualified psychologist, a career counsellor of 20 years' experience, or a gifted speech and drama coach, that is all very well, but if that is *all* they have, it may not be enough. In an ideal world, your coach will be perceptive/empathetic, inspirational, a *superb* communicator, have ongoing professional dealings with a spectrum of organisation types, the appropriate qualifications and a breadth and depth of experience. Rare fish indeed. It's your money, your time, your career and your make-or-break interview – shop around. A referral from someone you trust on your network is worth 10 times as much as a slick advertisement in the Yellow Pages or a good sales pitch on the phone. People can be quite shy in admitting that they have used a career management service – encourage them to share their experiences, good and bad, and make your choices from that base.

There is nothing phoney or duplicitous about practising for an interview – if you had a spoken part in a play, you would rehearse for *weeks*. Getting the unfamiliar language of the interview flowing smoothly from your mouth takes a lot of practice; you have to get the lexicon of the interview into your vocal memory. The greatest public speakers all rehearse extensively in advance of an important event. Chances are, if you think someone is excellent at talking off the cuff, they have probably put a *massive* amount of work into their speech (see page 41, Fanatics).

Take the time and have the humility to recognise that you *must* practise. If you find yourself getting stuck or coming up short in that practice, further have the humility to call for help. You take your cat to the vet if it's sick and your PC back to the shop when it's not working to your satisfaction. Why would you not seek expert help in something as important as a significant career opportunity?

Chapter 8

NEGOTIATING REMUNERATION

> *Quality is remembered long after the price is forgotten.*
>
> **MOTTO OF THE GUCCI FAMILY**

Salary negotiation is one of the most delicate parts of the whole job search process, and it is at this stage that many candidates inadvertently disqualify themselves. In every selection process, you will be asked, '*How much do you want?*' at some juncture. What they are, in effect, asking you is, '*What do you think you are WORTH?*'

Or, put another way, '*Do you have delusions of grandeur (or no self confidence), are you going to be impossible to manage, or are you a total wuss that I can micro-manage into an early grave?*'

QUESTIONS WITHIN QUESTIONS

What a lot you can reveal with the answer to a predictable, relatively innocuous question! Another thing you reveal in this answer is whether you told the truth in response to earlier questions (particularly those probing your motivation and enthusiasm). Naturally enough, the best response is to not directly answer the question at all, but rather to turn it back on the interviewer: '*Well, I'm not sure. Obviously, in an ideal world, I'd love to be coming in somewhere in the top half of your scale, but I presume that you have guidelines for what the starting salary should be for someone of my experience and qualifications, so what do you think I would be worth?*'

FIRST LAW OF NEGOTIATION
TRY NOT TO STATE YOUR OPENING POSITION.
IF AT ALL POSSIBLE, MAKE THEM SAY A NUMBER FIRST.

You should practise this in role-play with friends and relations, so that you get good at batting the ball firmly but politely back into their court. (Of course, you cannot play this sort of crude game for a senior level post. Your head-hunter/network should have given you a clear picture of what is on offer and your reputation and the organisation you work for should have done the same for the interviewer.)

MENTIONING MONEY AT THE WRITTEN STAGE

Some advertisements will specifically instruct you to 'submit a full CV and details of references and current salary' as part of the screening process. Unless the role is in public service and you will be disqualified for not doing this, I would not recommend showing all of your cards in this way this early in the process (see page 177, Managing Your References).

However, sometimes it can be to your advantage to kill off time-wasting placement agencies or employers by including some information about your package. If you are just about scraping by on your salary of £XXX, then obviously it is a complete waste of time applying for a job that turns out to pay £XXX minus 20 per cent. Employers, too, are very interested in what you are currently paid as it is a key indicator of your perceived worth in the marketplace.

So if they ask for these details at the written stage of the selection process, for very junior positions I would say okay, include them. For mid-ranking jobs, you should mention that your current package is '*competitive*' and that your expectations on that front are '*negotiable*' or '*to be discussed at interview*'. For more senior roles, it is probably to your advantage to mention your current package in broad strokes or to highlight the *range* of your expectations for the next move: '*My total package with*

Widgets Inc. in recent years has been in the range of £XXX to £YYY. Given the pivotal nature of the Operations role in Gidgets Inc., I would expect that the remuneration on offer would be of a similarly competitive nature.' This quickly cuts to the chase and means that you will not be wasting time running after low-paid jobs that have been dressed up to look more senior in the advertisement.

CURRENT PACKAGE?

In many instances at first interview, the other side will not directly ask you what your expectations are; they may just inquire as to the level of your current salary/package. Still a sticky moment. Most candidates at junior to mid-level exaggerate at this point and interviewers have learnt to automatically deduct 10–15 per cent from the figure that you mention, *especially* if your body language gives away the lie (see page 288, Body Talk).

If you are currently underpaid and this is a major factor in your reason for leaving your present organisation, then you will have to talk up the package that you are on. Maybe you are about to have a salary review? A new bonus scheme is being introduced that is going to significantly improve your current take-home situation? There's a company-wide negotiation being rubber-stamped at the moment, which will give you X per cent more than your current number and your next review will improve that by a further Y per cent? *That's* your starting point, *not* the number that you are on today (this holds true for mentions of your package in writing too – see above).

It is also imperative that you find out what the norm is in your target organisation, so that you don't (a) give yourself away too cheaply or (b) inadvertently disqualify yourself from the process by mentioning what they regard as a staggeringly large figure:

- **Placement agencies** (particularly the larger ones) frequently conduct salary surveys. For senior positions, your liaison person should be able to give you a hard number. If they can't, tell them to go away and get one.

- You will find this kind of material in the business sections of the broadsheet **newspapers** on an occasional basis. This will be somewhat generic and may not include remuneration details for the role-type that you are applying for, but a little educated deduction should have you in the right ballpark.
- Use any contacts you have in the **Human Resources** world. They frequently conduct benefits surveys to ensure that their organisation is in line with market norms. Talk to your network – someone may have at least a scale or range that you can work to.

This information is not hard to get hold of, so don't be caught out for the lack of it.

WHEN TO TALK ABOUT MONEY

As a general rule of thumb, you shouldn't raise the subject of remuneration first. The exception to this is if you are dealing initially with a placement agency – in which case, ask away. But once you are talking directly with the employer, it is appropriate to let them raise the subject. More to the point, when *they* start talking about money can be a useful 'tell' as to their attitudes and motivations. If they introduce the negotiation very early, it may be that they are less interested in getting the best possible person for the job and more concerned with keeping the hire cheap. If they introduce it very late in the process, it's a better sign but they may be hoping to lull you into a false sense of security and then yank the carpet out from under your feet when you are more than half-committed…

SECOND LAW OF NEGOTIATION
DON'T BACK YOURSELF INTO A CORNER.
NEVER SAY A HARD 'NO'.

If you are disappointed (or insulted!) by the figure that they mention, you have two options: (a) snort derisively in their faces and say something along the lines of, 'Pay peanuts, get employees with simian characteristics. Come on – get real' or (b) don't confront – say that the figure is way lower than it should be and you will go away and come back with a counter-proposal (which will be based upon your research and should be very difficult to argue with).

THIRD LAW OF NEGOTIATION

IF YOU HAVE TO SAY 'NO', BE PREPARED TO WALK AWAY.

SHOW ME THE MONEY!

How much you will and won't move for is a critical milestone on your road map for the job-hunt. That being said, it can be worth your while to look at an holistic picture. If your target organisation pays a little less, but really invests in its employees, it might be worth giving them at least a few years of your time. Maybe you want to gain a further qualification and they have a particularly generous reimbursement programme for employee education. They might do something very creative on car expenses that leaves you considerably better off over the course of a year than your existing package. Their bonus scheme is way better than your current one and you have always been good at hitting targets…

Don't be closed- or narrow-minded on this. Drawing a line down the middle of the page and comparing your total net worth in your current role with what's on offer is more than a clichéd or cursory exercise – it is a vital one.

REMUNERATION IS NOT THE SAME AS SALARY

Another common mistake made is to restrict the discussion to salary alone. Do not fall into this trap. When you are discussing your total remuneration package, you should include:

- Bonuses
- Stock options
- Profit sharing
- Working hours – do they offer flexitime/part-time work/job-sharing schemes?
- Overtime rates or time *in lieu* if they don't offer overtime
- Pensions (is it contributory or non-contributory, do they operate AVCs?)
- Health and other insurances (do they cover just you, or your family too? Death benefits for your family?)
- Car, mileage rates, car allowances (if they provide a car, how often is it replaced?)
- Travel allowance – could be very important if you are looking at a lengthy daily commute
- *Per diem* and overnight allowances
- Frequency of salary reviews
- Subscriptions to publications
- Memberships to professional bodies, sports or health clubs
- Training and personal development
- Further education
- Leasing arrangements
- Preferential loans

The list is long and depends on the type of organisation that you are about to join. Time to think broadly and get creative!

HAVE A CLEAR OBJECTIVE

As in any negotiation, you should also have a very clear picture of your objectives; in this case your minimum figure. Calculate how much you actually **need**, how much you **want** and how much you'd really **like** (more lines in the sand!). Employers tend not to be interested in how much it costs you to live, but if you can talk in concrete terms about your fixed outgoings (rent/mortgage, utilities, groceries, insurances, savings) it immediately becomes obvious that you are not being frivolous in the negotiation.

FOURTH LAW OF NEGOTIATION
DON'T NEGOTIATE WITH UNDERLINGS –
NEGOTIATE WITH THE PERSON WHO HAS THE
ULTIMATE POWER TO SAY 'YES' OR 'NO'.

This is very important. If you go into a garage to complain about the quality of the repairs done on your car, you don't talk to the guy with grease under his fingernails – you talk to the guy in the suit. In a negotiation on your salary and benefits, DO NOT engage with someone who can say, '*I'll have to get back to you on that.*' One of the keys to successful negotiation is that both sides have the same amount of thinking time. If you let the other person out of the room to talk to a boss, that means they have two to three times your thinking time. You will be up against the negotiator, the decision-maker and probably at least one other player from their side. Three brains to one? I'm not betting on you. As soon as someone tries the '*I'll have to get back to you on that*' line on you, it is imperative that you get past that person. Make this a deal-breaker if you have to, but talk directly to the ultimate decision-maker.

'WE COULDN'T POSSIBLY...'

Irrespective of the level of the player, a stock line used by negotiators on the employer side to keep your entry package low is, '*Oh, we couldn't possibly do that. It wouldn't be fair on the other staff'* OR *'Everyone would want that if we gave it to you.'* Human Resources professionals are particularly prone to trotting out this one.

Bull! Your immediate answer to this kind of jaded nonsense should be, *'Are you seriously trying to tell me that there is no confidentiality in this organisation and that everyone's salary and package is an open book to everyone else?'* Watch them run for cover! Their stammering response is typically something along the lines of, *'Of course not, but you know how these things get out…'*

Your counter should be to smile pleasantly and say, *'Well, with respect, I see that as being an issue for you and your department. It only becomes my problem if it affects this negotiation. Are you going to let that affect this negotiation?'*

GOOD COP/BAD COP

Another common tactic used by employers is a 'Good Cop/Bad Cop' routine, whereby the person that you will be reporting to hands over the negotiation to a colleague, typically someone from Finance or Human Resources. Do *not* let this happen. The Good Cop doesn't want to harm her working relationship with you at the outset – hence the hand-off. Insist politely, but firmly, that you deal with your boss directly (as long as she has final say on your package) for the negotiation. She will ultimately be the person who decides your pay rises and who is aware of your value to the organisation. So it is not unreasonable to ask to deal with the person that you will be dealing with for the rest of your time in the organisation.

THE WRITTEN WORD

If you really want to join a new organisation and they are promising you the sun, moon and stars, get them to put *all* of the elements in writing. This is of particular importance if you have to take a step backwards on some aspect of your package, for whatever reason. An airy undertaking of, '*Oh, that's just a starting salary while you're on probation. We'll be raising that by XX per cent after six months*' for a fairly junior position is all very well; but if you make them write it into your contract of employment, you will quickly determine whether or not they mean what they say.

Any unwillingness on their part to put their promises on paper should set off alarm bells in your head. It is fair to say that the selection process involves a degree of seduction on both sides, but an employer who is unwilling to provide concrete reassurances on promises made is *not* going to respect you in the morning...

FIFTH LAW OF NEGOTIATION
IF YOU DON'T ASK FOR IT,
THEY'RE NOT GOING TO GIVE IT TO YOU.

Have a look at this little scale. It examines the ratio of earnings by CEOs of Fortune 500 companies to earnings by an average line worker in those companies over time.

1980	42:1
1990	85:1
2001	411:1

Do you think those CEOs got that kind of disproportionate pay rise without asking? Maybe the boards of management of all of those companies, in their infinite wisdom and mercy, decided to just *hand over* the cash? If you think so, I have a bridge that I want to sell you...

One thing I have noticed about senior players over the years is that they have the self confidence to ask for items in their remuneration that would make you or me blush to the roots of our hair. Examples:

- A Chief Financial Officer who demanded that a six-figure severance package be put in place, '*just in case things don't work out in the first 18 months*'.

- An ex-pat Marketing Director who insisted that the company pay for 12 first-class flights per year for him and his family of four! (Naturally, the money was paid as part of his annual bonus and the Director flew back and forth only a few times a year, and travelled economy.)
- A Regional Personnel Director who asked for, and got, a car and full-time driver and the company had to pay the driver's rent so that he could live in the gate lodge of the Director's home. The Director lived less than 10 miles from the regional headquarters.
- Just take a gander at what Dennis Kozlowski was paid even when he knew that all was not well in the state of Denmark (Tyco).
- Enron's Ken Lay has a pension of $900,000 per annum, agreed way back when...
- *Time Magazine* reports that CEOs at major US corporations took an average of a 15 per cent increase in total direct compensation from 2001 to 2002. Did you get anything like that much?

> 'Never let us negotiate out of fear, but never let us fear to negotiate.'
>
> JOHN F. KENNEDY

You may not have the *chutzpah* (or downright gall) to ask for perks at that level, but, at the very least, you should know what the going rate is. Know what you are worth. Know what they can *afford*. Decide how much you want. And then ASK!

Chapter 9

AFTER THE INTERVIEW

We have not yet reckoned our debt.

FROM WINSTON CHURCHILL'S OBITUARY

The interview process does not finish (for you or for them) at the concluding handshake. They will be doing the talking-about-you-behind-your-back thing for some time after you leave and you should also use the time immediately after the interview to your advantage. Almost everyone, even the poorest candidate, operates a countdown schedule coming up to the interview. You should learn to continue that schedule in the aftermath.

First and foremost, remember that the interview is not over until you leave the building. Many interviewers (or an administrator/receptionist) will chat with you or stay with you right to the front door, so **do not relax** just because you've been told the interview is over. It is amazing what people will let slip once they believe that the process has concluded. Don't let go! Not your body language, not your confidence, not your tone, not your professionalism. Everyone you meet in the building is forming an opinion of you, so be mindful of holding it all together until you are out of the building, out of sight and out of ear-shot.

All too often, an interview does not result in a job offer. The reasons why are rarely based on core competencies or qualifications. It may be that your experience isn't as close a match as they inferred from your CV, or that your personality/style will not be a good fit with the organisation. For more junior positions, the points above also hold true, but experience has shown me that most people simply talk themselves out of the job (see page 155, Getting Ready to Talk About Yourself).

Interviews are necessarily stressful occasions, but if you are failing as often as not *and* not learning anything from them, you are putting yourself through the hoops for no good reason. EVERY interview that you attend is an opportunity for you to learn something that can improve your chances later in your career (see page 145, Learning Curve 4).

THANK YOU

As soon as the interview is over, and no matter how you feel it went, write them a thank-you letter. They must receive this no more than 36 hours after your departure. This is an entirely appropriate (and still, amazingly, rarely utilised) move – it certainly won't change their minds if they weren't going to give you the job anyway, but they will be impressed by your professionalism and courtesy. You will stand out from the crowd and they may keep you in mind for future positions. Occasionally, this note can also be used as an opportunity to follow up on a question to which you just didn't know the answer during the interview – if so, include your response in your thank-you (see page 284, Clangers). You can send your thank-you by e-mail, but I prefer a crisp printed letter – it is just that little bit more personal.

WHAT WAS SAID?

So, the interview is over. You have just been through a live-fire exercise and they have given you the blueprint for what it is potential employers are concerned about when they meet *you* for the first time.

- Once you are out of sight, start notating *everything* that was said in the interview room. Their questions. Your responses. Clangers that you dropped. Their answers to your questions. All of this is immediately pertinent.
- Take particular note of questions that you answered poorly, or that you weren't able to answer at all. Incomplete or fizzle-out answers.

Answers that you had practised but that you just didn't deliver well on the day. Things you wish you had said, points you should have made.

- A useful *aide-mémoire* for this is a Dictaphone®. Alternatively just scribble your thoughts down in a notebook. Keep doing this for 72 hours after the interview – little details will occur to you for about that long.
- Transfer all of this information in a structured way on to your computer. This forms the core of your job-hunting database.

DEAR JOHN...

- Didn't get the job? Let's find out why. Write to thank them (again) and express your disappointment and your continued interest in future positions, but also to mention that you will be following up to get feedback on your performance.
- Freedom of information came to Sweden in 1766, in 1919 to Finland, in 1966 to Denmark and in 1970 to Norway. In 1981, the Council of Europe put out Recommendation No. R(81)19. Check how the ensuing 2002 EU Directive affects you if you are dealing with a public service body. Once you know your local rights, get specific – ask them where you fell down under these headings:
  - a) Experience
  - b) Qualifications/Training
  - c) Personal attributes
  - d) Performance at the interview itself.
- Your tone throughout the feedback process must be totally non-threatening, but politely insistent. You are looking for their help in furthering your career – say so.

TALK TO WINNERS

Once the dust has settled, a very useful person to talk to with regard to a disappointment at interview is the person who got the job ahead of you. Send them a congratulations card. Follow up shortly afterwards and offer to buy them lunch or a drink after work. Explain why you want to meet them and gently ingratiate yourself. This is not as difficult as it sounds and can pay great dividends.

You can get a tremendous insight into an organisation from someone newly hired and you should try to maintain some degree of contact with that person over time — you may be competitors, but you can also feed off each other. Just make sure that you give them a reason to want to meet you/talk with you again. People will tolerate a symbiotic relationship, but will be quick to dismiss someone who brings nothing to the party (see page 168, Networking).

> 'It's not what they say about you that matters... It's what they whisper.'
> ERROL FLYNN

If your current approach is not working, start by assuming that the blame lies with yourself and go looking for that whisper — the one that will make a difference the next time.

FACE-TO-FACE 3 (ELEMENTS IN THE MIX)

Chapter 1

PANEL INTERVIEWS

> *A committee is a group of men who individually can do nothing but who,*
> *together, can decide that nothing can be done.*   **FRED ALLEN**

Almost all educational, Public Service/Civil Service (and many large insti-
tutional private sector) interviews are conducted by a panel of three to
nine interviewers. In the past, this process was often poorly conceived,
the interviewers were inadequately trained and prepared and the questions asked were inconsistent, often bearing no apparent relation to the
requirements of the job being discussed. Most dispiritingly, many candidates emerged from a short *pro forma* interview convinced that the job
was 'already gone' before the selection process had even begun.

TIMES THEY ARE A-CHANGING

With the roll-out of Freedom of Information legislation and strategic
management initiatives to bring public services more in line with the private sector, this process has had to be somewhat cleaned up.
Competency-based interviewing (CBI) is becoming the norm (see page
228), with comprehensive note-taking and scoring against a common set
of questions. The interviewers on the panel are given a much tighter
brief than in the past and more time to discuss and score each candidate. A Human Resources professional will usually be present to ensure
that the interview is conducted appropriately and in compliance with
Employment Equality legislation.

The process of sitting across a table from a group of inquisitors is still fairly off-putting though and you will typically have very little time in which to make your points. Public sector interviews tend to be *much* shorter than their private sector equivalents. This is where your structured approach and interview mapping (see page 193) really pays off – if you have a clear, accurate picture of what the role entails, you can crystallise your areas of excellence and strength for that role and really *sell* yourself, even in an abbreviated interview.

ENTITLEMENTS AND FOLLOW-UPS

It is important to realise that you are now entitled to concrete feedback on your performance, specifically on areas in which you were perceived as being weak. For Public/Civil Service roles, you may also be entitled to a transcript of the questions asked, the notes taken and scores assigned to each of your answers. If psychometric or other testing is used as part of the selection process, you are entitled to see the results and receive an explanation of what those results mean (see page 307, After the Interview).

POINTERS FOR PANEL INTERVIEWS

- Find out the names and titles of the interviewers, in advance of the interview if possible.
- Sit opposite the middle person in the panel – ask to move your chair if necessary.
- Answer the person who has asked you the question – spend most of your eye contact on that individual, but occasionally sweep across the others to engage their attention.
- Don't be afraid to ask for clarification on a question. On a broad topic, they may be interested in one small area which you could easily skip over. Ask.
- If you are a naturally quick talker, moderate your pace even more than usual.

- Likewise, if you are prone to speaking in long sentences with sub-clauses, abbreviate your style to a more 'bullet pointed' approach. This will require a great deal of practice, but it does pay off.
- '*Do you have any questions for us?*' If senior management are present, you can use this as an opportunity to show the quality of your preparation and thinking. If not, you can use it as an opportunity to slip in an extra Nugget or two: '*We didn't really cover the area of XXX in the course of the interview. I'd just like to mention my involvement with YYY...*' (see page 219, Asking Them Questions).
- If there are no policy-makers in the room, limit your questions to housekeeping details – when will you hear back, what's the next stage and so on.
- Thank each of the interviewers (and the stenographer, if there is one) individually as you leave.

If you feel that the selection process has not been conducted fairly, you are entitled to make some pretty big waves these days; but, of course, that can have a major impact on your long-term career prospects – a difficult judgement to make and one on which you should definitely seek professional advice first.

Chapter 2

LEARNING CURVE 6 – LACK OF CONFIDENCE

Think of the poorest person you have ever seen and ask if your next act will be of any use to him.

MAHATMA GANDHI'S EPITAPH

Jean, early 30s, single, arts degree
Jean was applying internally for a Head of Administrative Services role in a Third Level institution. She was not confident facing up to the interview process for a number of reasons:

• She had not sat an interview for more than eight years.
• She had a real problem in talking about herself in a positive light.
• She had heard on the grapevine that the position was effectively already filled.
• Last but not least, the prospect of a one-hour, five-person, formal panel interview was very daunting to Jean. (Many candidates find the physical situation of sitting across a table from three to nine interviewers very intimidating.)

Jean had always been very effective in her job performance, so effective in fact that she had been asked to step up as Acting Head of Service while the incumbent was on an extended period of sick leave which ultimately led to resignation on grounds of ill-health. Despite her obvious advantages for the role (intimate knowledge of all the nuances of the Department, proven track record and *total* commitment to the organisation) and her very real ambition for the position, Jean had, in her own head, virtually talked herself out of the job.

The initial part of the consultation centred on the politics of the Department and the backgrounds and personalities of the likely interviewers. On that basis, we put Jean through an arduous mock interview with frequent stops for feedback. Jean's reluctance to portray herself in a positive light and her unwillingness to take credit for significant accomplishments became the focus for the next part of the consultation. She was taught to stop looking at things from her own perspective and to start thinking like the interviewers she would be facing. On a second run-through of the interview, she was tangibly more focused in her answering and was starting to come out of her shell. We recommended ongoing vocal practice prior to the interview to ensure her comfort with talking about her strengths.

Jean's interview stress manifested itself most obviously in her speech. Her voice would alter in pitch when she was not on comfortable ground and her breathing became very shallow, resulting in her having to gulp in air halfway through a sentence. This had obvious negative connotations and detracted significantly from her credibility as a potential Head of Service. 'I'm not at all like this when I am on the job,' Jean told me. But this would not matter to the interviewers – they would presume that her interview behaviour would carry through into her performance of the job. We helped her start to rectify this problem with some breathing and postural exercises and physical mnemonics.

Jean's other concern was for her appearance – she habitually wore smart but comfortable clothes to work and did not feel that these would make a strong enough impression at the interview. She wanted to walk through the door of the interview room and make a big impact on the interviewers, but was afraid of making poor choices in her 'makeover'. We arranged a short-notice appointment with our style specialist who worked closely with Jean to ensure optimal professional impact.

Jean secured the position in open competition and was privately told by one of the interview panel afterwards that there had indeed been a preferred candidate and that she was initially not being considered as a serious applicant, but that her obvious insight and confidence in performing the job had shone through at the interview.

LEARNING POINTS:

- Being the **internal candidate** for promotion has obvious **advantages** – you may know some or all of the interviewers, you have a demonstrable track record, you are aware of the key issues and you will know the political hot-spots to avoid.

- But there *are* **disadvantages**, most notably that the selection board may have preconceived notions about you and may be aware of your weaknesses in a way that a truly objective interviewer could not be.

- You cannot, and must not, hide your light under a bushel. If you have **strong points** and successes to your credit, you must, *must*, MUST learn how to get them across at interview. All too often, I meet strong candidates who find it almost impossible to push themselves forward in this way. Overcoming this can be an agonising process for these clients and I have found that learning to take the interviewer's perspective is a crucial watershed in getting comfortable with this approach (see page 54, Who Matters?).

- Some measure of **stress** prior to and during interviews is normal and healthy – at the very least, it indicates that you are taking the process seriously. However, if that stress becomes a paralysing impediment to your performance, you need to take steps… (see page 372, Stress, and page 390, Breathing).

Chapter 3

LEARNING CURVE 7 – DISCRIMINATION

> *All animals are equal, but some are more equal than others.*
>
> **GEORGE ORWELL**

Kathy, late 20s, engaged, science degree

Fortify had helped Kathy to secure a position in a Public Service organisation some years previous to this case study. She had remained in contact with us through her settling-in period in the new job and had also used us during a difficult period when she was in a conflict with a bullying colleague. Now, a significant promotional opportunity had arisen and Kathy came to me for advice on dealing with the politics of the situation.

Kathy knew, from the internal grapevine, that the organisation had a history of passing over female candidates and that the gender split at a senior level was 85 per cent male, 15 per cent female. Furthermore, the organisation was notorious for promoting on the basis of political manoeuvring rather than straightforward ability. The introduction of performance management standards and open competition on the basis of merit was designed to redress this sort of 'old school tie' attitude and bring the Public Services more in line with the private sector, where promotion is more likely to be on the basis of the best person for the job. In Kathy's organisation, these management initiatives had done little as yet to impact on the old state of affairs and culture.

Following the initial consultation, Kathy elected to pursue a 'drip-feed' strategy. She discussed her intention to apply for promotion with her immediate superior and with the next two levels of management over the course of a few weeks. She also approached the Personnel Department to discuss the organisation's poor track record of promoting women. In each instance, Kathy was entirely professional and behaved in a non-threatening way. She had definite objectives set out for herself for each of the meetings and gained valuable insight into the intricacies of the selection process in her Department.

When the promotions were announced, Kathy had her application already primed and had mapped her key skills and experiences out against the requirements of the more senior role. Not surprisingly, she was called to interview and arrived with an agenda of key points to discuss and deliver to the interview panel. Faced with a highly qualified, capable and articulate candidate who had anticipated all of the key areas of competence and the core issues affecting the organisation, the Selection Committee scored Kathy in the top five per cent of the numerous candidates that they had interviewed and she was promoted shortly afterwards.

LEARNING POINTS:

- Kathy learnt from her early experiences in gaining a job that **preparation is everything**. Interviews are, by and large, very **predictable** and, with strong preparation, you can be ready for most lines of questioning – to take some control in the interview and be able to answer the questions to your best advantage (see page 193, Interview Mapping).

- In any large organisation, **politics** are going to be a very important component in your career progression. Merely working hard and keeping your head down may not be enough to get you noticed, particularly in a 'jobs for the boys' culture.

- Politically, you need to be (a) aware of future opportunities and (b) putting your name up on the radar screen of 'those who count'. Both of these measures require you to be thoroughly plugged in to the **grapevine** in your organisation.

- The **Glass Ceiling** is real and very hard to break through – it doesn't take a genius to look around the corridors of power and notice the gender inequity. If you are a genuinely strong candidate and feel that you may be discriminated against in an upcoming competition for promotion, you need to know your rights and you need to make management aware of the consequences of pursuing this (illegal, by the way) course of action. Management in any organisation will not react until it feels a strong stimulus – usually pain – so you need to be prepared to take on this battle in an unrelenting, but structured and goal-driven way.

Chapter 4

PLATFORM TESTS

> *All speech, written or spoken, is a dead language, until it finds a willing and prepared hearer.* **ROBERT LOUIS STEVENSON**

Certain jobs have a large element of stress, 'performance' or dealing with the public at their core – airline cabin crew, training and development positions, solicitor, lecturer and customer service roles would be good examples. An emerging trend in the recruitment process is to put the candidates through a Platform Test as a 'weeding-out' exercise prior to the commencement of interviews – there is no point in wasting time interviewing someone who does not have the composure to survive in the environment.

In the past, candidates were put through a deliberately contrived 'Stress Interview', but this approach has fallen into disrepute, as interview performance is such a poor predictor for performance on the job and this method did not reliably identify the optimal candidate.

DISTINGUISHING YOURSELF FROM THE HERD...

The Test can take a number of formats, but typically you will be performing in front of a deeply unsympathetic audience of your competitors for the job (this won't happen in senior roles, for reasons of confidentiality), plus a number of moderators or observers from the organisation that is recruiting. Examples:

- Deliver a short presentation, using visual aids, on a subject set in advance (or sometimes on the day) by the moderators (see page 326, Public Speaking at Interviews).
- Stand up and talk about yourself for three to five minutes.
- Argue your case on a range of issues thrown at you by the moderators/observers.
- Tell a joke, sing a song, perform your party piece.
- Arrive at a team answer for a series of tests/questions/issues.

EVALUATION CRITERIA

Any one of the above is a very gruelling exercise and the moderators/observers will be appraising you on a range of criteria:

- **Poise** – do you keep your cool, do you take umbrage if someone disagrees with you, suffer from flop-sweats, or retreat into your shell altogether and withdraw from the process?
- **Listening** – particularly important in team or discussion settings. Can you listen effectively and make use of what your competitors (or the moderators) are saying?
- **Advocacy** – how effectively do you deliver your presentation, tell your joke or argue your case?
- **Tenacity** – do you clam up, or give up easily just because someone heckles you in Q&A or makes a better point? (And would you, therefore, do this on the job…?)

THE NAME OF THE GAME IS...

The overriding concern will be your **professionalism** in the face of this gut-wrenching stress. If you have been given something to prepare, how well did you research and present it? If you are thrown in at the deep end, how confidently do you portray yourself? Some useful tactics:

- Position yourself in a power spot/seat where you can observe both your competitors and the interviewers. Read their faces. Read their body language. Modify your approach accordingly as the test proceeds.
- Bring a notepad – jot down the names of your competitors and of the observers against a sketch-map of the room. Few people bother to do this and your ability to address people by their names will stand out.
- In a group discussion setting, vary your approach – don't always be the first to speak, but don't *always* let others speak up ahead of you. Be aware of your preferred style in group settings and work on your back-up style(s) (see page 252, probes on teamwork in The Nightmare Interview from Hell).
- If you have to deliver a presentation, go overboard on your research, your visual look and feel and your level of rehearsal – you can never be too prepared (see page 326, Public Speaking at Interviews).

If I asked you, right now, to jump up and tell me your life story in three minutes plus tell a joke for another minute or two, you probably wouldn't do it to your (much less my) satisfaction. Think about it for 20 minutes and you could probably do it quite well. Okay, so then I stick you in a room with a hostile or uninterested audience and you'll almost certainly get a bit wobbly again.

Your life story in this setting is quite a different pitch from your Opener (see page 209, Introducing Yourself Well) for the interview – typically you will talk more about your family, your education and your hobbies. You are not there to endear yourself to your competitors; that would be virtually impossible. You want to transmit confidence and aplomb under these weird circumstances to the moderators, which will have the beneficial side effect of putting your competition off their stride. So, a bit of humour, a nice anecdote or two and a flowing chronology are the main ingredients. Do this well and you will definitely unnerve the people who have to come after you.

If you are asked to tell a **joke**, keep it safe – no sex, no religion, no politics. Situational humour or jokes about the human condition are fine. You should have at least two funny stories polished and ready to go at a moment's notice.

An **off-the-cuff** presentation is a very tricky business indeed. Typically, you are given a topic and either a flip-chart/some overhead transparencies and pens or access to a laptop computer, and you will have anything from 15 minutes to an hour to prepare. Work with a pencil and paper first. What do you want to convey in your 10–15 minutes? Narrow it down to just a few clear messages (there might be only one) and then you can structure your Beginning, Middle and End.

Less is more for **visual aids** and this is particularly the case when those visual aids are hastily constructed. Use a small number of words and images on each aid and draft your notes out on paper using large letters that you can read from a distance. The off-the-cuff presentation is a *hideous* test, so set yourself apart by trying to determine what the moderators' primary concern is. Is it about the quickness of your mind and the number of ideas you can come up with in an abbreviated timeframe or is it about being able to respond nimbly to changing circumstances in the manner in which you present?

The most useful thing you can do in a Platform Test situation is to *know what is coming*. If you are caught by surprise with a request to step up and perform in some way, it is obviously not to your advantage. Find out how this organisation recruits, what tricks and traps they use. Exhaust every avenue on your network until you have at least *some* idea of what you are likely to be hit with.

Chapter 5

PUBLIC SPEAKING AT INTERVIEWS

> *We had snakes in* **Raiders of the Lost Ark,** *and bugs in* **Indiana Jones and the Temple of Doom;** *but supposedly man's greatest fear is public speaking. That'll be in our next movie.* **STEVEN SPIELBERG**

A selection interview is a public speaking exercise and one which most people dread. And as if an interview wasn't bad enough, candidates nowadays are increasingly required to make a formal presentation as part of the selection process. For teaching, training and many sales positions, recruiters will want to be satisfied as to the quality of your presentation skills and will test you accordingly. Some organisations (airlines, training and law firms) are using the so-called 'Platform Testing' method (as discussed in the previous chapter), whereby you have to make your pitch to an audience consisting of unsympathetic moderators and your competitors for the job. This is obviously highly stressful and is designed to eliminate candidates who cannot operate under difficult conditions. Finally, most senior management positions will require candidates to deliver one or more presentations during the selection process highlighting their approach, vision and mindset.

You can be asked to spontaneously step up to a flip-chart with a pen and outline some of your ideas – or the organisation may notify you in advance that they want you to make a structured 10–60 minute presentation using visual aids. The interviewers will be measuring you in a number of ways:

- The quality, depth and structure of your ideas – **content** is always king.
- Your **comfort** level when you are on your feet – eye contact, posture, gesturing and holding your audience's attention.
- Your **technical** ability in a presentation setting – positioning, effective use of presentation software, use of equipment, bridging from one slide/idea to the next.
- Your ability to work within set **guidelines** – relevance, structure (again!) and timing.

Remember, a presentation is one of the few aspects of the face-to-face stages of the recruitment process over which you have TOTAL control (there's that word again). Exercise that power. Studies demonstrate that 66 per cent of people in the developed world are clinically sleep-deprived. Experience suggests that a large percentage of people make up for their lack of sleep when they are forced to sit through a poor presentation. Your ideas may be top-notch, you may have the latest software, the best projection equipment and plush surroundings to present it all in; but if you do not put pertinent information across in a way that is interesting to your audience, you might as well be handing out sleeping-pills and water to wash them down with.

Holding an audience's attention is hard enough under normal circumstances, but it becomes vital when you are on your feet as part of an interview/selection process. Effective presentation is, at its essence, a simple business, but I won't pretend that it is an easy skill. Delivering a below-par performance due to arrogance, complacency or lack of preparation is inexcusable and will cost you your chance for that plum job.

PRACTISE

Practise, practise, practise. If you had a role in a play that involved delivering a lengthy monologue, you would rehearse for weeks on end. Presentation and public speaking come naturally to almost no one. As you sit here reading this, if you can't give yourself a fat 9 out of 10 for your ability with this skill, you need to get really serious about this, swallow a great big wedge of humble pie and free up time in your diary to practise *every* presentation you make (see page 41, Fanatics). The people watching and listening to you in a recruitment presentation will be scrutinising *every* nuance and will miss *nothing*. If you betray yourself and blow your chance for the want of a few more hours of diligent preparation, you will feel very foolish afterwards.

DELIVERY

Really deliver your ideas with conviction and passion – don't just read them out. Nobody is impressive when they are looking down – it is a sign of subservience, lack of confidence and defeat (see page 288, Body Talk). Why do you think politicians use Autocues? By all means, have your speaking notes in your eye-line, but if you constantly need to refer to them, then you haven't *practised enough*! End of discussion. Speaking notes are particularly useful if you are interrupted by a question and lose your thread in the presentation. But they are not, and should not be, a crutch. How could you inject any enthusiasm/emotion/conviction/ passion into a role in a play if you couldn't remember your lines?

VOICE

The intonation/inflexion of our voices is what distinguishes human beings from Daleks. Pacing, pauses and the pitch of your voice can all help to get your message across more effectively. Try this exercise: pick seven states of mind (happy, sad, inquisitive, loving, etc.) and write them down. Then read out the days of the week to a friend (who has their eyes closed) using one state of mind for each. If your friend can't iden- tify at least five of the emotions you are trying to convey, you need more practice.

LANGUAGE

Appropriate terminology for your audience is vital. This can sometimes necessitate deviating from your intended wording and pitching it to a higher level or dumbing it down on the spot, which obviously requires a real mastery of your subject. Presentations aren't about you – they are about your audience. Their needs. Their concerns. Poor presenters invariably lose sight of this. Nothing is more off-putting than someone who is having a marvellous old time, basking in the spotlight, loving the sound of her own voice and ploughing through her pet subject. I have met vast numbers of egocentric presenters – they invariably come down off the podium breathing heavily and saying, '*Well, I think that went **very** well, don't you…?*'

BODY LANGUAGE

Keep gesticulation to a minimum. The 'less is more' adage really holds true in presentation. This includes shifting from foot to foot, fiddling with a pointer, shuffling notes, jiggling your keys in your pocket, taking your hand in and out of your pocket. An occasional gesture for emphasis will have much greater impact than ongoing, distracting movements (see page 288, Body Talk). You don't have to be a statue, but you should try to become aware of your movements and of the impact that they have on your audience. The CEO of a company in the UK used to rehearse his presentations while standing naked in front of a mirror. Are you that brave?

CONTENT

All the skill in the world at presenting is not going to lift your performance if your content is poorly researched, inappropriately pitched or doesn't pertain to a need/concern of your audience. So, for any presentation, but particularly one that is part of a selection process, you should be 100 per cent mindful of the following:

1 Define your intentions/objectives on a scale with INFORM at one end and PERSUADE at the other. Think about *why* you have been assigned this topic. Are they looking for new ideas? Checking your ability as a researcher? Deliberately choosing a controversial subject to see where you stand?

2 Gather your data – a good rule of thumb is to have three times more material than you need for the time allotted and then start trimming. Never, EVER pad out a presentation.

3 Structure your materials and give your audience an overview of the content – a recurring agenda slide or progress bar can be very useful for this. Beginning, middle, end. Contents, body, summary. Bad presenters invariably stray from the simple approach.

4 Decide whether you will be taking questions as you go along or when you finish.

5 Anticipate questions as you draft and rehearse your presentation and if the answer is going to be complex, prepare a back-up slide (or slides) for use in the Q&A session.

6 Few things irritate an audience more than a presenter who is oblivious to time. Have a watch or a clock in your eye-line and work to milestones – you should be at point X after five minutes, point Y after ten, etc. If you are running long because of an interruption, immediately notify your audience and apologise. Then trim one or two of your explanatory points to try and make up at least some of the time – I have gritted my teeth once too often to the phrase, '*I'm way over my time, aren't I?*' (usually accompanied by a vacuous grin and a shrugging of the shoulders by the presenter).

> 'Most bad story-telling is beginning, muddle and end.'
> PHILIP LARKIN

Think back over the good presentations you have attended in your career. They consistently involved a properly thought-out, well-pitched message that ended with a few minutes to spare – professionalism personified.

NERVES

You *want* to have butterflies in your stomach before your presentation. If they are not there, it is a sign that you are either too complacent or that you just don't care. A degree of *Fight or Flight* (see page 372, Stress) is normal, healthy and desirable as you get ready to speak. If you have constructed your presentation carefully and rehearsed professionally, the nervousness should *galvanise* you into a more effective performance. If you have not, it can *paralyse* you. We have all felt sympathy for the tongue-tied Groom or Father of the Bride at the wedding dinner and clapped at their abysmal jokes. Don't expect the same degree of understanding from a professional audience.

PRACTISE

This is not a misprint. Practise. Really. Swallow your pride and REHEARSE! For an important presentation, I recommend a ratio of 30 minutes of practice for every minute that you will be on your feet. For a really crucial pitch, I would double or triple that. If you have been asked to speak for 15 minutes, you should be confident that you can wrap things up at 14½, and that kind of polished accuracy does not happen without a disciplined approach and assiduous rehearsal.

There is no excuse for bad presentation. In almost every case that I have witnessed, poor presentation is a manifestation of selfishness, arrogance and downright aggression – '*I couldn't give a damn about you, the audience. I am up here, doing my best* (invariably untrue) *so just sit there, shut up and let me plough through this thing.*' I have coined a word to sum this attitude up – it is COMPLARROGANCE.

Top-end presenters cannot afford the luxury of complacency or arrogance. A CEO who blows it in a presentation to the financial community risks a significant drop in share value with all the resultant miseries and woes. She cannot '*wing it*', cannot '*regurgitate it*', cannot '*hope for the best*'. She cannot fall back on the most common excuse that I hear: '*Oh, I get stale – I'm more effective when I'm not over-rehearsed.*' No such luxuries here, just hard work and humility, because she has to be relevant, comfortable, credible and memorable every time.

Objective help and training can make a huge difference to your effectiveness in a crucial presentation. But a good place to start is by paying closer attention when you are in the audience at presentations, both good and bad. Learn from excellent presenters, but also by avoiding the mistakes of bad ones. It is said that there are three types of public speakers – those that inspire, those that aspire and those that perspire – which would you like to be? Which would you *hire*?

Chapter 6

LEARNING CURVE 8 – PRESENTATION

> *You can put wings on a pig, but that doesn't make it an eagle.*
>
> **WILLIAM JEFFERSON CLINTON**

John, late 30s, business degree, married, two children
John came to *Fortify* looking for help in two distinct areas. There was an excellent position at a senior level coming up shortly in his sector but his CV was totally out of date and old-fashioned to boot. He also knew that he would have to make a presentation as part of the interview process (he was confident that he would be called to interview if he could scrape together a decent CV in the meantime) and he needed advice on both the content and delivery of that presentation.

John's CV was what we call a **telling** document – it gave the reader a great deal of basic information about his responsibilities and progression (he had been with the same company for almost 15 years). But the CV did not adequately **sell** him to a potential employer. The first consultation focused in on this and John spent nearly three hours at our offices in the 'hot seat', being grilled on his accomplishments, contributions and the skills he had developed on the job – he later described the experience as being *'like having teeth pulled'*. He had not considered portraying himself in this light before and the session concluded with a much stronger document that left the reader in no doubt as to John's considerable abilities and the tangible benefits to having him on board.

John had also roughed out some ideas for a 20-minute presentation, but was not happy with either the content or the structure.

Furthermore, he was unfamiliar with modern presentation software and wasn't in a position to ask his secretary for help. Working with *Fortify*, he honed the talk to a precise 18-minute delivery, trimming all of the unnecessary detail and focusing in on his vision for the future and the regulatory changes that were going to impact on the sector. Over the next several weeks, he further refined the content on the basis of research suggestions from us and became very polished in his presentation technique following repeated dress rehearsals. We served as Devil's Advocate during this rehearsal process, constantly interrupting John with difficult questions and providing objective feedback on every aspect of his performance. (He was also able to apply some of this feedback to his preparation for the interview.)

John was called for interview as expected. He performed well and was called back for the second interview, at which point he made his presentation. Following two more interviews, he secured the position ahead of stiff competition.

LEARNING POINTS:

- An **out of date CV** can lead to a last-minute panic when an opportunity arises in your desired sector. It is worth **jotting down** any moves or changes in responsibility that you make in your career. It is also worth noting accomplishments/achievements as they happen – too often we forget about these with time (see page 45, Tools of the Trade).

- Your CV has just one job to do – get you to interview. It is not a life history, nor should it be a delineation of the minute details of every job you have ever held. Every word in your CV should be **selling** you to a potential employer. If it is not – delete the word. Far too many CVs are full of untargeted, irrelevant waffle. Make sure yours isn't.

- **Presentations** have become an increasingly common requirement in the selection process. Organisations use them to gather ideas and to determine what competitors are doing in the market. Interviewers use them to specifically assess your ability in this vital skill, to get a sense of your level of professionalism/intelligence and also to see how you perform under pressure.

- Most candidates spend **too much time** on the presentation and not enough on preparing for the interview. This is an easy trap to fall into and can leave you lost for words in a difficult question and answer session. Map your time out (see page 18, Managing Time Effectively) and strike a **balance** between the areas you need to prepare for.

PART 6

I THINK I WANT TO DO SOMETHING DIFFERENT WITH MY LIFE

'I HATE MY JOB'

> *Equity – Integrity.*
>
> **MARSHALL FIELD'S EPITAPH**

'I hate my job.'

'I get headaches on Sunday night just thinking about going back in to work on Monday.'

'If only I could win the Lottery.'

'I'm starting to feel like I'm working in a pressure cooker.'

'Sometimes I wish the alarm clock just didn't work.'

I hear stuff like this a lot. Too much. Far too many people make career choices in their teens on the basis of scholastic aptitude and end up getting locked into a direction and dreading the alarm clock ringing every day. We get to make very few choices that really matter in this life. Where we live, with whom we live and what we do to pay the bills are three of the really big ones. The shelves in your local bookshop are *groaning* with volumes on the subject of decision-making for life. Why? Because experience shows us that human beings don't seem to be very good at making sound choices.

Decisions taken quickly turn out to be bad ones about 60 per cent of the time. Just look at the statistics for marital breakdown (and *that's* not exactly a decision that most people enter into lightly), and I suspect that the numbers for career dissatisfaction are much higher and would result in a much greater rate of career change were it not for the golden handcuffs that many jobs become. If you are happy in your job, whoopee for you and skip this section. If not, read on…

SIMPLE MATHEMATICS

You spend a lot of your adult life asleep. You also spend a hell of a lot of it at work. If you sleep 7½ hours a night, work for 40 hours a week (only 40? Lucky you!) and commute an hour each way Monday to Friday, that's 31 per cent of your week asleep and another 30 per cent working/commuting every week. Roll those numbers out on an annual basis and you get:

48 weeks x (40 + 10) = 2,400 hours a year working
and commuting.

For how many years do you intend working? For how many years will you *have to* work? 20? 30? 40? 45?

2,400 hours a year x 20 years = 48,000
2,400 hours a year x 30 years = 72,000
2,400 hours a year x 40 years = 96,000
2,400 hours a year x 45 years = 108,000

Rounding off, that's 50–100,000 hours of your life, working from our rather conservative numbers of a 40-hour working week plus a 10-hour commute. (By the way, if you sleep 7½ hours a night, you will spend a further 55–123,000 hours of that 20–45 years out cold.)

LIFE IS SHORT

My point is this: when you wake up next Monday morning from your 7½ hours, wouldn't it be great if you were looking forward to getting out of bed and going to work? I don't happen to subscribe to the *Life is hard and then you die* school, but I do recognise that life is *short*. Go back to the Three Phases Model – far too many people in this world pass their time in the Earning years with no real eye on the future. Mark your age on the plot opposite. How far along are you in the Earning years? Twenty in and twenty to go? Just started but not happy? Too late to go back? (Incidentally, it's my belief and experience that it is *never* too late to revisit your choices in life.)

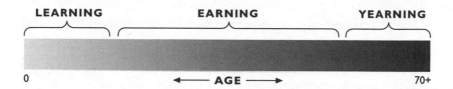

This is not a rehearsal. Irrespective of your beliefs about the existence or otherwise of an afterlife, every minute that you waste of your time on this planet is just that – wasted. It's called 'The Present' because it is a GIFT! Don't waste the gift. Find what makes you happy and do it (or be it), but don't throw it away. The Yearning years can be a very *loooong* time if you are constantly harking back and saying, '*I wish, I wish... if only, if only.*'

WHY WE BECOME UNSETTLED

If you have arrived at a point in your career and have realised that your working life is just not making you happy, or worse yet, that it is actively making you miserable and unwell (see page 372, Stress), then you need to do some *serious* reflection on your past and some even more serious crystal ball-gazing about your future.

We set out on a road when we enter the schooling system and our lives take on a rhythm from that road. Young children have no sense of time. The phrases '*in a minute*', '*later*' and '*in a few days*' are interchangeable in the mind of a pre-school child. Once that child enters the 'system', time becomes a very important, and constantly measured, factor in their lives. (Interestingly, a sense of time is one of the first things you lose when you contract Alzheimer's Disease – it is a higher brain function that is *utterly* irrelevant for your survival. Back in the caves, no one knew exactly what time it was and no one was ever late for a meeting.)

Nevertheless, the child soon learns about time and his day develops a relatively unvarying schedule. The child then learns about weekends, then mid-term breaks, then holidays… The year takes on a pleasing 'security blanket' feel:

- School starts when the leaves turn brown and the trees go to sleep for the winter. (Unless you live in the Antipodes.)
- At weekends, you don't have to go to school and you can play all day at home with your friends and family.
- There is a lovely mid-term break at Hallowe'en/Guy Fawkes Night.
- There is a long break for Christmas and you decorate the house and get lots of presents.
- Another mid-term break in the spring…
- Easter Bunny…
- Very long break in the summer, maybe with a family holiday.
- School starts when the leaves turn brown…

HORIZONS

The sense of security engendered by the education system derives from (a) not having to pay the bills (worries? what worries?) and (b) life having horizons. Horizons are very important to human beings. We can tolerate almost anything if we know that it is finite – a 5 km walk, a course that we hate, a tough exercise class, a 9-week boot camp, a project that we are not enjoying…

The problem is, when you enter the Earning Years, those horizons tend to evaporate. Many people find the transition from the education system to the tax net very unsettling – *simply because there are no more horizons*:

'The only certainties in life are death and taxes.'
'Well, that's me set up for life then.'
'Life is hard and then you die.'
'Well, now I have my permanent, pensionable job.'
'This vale of tears.'

I believe that bleak humour and religious clichés were developed purely to enable intelligent people to cope with the many foolish and unpleasant facets of the Earning Years — because without that ability to sublimate, cope and stick with it, the whole edifice of working for a living and being a valuable member of society would come tumbling down.

WORK ETHIC?

Work used to be equated with prayer. In this 'vale of tears', the God-fearing, self-motivated worker used to jump out of bed every morning raring to go to work. In effect, he was praying by working. But as church attendances declined, job security became a thing of the past, family values continued to be supplanted and a higher percentage of relationships failed than succeeded; one fine day, our no-longer-God-fearing worker decided to stay in bed.

People now feel less of a moral compulsion to work and be productive than at any time in history and this is mirrored by dwindling attendance at religious services all over the developed world. No one can deny that the pressure to perform and succeed is at an all-time high (although every generation since the caves has probably thought that); but

> 'Sure, I could get up at dawn and drive an hour in traffic to a job I hate; that does not inspire me creatively whatsoever; for the rest of my life. Or, I could wake up at noon and learn how to play the sitar.'
> **BILL HICKS**

now that the job-for-life covenant is shattered, the sacred bond between worker and employer has also been consigned to the history books.

Today, people work to get rich, to stay afloat, to meet payments, to have a bit of fun with their colleagues, to be fulfilled, to be recognised, to meet exciting people, to travel the world at somebody else's expense. Companies have had to invest *enormously* in security measures to prevent their employees from pilfering, embezzling or sabotaging them. Very few of us work for work's sake. The work ethic? The moral obligation to work? Loyalty to the company/organisation above all else? Gone.

I have counselled thousands of people through career moves and only a handful of them have stated that they would stay in the same job in the same organisation if they were financially independent. Who said that work is a four-letter word? They were not wrong.

TURN-ONS AND TURN-OFFS

So it really is imperative that you identify work that you will find fulfilling in the medium to long term. Just because you are good at something does not necessarily mean that you enjoy it – something that comes at the top of your hate list about your last job may be the very thing that is a significant area of skill or expertise for you and may also be a very marketable and transferable skill for your job search. So for now, you need to set aside thoughts of your capability at the items on the list below.

Rate each of the following activities from one to WOW! Assign a WOW! to a fantasy or ideal activity. Limit yourself to just a handful of these – or there may be none at all.

Remember this is purely about **Like/Dislike** – not about whether you are any **good** at the item. So think of each item as: '*If a large part of my job involved…*' and score it accordingly.

Acquiring new skills/information	I	2	3	4	5	6	7	8	9	WOW!
Mending/Repairing things	I	2	3	4	5	6	7	8	9	WOW!
Working at night	I	2	3	4	5	6	7	8	9	WOW!
Running my own business	I	2	3	4	5	6	7	8	9	WOW!
Clinching a deal	I	2	3	4	5	6	7	8	9	WOW!
Working at a desk	I	2	3	4	5	6	7	8	9	WOW!
Decision-making	I	2	3	4	5	6	7	8	9	WOW!
Working as part of a team	I	2	3	4	5	6	7	8	9	WOW!
Conducting research	I	2	3	4	5	6	7	8	9	WOW!
Solving personal problems	I	2	3	4	5	6	7	8	9	WOW!
Working 60 hours a week	I	2	3	4	5	6	7	8	9	WOW!
Working with music	I	2	3	4	5	6	7	8	9	WOW!
Arguing my case	I	2	3	4	5	6	7	8	9	WOW!
Selling	I	2	3	4	5	6	7	8	9	WOW!
Dealing with others by phone	I	2	3	4	5	6	7	8	9	WOW!
PR, promotions, publicity work	I	2	3	4	5	6	7	8	9	WOW!
Inventing and conceptualising	I	2	3	4	5	6	7	8	9	WOW!
Team leading/Facilitation	I	2	3	4	5	6	7	8	9	WOW!
Participating in meetings	I	2	3	4	5	6	7	8	9	WOW!
Questioning/Inquiring	I	2	3	4	5	6	7	8	9	WOW!
Working out and about	I	2	3	4	5	6	7	8	9	WOW!
Working 40 hours a week	I	2	3	4	5	6	7	8	9	WOW!
Operating high-tech equipment	I	2	3	4	5	6	7	8	9	WOW!
Working with numbers	I	2	3	4	5	6	7	8	9	WOW!
Persuading people	I	2	3	4	5	6	7	8	9	WOW!
Investigating/Digging for the truth	I	2	3	4	5	6	7	8	9	WOW!
Working for a big organisation	I	2	3	4	5	6	7	8	9	WOW!
Dressing formally for the job	I	2	3	4	5	6	7	8	9	WOW!
Customer service	I	2	3	4	5	6	7	8	9	WOW!
Working primarily with my hands	I	2	3	4	5	6	7	8	9	WOW!
Working in politics	I	2	3	4	5	6	7	8	9	WOW!
Performing routine tasks	I	2	3	4	5	6	7	8	9	WOW!
Writing	I	2	3	4	5	6	7	8	9	WOW!

Caring for people/animals	1	2	3	4	5	6	7	8	9	WOW!
Designing things	1	2	3	4	5	6	7	8	9	WOW!
Working with machinery	1	2	3	4	5	6	7	8	9	WOW!
Working part-time	1	2	3	4	5	6	7	8	9	WOW!
Playing sports	1	2	3	4	5	6	7	8	9	WOW!
Being on a succession of projects	1	2	3	4	5	6	7	8	9	WOW!
Wearing a uniform	1	2	3	4	5	6	7	8	9	WOW!
Working from home	1	2	3	4	5	6	7	8	9	WOW!
Working irregular hours	1	2	3	4	5	6	7	8	9	WOW!
Repetitive, predictable work	1	2	3	4	5	6	7	8	9	WOW!
Teaching	1	2	3	4	5	6	7	8	9	WOW!
Being closely supervised	1	2	3	4	5	6	7	8	9	WOW!
Working for a small organisation	1	2	3	4	5	6	7	8	9	WOW!
Supervising others	1	2	3	4	5	6	7	8	9	WOW!
Reading	1	2	3	4	5	6	7	8	9	WOW!
Acting as a consultant	1	2	3	4	5	6	7	8	9	WOW!
Travelling a lot of the time	1	2	3	4	5	6	7	8	9	WOW!
Labouring	1	2	3	4	5	6	7	8	9	WOW!
Co-ordinating large events	1	2	3	4	5	6	7	8	9	WOW!
Negotiating	1	2	3	4	5	6	7	8	9	WOW!
Working with fashion	1	2	3	4	5	6	7	8	9	WOW!
Working with money	1	2	3	4	5	6	7	8	9	WOW!
Dressing informally	1	2	3	4	5	6	7	8	9	WOW!
Listening to people	1	2	3	4	5	6	7	8	9	WOW!
Working with children	1	2	3	4	5	6	7	8	9	WOW!
Social/Community work	1	2	3	4	5	6	7	8	9	WOW!
Working with old people	1	2	3	4	5	6	7	8	9	WOW!
Singing, acting or performing	1	2	3	4	5	6	7	8	9	WOW!
Working outdoors	1	2	3	4	5	6	7	8	9	WOW!
Working with professionals	1	2	3	4	5	6	7	8	9	WOW!
Altruistic work	1	2	3	4	5	6	7	8	9	WOW!
Working by myself	1	2	3	4	5	6	7	8	9	WOW!
Other…?	1	2	3	4	5	6	7	8	9	WOW!

This should give you a good idea of what your Turn-ons (and perhaps more importantly your Turn-offs) in the workplace are. List the top seven of each here:

MY TOP 7 TURN-ONS	MY TOP 7 TURN-OFFS
I.	I.
2.	2.
3.	3.
4.	4.
5.	5.
6.	6.
7.	7.

What is this polarised list telling you about the sort of work you are doing now? Is it right for you, good for you, *great* for you? What is the list telling you about the sort of work you should be doing, going forward? As I have said before, you don't have to be bouncing out of bed on a Monday morning clicking your heels together with delight at the prospect of going to work, but if you are dreading it, or if you are utterly indifferent to it, that is not a good thing. So what makes you happy? A good way to discover this is to look at what has made you happy and satisfied going back through your life.

HIGH POINTS

Now I want you to list a bunch of high points from your life – include professional, personal and academic experiences that you look back fondly upon. If you find this exercise difficult (and many people do), try this method of dredging up good stuff from your past: buy an A6 or pocket-sized hardback notebook and keep it within reach at all times. On the first page, write a heading of **Reception, Junior Infants** or **Kindergarten** – whatever your first year of formal education was called. Write the title of each successive academic year on the following pages – one per page. When you get to the end of your years of formal education, switch to calendar years as your header. (We tend to remember our Learning Years as the Academic year rather than the calendar.)

Now, your exercise is to fill in a *minimum of three* great moments for each of your Learning Years and a *minimum of six* for each of your Earning Years. What made you happy? What do you look back proudly or fondly upon? What kind of things used to make you happy? Do they still? If not, why not? What has changed? A very good idea to help you complete this exercise is to talk with people – old friends, family and colleagues in particular.

CLOUDS

If there is a major negative item or event that cast a cloud over a whole year, or years, you should write it at the bottom of the page – a major illness in the family or in yourself, loss of a parent or loved one, a stressful break-up, an unhealthy relationship. These can be life-changing events and it is useful to pay heed to them and to the impacts that they had upon you.

HELPING HAND

Make no mistake, this is not going to be easy, but here are some memory-joggers, some of which may cause a smile as you go through this process.

- **Birthdays**: What kind of cake? What kind of party? Any memorable presents?
- **Family occasions**: Anniversaries, weddings, birthdays, parties, gatherings.

- **Christmas**: Where did you celebrate? What presents did you give/receive?
- **First Times**: First dates, first kiss, first sex, drink, drugs, bicycle, car, driving. First time away from the nest, going abroad, trying new foods. New sports, new hobbies, great new books, music, films, plays or concerts. First job, first boss, first colleagues, first office romance, first pay-cheque. Get the idea?
- **Pastimes**: Sports or activities you enjoy(ed). Stuff you were *good* at. Hobbies you tried and dropped. Fads. Stuff you were just *rubbish* at, but still enjoyed. Prizes, events, tall tales of derring-do, m-e-m-o-r-i-e-s!
- **Mastery**: Anything new you learned or gained expertise in.
- **Close friends**: Where did you first meet? How did you hit it off? Crazy moments? Stuff you got away with? Times you were caught?
- **Relationships**: List all your boy/girlfriends in chronological order. Give them marks out of 10 under any headings you choose! What about unrequited loves? Remember them too and any good stuff you can link back to that time.
- **Partner**: How did you meet/mate/fall in love? How did you cement the relationship (who asked who, where and how)? Did you marry? How?
- **Kids**: Include some of the *big* highlights here.

Going right back to the beginning of the Learning Years like this will help you to form strong associations with the good moments from later years. You should have an embarrassment of High Point riches to select from. Pick your top seven or so and fill in the section below. Now look at those high points and see if any of them correlate to your top seven Turn-ons from above. Then check and see if the skills that enabled you to experience those high points appear on your Skillbase list from the 360° exercise in Part 2: Chapter 4.

HIGH POINTS	TURN-ONS	SKILLS
1.		
2.		
3.		
4.		
5.		
6.		
7.		

Review your accomplishment list from the 360° exercise – do any of those achievements appear here as a high point or turn-on? This is not a hard-and-fast inventory of occupational interests, but a picture should be starting to emerge and you can build on that as you proceed to the next exercise.

Chapter 2

THREE ROADS

It is a rough road that leads to the heights of greatness.

LUCIUS ANNAEUS SENECA

If you have woken up one fine day to discover that you no longer enjoy your job, the decisions that you need to make next are simple, but by no means easy. And the further along in the Earning Years you are, the harder those decisions become, as there are more demands and constraints placed upon you and your thinking.

One of the difficulties in changing career is that you have to take a leap that involves some degree of faith in order to do it. You can't dip your toe in the water of a new career – what employer would allow you (or pay you) to do that? So before you leap, you have to be *sure*. You need strong Supporting Evidence (see page 199) in order to make any important decision. For your career decision, you need to have completed some very heavy thinking indeed before you jump ship.

'Never test the depth of the water with both feet at once.'
BUMPER STICKER

CHEESY MBA ANALOGY – 'WHERE'S MY OASIS?'

Imagine you have come to the end of the road you are on and a desert stretches out in front of you. Hundreds of footprints lead in every direction and you don't know which set to follow. You know that there is a perfect oasis somewhere out there in the distance. But those blobs on the sand could be anything – an oasis, a mirage, a pile of camel-dung. If you could get in a helicopter and fly out over the desert, you could see where the real oases are. You could touch down and sample the water and the dates and decide which oasis you liked best. Then, when you flew back to the end of the road, you would have a clear bearing on which way to travel forward...

Career planning is very difficult to do from *Now* to *Then*. It's much easier to decide on your 'Then' picture and reverse-engineer your way back to '*Now*' (see page 363, Ten Year Plan). So, let's think about Three Roads you could travel next:

1. PROBABLE/OBVIOUS

This is the job move that no one will have a problem with you making. Not the next employer, not a recruitment consultant interviewing you, not your mother, nobody. It is a fairly obvious next step for you. It is safe and predictable, perhaps it is even pre-determined to a certain extent. It is a logical choice, given your educational and experiential background. No one will raise their eyebrows and say, 'Well, I didn't see **that** move coming' when they hear about your going down this Road.

See if you can slot something (that is not *too* objectionable to you) into the box on page 354 and then think of three pluses to that move and two possible minuses. If you can't, that's fine. Park it for now and come back to it.

2. FINANCIAL INDEPENDENCE

If you had a legally acquired large-number-divisible-by-a-million sitting in your bank account in the morning, what would you do? (Would you be reading this book?) Let's get past the buying a house and a big car and going on holidays stuff. Let's say you've done all that and you still have wads of cash in your account. Enough so that you never need to get out of bed and go to work again. (This is known in polite circles as '*Arrogance Money*' and in somewhat less polite circles as '*Fuck-You Money*'.) What would you do to keep the grey cells ticking over? What would you do to stay sane? Would you work? Would you do something voluntary or altruistic? Would you educate yourself further or would you dabble in something?

Let's presume for a moment that you are going to do *something*. But, whatever it is you might want to do, security is not an issue – you don't need to make a living from this, you just need to *enjoy* it. No idea, industry, field or role is too wild. Maybe you had some crazy hankering years ago. Write it down. Write down the five pluses to doing it. (I am presuming at this point that there are no minuses.)

3. AN ODD MOVE

We tend to get pigeon-holed in this life. We talk about what we *are* rather than what we *do*. So, if you still had to make a living (bummer!) and wanted to make a change, have you *any* idea(s) as to what that change might be? Again, this might be an old fantasy or a career aspiration that you had to regretfully let go. It might be a service industry that you became aware of yesterday or a job you saw advertised last week. You might know nothing about it, but you're curious. Jot it down and think about the upsides and downsides…

PROBABLE/OBVIOUS NEXT MOVE	'IF I HAD £X MILLION IN THE BANK...'	ODD/UNEXPECTED MOVE
Plus:	Plus:	Plus:
Plus:	Plus:	Plus:
Plus:	Plus:	Plus:
	Plus:	Plus
Minus:	Plus:	
Minus:		Minus:
		Minus:
		Minus:

FILTERING OPPORTUNITIES

When you have too many options/opportunities/projects to deal with, you may have difficulty in choosing just three roads to examine. There is no harm in having a lot of options at the outset, but experience has shown me that you can't really get serious about more than three at a time and so you may need a method of identifying the best of those going forward. The questions which will really help get the ball rolling on this are:

Is this option/opportunity/career path/project...

1 **Desirable**? (*Does it fit in with my short-term needs and my long-term objectives?*)
2 **Viable**? (*Will it do anything for me? Is it sustainable at least in the medium term?*)
3 **Likely**? (*Am I suitably skilled for this? Will the market allow me to do it? Is it too big a risk?*)

This **DVL** (Devil) questioning process will certainly trim down your number of options. I rarely encounter candidates who are this spoilt for choice on the career front: more often it will be someone who is at a loss to decide which of a number of projects to pursue and in what order. If you still have a bewildering array of choices, you will need to do more filtering on each one.

Do you have the **skills** to pursue each of the options? Get hold of a job description from an organisation or a pal in a Human Resources function and closely rate yourself against each of the requirements of the job. Are there other people out there who are better qualified, trained or experienced to do this?

Is the **market** likely to give you a chance to pursue each of these options? What are the likely impediments and how are you going to overcome them? Are there cost of entry issues? Will you have to re-train in order to be even considered for jobs of this nature?

Finally, are you *genuinely* **excited** about each of these options? Are they truly desirable given your current circumstances and future plans? (See page 363, Ten Year Plan.)

BARRIERS

There are real, concrete barriers to changing your career and there are imagined ones. Barriers that stem from a lack of experience or suitability for a certain type of work and barriers that stem from a simple lack of confidence. Barriers based on your not being able to pay the bills and barriers based on your not believing that you have any right to be happy…

The minuses in the boxes opposite are your first stab at identifying the barriers to your next move. Typical minuses in the 'Obvious' box might include:

- 'I'd hate to be doing the same old thing.'
- 'I get no satisfaction from it.'
- 'I loathe the kind of people that I work with.'
- 'Such-and-such an aspect of the job makes my skin crawl.'

- 'There are no advancement prospects in this line of work.'
- 'It's so boooring!'

In the 'Odd Move' box:

- 'They won't take a chance on me.'
- 'I'll have to spend a *fortune* on re-training.'
- 'I'll have to take too big a cut in pay to get my foot in the door.'
- 'It will take too long to gain a new qualification in that area.'
- 'My husband/wife would never let me do that.'
- 'My family would be so disappointed in me if I left the job/career that I'm in now.'

Look again at your middle box, the one that relates to a fantasy, wow-wouldn't-that-be-great activity — if only you could afford to do it. Delineate what is preventing you from doing that fantasy activity. Are the barriers tangible or imagined? Are they really insurmountable? Could you persuade an investor or a financial institution to take some degree of acceptable risk and support your venture? Why does the prospect of that risk frighten *you* so much?

If your activity is a definite no-no, if you *definitely* cannot make a living from it, maybe you can look at taking some element(s) of it into a new career. Talk to some creative thinkers in your circle about this. Dreams are not easy to come by; don't let yours die for the want of some time, attention and a little bit of innovative thinking.

LINES IN THE SAND

A useful follow-on to the Three Roads exercise is to decide in advance what you will and won't tolerate in your new career. Start by listing five elements or factors that *must be present* in your career for you to have a fulfilling working life. Do this for each of the careers you have identified in the Three Roads exercise.

PROBABLE/OBVIOUS ROAD – 5 ESSENTIALS:

1.

2.

3.

4.

5.

Account for each element – why is it important to you? On the basis of what positive (or negative) experience did you decide to include this element?

1.

2.

3.

4.

5.

FINANCIALLY INDEPENDENT ROAD – 5 ESSENTIALS:

1.

2.

3.

4.

5.

There may be some cross-over, or they may be exactly the same as the elements above – that's fine. Account once again for each element you have included.

1.

2.

3.

4.

5.

ODD/UNEXPECTED ROAD – 5 ESSENTIALS:

1.

2.

3.

4.

5.

Account for each element again.

1.

2.

3.

4.

5.

POTHOLES TO AVOID

Now that you have identified the good stuff, let's look at the obverse side of the coin – list three elements or factors that must *not* be present in your career (or in your next move). If these were a significant part of your new career, you'd be just *miserable*. These are your deal-breakers. Again, do this for each of the Roads. (You may have four or even five elements. If so, squash 'em in.) Go back to your Turn-ons listing in Part 6: Chapter 1 and have another look at your big Turn-offs.

PROBABLE/OBVIOUS ROAD – 3 UNDESIRABLES:

1.

2.

3.

Give a reason for your including each of the elements – why is it important to you that this factor should not arise in your next move? What made you think of it?

1.

2.

3.

FINANCIALLY INDEPENDENT ROAD – 3 UNDESIRABLES:

1.

2.

3.

Same again – justify your thinking.

1.

2.

3.

ODD/UNEXPECTED ROAD – 3 UNDESIRABLES:

1.

2.

3.

And again – why do these matter to you?

1.

2.

3.

BOUNDARIES AND FENCES ALONG THE ROAD

Are your Lines in the Sand common or different for all of the possible Roads? Should they be? Now you can start the more active (but still very much preliminary) stages of a job-hunt for any or all of the Roads with some key boundaries clearly marked. Those boundaries might include:

- **Finance** – the job has to pay you a certain minimum. You might split this out into a minimum ('What I actually need') and a fantastical maximum ('What I think I might be able to get away with') figure.

- **Location** – commuting is such a nightmare and can really add to your time away from home. Furthermore, it may not be feasible for you to move house, county or country to suit your career. Or travel all the time on the job. This is a major constraint and you should discuss it with those closest to you and clarify it early in your thinking process.

- **Organisation type** – you could work for Apple, IBM, Dell or HP doing *exactly* the same work, but only be really happy in one of the companies. Corporate culture is an enormous factor in people's satisfaction level with their career or job. Start digging to find out what you are really heading into and map it against your Lines in the Sand (see page 162, Research, and page 168, Networking).

- **People/Process split** – some people shy away from a lot of face-time with colleagues or customers while others would just curl up and die without it. Know which kind of person you are and how much of each you need.

- **Advancement** – most people want some degree of progress in their career. Make sure your new career has a defined progression path and that opportunities genuinely exist for that progression within your desired organisation or type of organisation.

NEXT STEPS

Now you are getting there. Sorry about all of the boxes, but you must be able to defend your thinking on this most important of decisions – if only to yourself. Now that you have identified three possible Roads to travel, delineated the required and undesirable factors in each and placed some boundaries around them, you can start your research on sectors, organisations and job types (see page 162, Research). Make sure you log your findings as you go and cross-reference them with your Ten Year Plan and your Lines in the Sand.

Chapter 3

TEN YEAR PLAN

> *Called back.*
>
> **EMILY DICKINSON'S EPITAPH**

If you have completed the Three Roads exercise and have decided what your Lines in the Sand are for each of those Roads, it will be useful to do a Ten Year Plan for each of the possible careers you have identified. Even if you are *deliriously* happy in your present career and are not going to move, you need to map out where your professional life is going. It's just ink on paper at this stage, so take the time and give it a try.

Life planning and career planning are inextricably connected. I always start the planning process with a client's personal life, because (a) it is *way* more important and (b) it is usually easier to envisage your personal future, or at least your desires for that future. So I recommend that you take the following pages in order. Lots more box-filling here. Sorry, but it is important – you wouldn't build a house without a full set of plans would you?

CURRENT PERSONAL CIRCUMSTANCES

Are you
Single/Engaged/Married/Separated?   _____

Do you have a Significant Other?   _____

Offspring?   _____

Living with your parents?   _____

If not, do you own your property
or are you renting?   _____

Is your current home urban/suburban/rural?   _____

How is your social life? (give it marks out of 10)   _____

How would you rate life overall?
(including your career)   _____

What is your no.1 priority in life right now?   _____

What about no. 2?   _____

What is your current Standard of Living (SOL) Index? Measure this against the role-model of your family's SOL, giving them a score of 100. So, if you live half as well as your parents, your SOL Index is 50...

_____

How important is material comfort to you?
(marks out of 10)   _____

PERSONAL CIRCUMSTANCES
10 YEARS HENCE

This is aspirational stuff. How do you want to be living in 10 years from now? What kind of home life do you want to have and what kind of (material) standard of living do you want to enjoy? What will be the substantive changes between the way in which you live now and the way you want to be living then?

...Remember – this is not an exercise that has to be grounded in realism. It is an exercise in *desire*. In your ideal, fantasy world, how would you be living?

Will you be Single/Engaged/Married/Separated?   _____

Will you have a Significant Other?   _____

What sort of person will your Significant Other be? (if applicable):

    Education level   _____

    Occupation   _____

    Working for Self/Organisation   _____

    Most important attribute   _____

    What will he or she bring out in you?   _____

What about kids?   _____

Private or State schooling for kids? (if applicable)   _____

Will you own property or will you be renting?   _____

Will your home be in an urban/suburban/rural area?   _____

How active a social life do you want to have?
(marks out of 10)   _____

How will it be different from your social life today?   _____

Score your life – how great would you like
it to be? (1–10)   _____

What do you expect will be your no.1 priority
in life?   _____

No. 2?   _____

What SOL Index do you want to have in
10 years' time?   _____

When you have your 10-year destination decided, mapping out milestones along the way is much easier. Now it's time to move on to your Professional Life. (At last! We finally got there! Admit it – you were beginning to wonder…)

CURRENT PROFESSIONAL CIRCUMSTANCES

These questions pertain to your current job. If you are currently unemployed, answer as though you were still in your most recent job.

Are you working Full-time/Part-time/Casual/Retired?   _____

How many working hours in a typical week?   _____

How many hours commuting time?   _____

Do you work for yourself or for an organisation?   _____

Type of business/work/job title   _____

Salary (including bonuses)   _____

Benefits   _____

Do you work with people/processes/both?   _____

What (if applicable) is the split (50/50, 70/30)?   _____

What would be your ideal split?   _____

Customer type: corporate/consumer/both   _____

Which do you prefer? (if applicable)   _____

If there are 10 rungs on the ladder, where
are you now?   _____

Do you work solo/in a team/both?   _____

What's the split (50/50, 70/30)?   _____

What would be your ideal split?   _____

Score your current job satisfaction?
(marks out of 10)   _____

What is your no.1 priority in your job right now?   _____

What about no. 2?   _____

What's the first thing you would change
if you could?   _____

Second?   _____

PROFESSIONAL CIRCUMSTANCES 10 YEARS HENCE

More aspirational stuff. Typically, this is much harder to pin down, but that's okay at this stage. What we are looking for here are the broad strokes. If you can paint a tighter picture than that, lucky you – it will make all the other parts of your life and career plan fall into place much more easily. If there are elements you can't envisage or complete at this stage, park them and come back later, but don't give up too easily.

Remember, once again this is **aspirational**. This is a Utopian picture of what you would really **like** in your career in ten years' time, NOT necessarily what you think is likely to happen...

Will you be working full-time/part-time/
casual/retired?   _____

How many working hours in a typical week?   _____

How many hours commuting time?   _____

Working for yourself or for an organisation?   _____

Type of business/work/job title   _____

Salary (including bonuses)   _____

Benefits   _____

Further qualifications gained?   _____

Further training/upskilling?   _____

Will you be working with people/processes/both?   _____

What's the realistic split?   _____

Customer type: corporate/consumer/both   _____

If there are 10 rungs on the ladder,
where will you be?   _____

Will you work solo/in a team/both?   _____

What's the split?   _____

Score your job satisfaction (marks out of 10)   _____

What will be your no.1 priority in your career?   _____

What about no. 2?   _____

Any big changes left to be made in this role?   _____

What (if any) is your next move from here?   _____

NEW HORIZONS

How long is your planning horizon? A week? A month? A year? 'No plan survives first contact with the enemy' is the old saying trotted out by military personnel and management consultants the world over. But without a plan, what chance is there that you will survive? If you are up against a well-trained enemy who has an overall strategy, contingency and fall-back plans and a real desire to win (see page 38, The Bogeyman) and you have none or only some of the above, it doesn't matter whether you are competing in a job-hunt, a large-scale military conflict or a game of tiddlywinks – you are, in all probability, going to lose.

If you don't have a plan, ask yourself why. There is no good reason you can give here, there are only excuses. Sit down and think about what you want out of life. For yourself. For your family. For your career. For your self-esteem. If you are afraid of failing, put a plan together anyway and *don't tell anybody*!

I accept that there are no certainties in this world. I accept that any plan you write will be obsolete before the ink is dry, but think of it like a bus schedule – no one expects the bus to arrive when the schedule says it will. The schedule is merely there to tell you how late (or early) the bus is and, by extension, how pleasantly surprised or angry to be.

HUMAN NEEDS

Abraham Maslow wrote his classic paper on human motivation in 1943, seeking to identify and clarify the key drivers for mankind. Unusually for a psychologist, he did not study patients with neuroses and psychoses – he studied the luminaries of his time. On that basis, he propounded his Hierarchy of Needs model, which asserts that humans tend towards love and growth.

On the top of this pyramid is **Self Actualisation**, which Maslow defined as 'the desire to… become everything that one is capable of becoming'. Content, complete, at peace. Buddhists refer to this as 'Enlightenment'. The steps and needs on the way to self actualisation are:

- **Physiological** – the basic animal needs of food, water, sex, shelter.
- **Security** – bringing order out of chaos. A home. Law and order. Adequate finance to support the physiological needs on an ongoing basis.
- **Belonging** – these are love needs. Steady relationships. Family. A group of friends. A club, society or team. Humans are social animals and need to feel loved and needed.

- **Recognition** – these are esteem or ego needs. One needs self esteem in order to face the world, but one also needs affirmation from others – friends, family, society, colleagues. This need can sometimes manifest itself as an abuse of power. It is a very important driver but, as with the others, is dependent upon the lower needs being satisfied. Someone who is worried about where their next meal is coming from is not too concerned about how they are perceived by society…

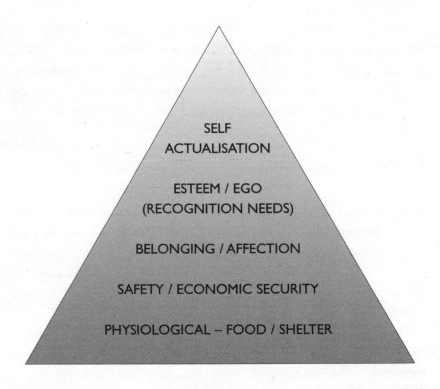

Where are you on the pyramid and where do you want to be? Without a plan, how can you answer that question? So, go on, treat yourself. Make a plan. Just a little one. Tear it up and make a new one in a week's time if you want, but *make a plan*. I wasn't kidding about Bogeymen – they are out there and they want the jobs that you want. If they are working off a plan (and they *are*) and you are not, you will be dead in the water before you begin.

Life was much simpler in the caves – you didn't have to get into this kind of cerebral stuff to survive. But we have come down from the trees, we have shed the animal skins and, short of a global thermonuclear war, I don't see us climbing back up there any time soon. This kind of thinking is a new survival skill and one that not many people are good at yet. See if you can get ahead of the evolutionary curve in managing your career.

Chapter 4

STRESS

DICTIONARY DEFINITION

Stress • n.

1 a state of mental, emotional or physical strain caused, for example, by anxiety or overwork. It may cause such symptoms as raised blood pressure or depression.

2 pressure or tension exerted on a material object and resulting in deformation or strain. ▶ physics the magnitude of this measured in units of force per unit area.

3 particular emphasis ▶ emphasis given to a syllable or word in speech.

• v.

1 emphasise ▶ give emphasis to (as syllable or word) when pronouncing it.

2 to subject somebody or something to experience mental or physical stress.

DERIVATIVES: **stressful** adj. **stressless** adj. **stressfully** adv. **stressfulness** n. **stressor** n.

ORIGIN: Middle English (denoting pressure exerted on a person for the purposes of compulsion): shortening of **distress**, or partly from Old French *estresse* 'narrowness, oppression', based on Latin *strictus*.

I don't usually like to start a discussion on any subject with a dictionary definition but, '*pressure exerted on a person for the purposes of compulsion*'? Yuck! That phrase makes me cringe. Does any of this sound in any way familiar? It may not even be someone else who exerts the pressure; in many instances, you do this to yourself...

LASH OUT OR LEAVE?

What is stress and what happens to you when you feel it? Stress is not something that is just in your head – it is a cascade of physiological (and psychological) symptoms, which can be brought on by a wide variety of causes. The normal reaction to an immediately stressful situation is for your body to manifest the **Fight or Flight Response**. Fight or Flight is a hard-wired, 'cave-man' response to a perceived threat and this response is automatic and involuntary – it is controlled by the sympathetic part of the autonomic nervous system (which controls your organs, blood flow and all of those other vital things that keep you healthy but that you don't even think about).

When you sense a threat, your hypothalamus (in the brain stem) releases the hormone noradrenaline, which in turn causes the adrenal glands above the kidneys to release adrenaline. This increase in adrenaline causes:

- The capillaries under your skin to close off so you won't bleed to death if you are cut (this has the effect of immediately sending your blood pressure sky high)
- A pounding heart (two to three times its normal rate)
- An increase in breathing rate and depth

- Oxygen-rich blood to be channelled to the heart, the brain and to the big muscles in the arms and legs (as a result, your face may go pale or very red)
- A release of blood sugar, lactic acid and cortisol to further help gear the body up to deal with the threat
- Your eyes to dilate so that you can see better; your sense of hearing is also sharper than normal
- A shut-down of the major functions of your body that are not necessary for immediate survival – digestion, your immune system, sexual function
- In extreme circumstances, the noradrenaline causes a sudden relaxation of the smooth muscles in the intestinal walls and excess bodily waste is violently eliminated to reduce body weight for flight.

All of this is designed to level the odds and get your body ready to either fight the perceived threat, or escape from it at *very* high speed. Psychological aspects of the response can include fear, feelings of dread or a sense of impending disaster. The body is typically exhausted very rapidly following a Fight or Flight episode and requires plenty of food and relaxation to recover (a process known as 'Rest and Digest').

PENT-UP

Fight or Flight is an absolutely *marvellous* response – as long as you are faced with something that truly threatens your life. However, our somewhat crude endocrine system has not changed since our days in the caves and, consequently, Fight or Flight is very often an *inappropriate* response to today's stressors.

There you are, in a major disagreement with your boss over the best way to proceed on a project. You *could* punch his lights out, but pleading that you were in a state of Fight or Flight is unlikely to cut you much slack with the Judicial System. You *could* run – no court case, but probably no job to go to in the morning either. So you have to sit there with your whole system *seething*, chock-full of chemicals that are effectively useless to you. Just look at the list of physiological responses above –

do any of them serve *any* useful purpose in the argument with your boss?

Repeated exposure will magnify and compound the effects of stress, because the existence of one form of stress has a tendency to diminish resistance to other forms. Stress can throw the digestive system out of kilter and frequently results in sleep disturbance. On a physical level, long-term stress brings about changes in the hormonal balance of the body. You can also become *conditioned* to react in a stressed way. (Remember Pavlov and his dogs? They became conditioned to the sound of the bell, so that they would salivate even when no food was present.) Does your heart start pounding *every* time you are called in for a meeting with your boss? Unless that boss is digging lumps out of your backside *every* time you have a meeting, this is an inappropriate and unnecessary stress reaction that you are putting your body through.

If this sort of circumstance happened only once in a blue moon, it would be fine. The problem is, it can happen every week. Every day. Three times a day. By the time you get home, you can be a physical *wreck*. And all this takes an enormous mental toll too. Anything that is overstrained will show wear and tear. A car engine over-revved. A hi-fi played too loud. You.

If you are feeling worn, you need to take *major* steps to prevent long-term damage. You need to:

(a) Determine if you are in fact suffering from stress and whether it is acute (in response to a one-off situation) or chronic (long-term).
(b) Identify what the major stressors in your life are.
(c) Develop coping mechanisms/corrective actions to minimise their effect.

AM I STRESSED?

Stress typically manifests in both feelings and behaviours. Fill in the following:

SENSATIONS/BEHAVIOURS:	OFTEN	SOME-TIMES	RARELY	NEVER
Tired, even though I've slept well				
Easily irritated/short fuse				
Short, fast breathing/butterflies				
Restless/fidgety				
Tense muscles in my back/shoulders				
Demotivated/lethargic				
Headachy				
Overeating/loss of appetite				
Cold, clammy hands or feet				
Over-reacting to situations				
Dry mouth/throat				
Feeling unattractive				
Hot and bothered				
Increased drinking/smoking				
Heart pounding				
Sleepless nights/tossing & turning				
Feeling powerless/overwhelmed				
Troubled, anxious, close to tears				
Indigestion				
Diarrhoea/constipation				

Look at the pattern. If you have a specific underlying illness (not stress-related) it can influence the model quite markedly. If you have no such illness then, hopefully, there are only a few 'Oftens' and 'Sometimes'. If they are the majority, there is trouble brewing.

LIFE EVENTS

This is the life events scale developed by Drs Thomas Holmes and Richard Rahe in the 1960s. It is the classic (often misquoted) list of occurrences that can contribute to stress with a value rating assigned to each one. Complete the list, including events that have occurred in your life in the past 12 months and totting your score as you go.

EVENT	SCORE	CUMULATIVE SCORE
Death of a partner	100	
Divorce	73	
Separation from partner	65	
Gaol sentence	63	
Death of a close family member	63	
Personal injury or illness	53	
Marriage	50	
Loss of a job	47	
Reconciliation with a partner	45	
Retirement	45	
Significant change to your health	44	
Pregnancy	40	
Sexual problems	39	
New family member	39	
Major business/work changes	39	
Change in your financial state	38	
Death of a close friend	37	
Arguments with your partner	35	
Large mortgage	31	
Foreclosure of mortgage/loan	30	
Change in responsibilities at work	29	

EVENT	SCORE	CUMULATIVE SCORE
Child leaving home	29	
Trouble with in-laws	29	
Outstanding personal achievement	28	
Partner beginning or stopping work	26	
Child starting or ending school	26	
Change in living conditions	25	
Change in personal habits	24	
Trouble with manager/employer	23	
Change in working hours/conditions	20	
Moving house	20	
Change in schools	20	
Change in social activities	18	
Low mortgage or loan	17	
Change in sleeping habits	16	
Change in number of family get-togethers	15	
Change in eating habits	15	
Holiday (score each holiday you took)	13	
Christmas	12	
Minor infringements of the law	11	
CUMULATIVE TOTAL		

(Source: Holmes and Rahe, Social Readjustment Rating Scale)

SCORING IMPLICATIONS

300 or greater – unacceptable, risk of illness
250–300 – very high
200–250 – high
150–200 – medium
150 or lower – manageable

Can you do anything about the items on your list? Are there some recurring problems that you can start to bring to heel? Many people feel powerless in the face of ongoing stressors and point to external factors over which they have no control. Let me posit this thought: you may not be able to control the factors, but you *can* learn to control your responses to them.

Some of the biggest repeating stressors are people. Let's look at the people in your life and all of the associated angst that they can give you...

PEOPLE STRESS

Anthropologists tell us that there are typically about 30 people in our social circle that we really care about. This relates to the size of an extended family in a cave setting. Who are your 30 people? The people that you spend time with or spend time thinking about or talking to on the phone (if they are abroad, for example). This list of 30 will probably have a degree of cross-over with your network list, but there will probably be people who only appear on one list or the other. So take your time and list them below.

You may not have exactly 30 people. Anything from 20–40 is fine. If there are more than 40, you need to really think before you include them – a helpful visualisation tool is to put everyone on the steps of a four-tier ziggurat:

- The top step holds a maximum of **three** people plus you.
- The second step holds **eight**.
- The third step holds **twelve**.
- The fourth holds a maximum of **sixteen**. (Don't feel you have to completely fill this step.)

If, however, you find that you have more than 40 people who seem to matter to you, they are not all going to fit. If you *absolutely* had to, who would you leave off the list? If you were going to be stranded on a desert island with them all, who would you rather not have there? Who *really* matters in your life?

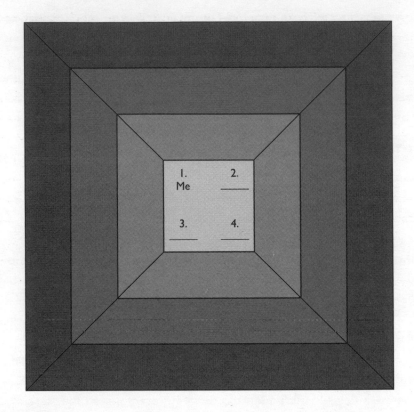

EVERYONE IN A COLUMN...

Now let's take the pyramid steps analogy a stage further. This is not a pleasant exercise. It may make you squirm or feel guilty or a little callous. It is *entirely* and unapologetically self centred. You will almost certainly not want to show it to anyone when you have completed it...

Some people are plain good for you — they bring out the best in you, you can really be yourself around them, they stimulate your mind, your body, your spirit and your humour. These are the people that you make time for (perhaps you wish you could make more), the people whose company you actively seek out and really enjoy. There is no downside to being around them. Put them in the first (+/+) column. Be ruthless.

The second (+) column is for the people whose time and company you really enjoy but, for whatever reason, not quite as much as when you are with the +/+ people. The third (−) column is for those people that you *have* to make time for – out of guilt, duty or moral obligation – but you don't really get much of anything back from them.

The –/– column is for people who are a part of your life, but who are something of a burden. Maybe they only call when they need a favour or have a problem they want to discuss. They probably never pay anything other than lip-service to you and your needs/life/concerns. We all have these people in our lives – family members, friends from way-back-when, brothers- or sisters-in-law that you have to be nice to, tiresome colleagues. Maybe you have developed evasion tactics to minimise your contact with these people, or maybe they are still a significant drain on your time. Time to name that problem – stick 'em in a column!

+/+	+	–	–/–

How does the spread look? Chances are, if you have a high stress rating, there will be more people in columns 3 and 4 than in the plus columns. Now think about this – in the last month, how much time have you devoted to people in the negative columns? How much of your precious time, time that you can never get back, have they *stolen*? How many of the 168 hours of next week will you have to devote to these people?

FLOATING OUT IDEAS FOR COPING...

There *can't* be any stock answers to dealing with your time-stealers, but I'm going to float out some ideas which may give you food for thought. The late, great Bill Hicks once said, '*I don't mean to sound cold, heartless, cruel or vicious, but I am so that's the way it comes out.*' If thinking about this sort of thing makes you acutely uncomfortable, fine – skip on to the next section. But if you are stressed-out, maybe some of this cold, hard thinking is just what you need to be doing...

1 **Old, needy friends**: '*We go way back*' '*There's a lot of history there*' – okay, fine. Let me posit two thoughts. (a) If you met this old, old friend *as they are now* in the pub tonight, would you give them the time of day? Would you really want to meet this whiny, needy person again? If not, why not? (b) If you stepped under a bus and got killed, would that old, old friend shrivel up and die or would they find some other person to fall back on to solve their problems? They depend on you and leech out of you because you give them permission to...

2 **Colleagues**: You know this person. They sit beside you at lunch, droning on. They send you endless joke e-mails. They prop up your door and do the, 'Woe is me' routine when you're trying to make a deadline. The simplest approach I have found is to develop a code-word with a sympathetic colleague who has line of sight to your office/work-space. That colleague phones you X minutes into the visit and you can shunt the time-stealer out of your office with an apologetic, 'This is going to take a while.' If the time-stealing

colleague is (for once!) involved in genuine work with you, you can use the code-word to indicate that the sympathetic colleague should call back in 20–30 minutes to save you. This solution will not succeed if the time-stealer works within earshot, as they can hear you hang up the phone and will be back like a shot. If this is the case, ask to be moved.

3 **In-laws/Cousins/Extended family**: You will need to gain agreement from your partner to limit your exposure to those in-laws that make your teeth grind. Likewise, have a chat with immediate family members to minimise the number of family gatherings. If there are a few members of the extended family whose company you really enjoy, form a clique and get good at linking arms and sitting together. This is crude, rude and obvious, but so what? Life is too short for this kind of nonsense.

> 'Friends are God's apology for relatives.'
> HUGH KINGSMILL

4 **Elder Lemons**: These are the really tricky ones. These are the relationships which are born out of duty, obligation and, in many cases, plain old guilt. Elder Lemons (parents, grandparents, uncles, aunts, etc.) tend to be *very* good at pushing our buttons and making us do things we don't want to do. They know where all the buttons are, because they have known us since we were children. You *can't* stand up to them – you just *can't*. All you can do is try and ring-fence the time to some extent. State your intended departure time when you arrive and make sure you have a good reason for departing at that time. Emotional blackmail is a terrible thing and we are all prone to using it, but none more so than the Elder Lemons. I hear a lot of clients blaming their miseries on their parents and elderly

> 'If you hate your parents, the man or the establishment; don't show them by getting wasted and wrapping your car around a tree. If you really hate your parents, out-earn them, outlive them and know more.'
> HENRY ROLLINS

relatives. Let me ask something really *horrendous* now – when your Elder Lemons are dead and gone, who are you going to blame for all of your woes?

NAME THE PROBLEM

Know who they are. Know how they do it – how do they get under your skin? Know how you *let* them do it. Then you are in a position to think about a coping strategy.

My **Number 1** time waster is:
I give time to this time waster because:
I would like to scale this back by:

My **Number 2** time waster is:
I give time to this time waster because:
I would like to scale this back by:

My **Number 3** time waster is:
I give time to this time waster because:
I would like to scale this back by:

JOB-HUNTING STRESS

So much for general stress. The very phrase 'job-hunting' causes nearly everyone's hackles to rise. The most common stressors that clients raise with me while they are job-hunting are:

- Lack of control
- Disappointments
- Interviews!
- Money problems
- Family issues
- Time management

> '**Most people are about as happy as they make up their minds to be.**'
> **ABRAHAM LINCOLN**

LACK OF CONTROL

This is a particular problem for people who derive a sense of security from controlling their circumstances (a nice way of saying 'Control Freaks'). In a job-hunt, there is a large degree of impotence at the outset. You cannot *make* a job advertisement appear in the paper. You cannot *make* someone take your call or call you back. You cannot *change* the prevailing conditions in the economy, sector or organisations that you are interested in working for. By and large, you have to sit and wait for your opportunity to arise and Viagra® doesn't help.

DISAPPOINTMENTS

Job-hunting is a rollercoaster of optimism and pessimism. No sane person enjoys rejection, and maintaining your focus and your positive approach in the face of continued indifference, rebuffs and downright rudeness can be very difficult. A structured approach can help you deal with the intellectual aspects of the disappointment, but the part that erodes your confidence over time is the emotional aspect (see page 145, Interview Fatigue Syndrome). If your self esteem dips significantly, if you stop believing that you *deserve* this job, someone is going to pick up on that – probably in an interview. Interviewers are like dogs and horses – they can smell fear (and desperation).

INTERVIEWS!

People just *hate* being interviewed. For many, it's the Spanish Inquisition nature of the process that they loathe. But for some, there is also the aspect of being the supplicant in the process. If you are very good at what you do, if you are highly motivated, well-educated and smarter than the average bear, it can be very demeaning to have to go, cap-in-hand, and give an account of yourself to someone that you know, in your heart of hearts, you're *better* than.

MONEY

If you are made redundant, you should have at least *some* cash to get you through the crisis and fund some sort of job-hunt. If your company collapsed, you were fired or your contract wasn't renewed, you have no such luxury. Budgeting for the job-hunt process is vital and there are entire books out there on this subject. If you are bad at money management, read one of these and stay on top of the situation. This is a pressure that you just don't need.

The other key problem with money running out is that it can force you to take a job that you normally wouldn't touch and that takes up so much of your time, you have none left to continue job-hunting… vicious circle or what? A whole range of bad decisions tend to get made when the bank account is empty. You may have to consider taking a pay-the-bills job in the interim, but try and make it one that doesn't eat up your whole week.

FAMILIES

Unless someone has been through the process of a job-hunt, they cannot have an appreciation of the impact that it has on you beyond the intellectual knowledge – there is no real emotional understanding. So, hand-wringing mothers, husbands who insist on giving unwanted advice instead of just listening, wives who don't realise how long the process can take, gung-ho fathers ('*Well in **my** day we…*'), and children who don't understand why you are not your usual cheerful self can all place additional strain on you.

TIME STEALERS

'Nuff said.

COPING MECHANISMS

Putting aside your long-term physical and mental wellbeing, any and all of the above can significantly detract from your ability to conduct an effective job-hunt. You have to learn to spot the patterns, know what effect they have on you and develop mechanisms that will enable you to deal with them. I have had clients who spent two nights in a hotel with the phone turned off to get away from *everything* coming up to a vital interview or presentation. Extreme? Definitely. Did it work? Was it worth it? For them – hell, yes! For you? Only you can answer that.

The most important aspect of learning to cope is *taking the time* to do so. The patterns of behaviour that we manifest when we are under stress are (a) instinctual – they stretch back through millions of years of evolution; and (b) learned – typically reaching back to childhood. Something which is that deeply ingrained will not be mended by any 'quick fix' approach. The list below is common-sensical, obvious and comprises elements that may help overcome not only job-hunting stress:

- Spot the signs and learn to worry about only those things that you can control. If you are getting palpitations because of a situation that is going to happen irrespective of your feelings, you are granting that situation/person far too much control. You can't control the situation, but you very much can control how you respond to it and whether that response is proportional or not.

- Use your network, your family, your colleagues and your friends – delegate *anything* relating to the job-hunt that you can.

- Manage the time available to you and build in 'me' time. If you are being pulled in 29 directions and always seem to be playing catch-up with your diary, you will quickly start to feel like a wet rag and lose all enjoyment for life. If you find that you can't relax and your mind and body are constantly whirring, trouble is coming.

- Learn how to relax properly and effectively – take a course in Relaxation Response.

- Re-learn how to breathe like a child — *T'ai Chi,* yoga, meditation (see page 390, Breathing).

- Bathe and exercise regularly. Feeling fresh and looking good are advantages that are so obvious they shouldn't need to be pointed out, but I meet pale, sweating, stressed-out job-hunters all the time. Successful people have an ineffable quality about them — they are *shiny,* they never seem to get hot and bothered. Learn to project that sort of swan-like demeanour — swans may be swimming away frantically under the surface, but all the world sees is the gliding elegance above the waterline. For human beings, this happens from the outside in and also from the inside out. Being fit, clean, groomed and in control of your time is a good start for the veneer. Taking charge of your emotions and your reactions to stressors is even better.

- Laugh regularly. Nobody enjoys the company of a joyless person.

- Desensitise yourself to situational stressors (like interviews, public speaking, cold calling).

It sounds so simple, doesn't it? It's almost trite. It's certainly very easy for me to write, I realise, but don't let the brevity of the list fool you. Read it again. Are you stressed? How stressed? Check your Holmes scale result or give your level of stress a mark out of 10. Remember the 10 Year Plan? Have you filled in 'Dead of a heart attack' as an aspiration? How about 'House-bound with clinical depression'? Or maybe our old friend, cancer? Is that on your wish-list? (I realise that modern medicine has not conclusively determined the increased likelihood of your developing cancer based on your rating on the Holmes scale, but there is just too much anecdotal evidence for even an empiricist like me to ignore, and the stuffiest oncologist you can find will agree that 'lifestyle factors' have an enormous part to play both in contracting and curing malignancies.)

I'm not fooling around here — read the damn list and start making time to do some of the things on it. If you have identified yourself as being significantly stressed, if that stress is coming between you and a beatifically happy existence, **get help**. No book can provide a tailored approach to dealing with and recovering from *your* stress. If the problem is serious, someone on your network will know a reliable professional who can help you regain control. The fix is not overnight, but it is not a question of months or years either. Cognitively breaking a habit or learning a new skill takes 21 days. Just three weeks of concentrated effort could make an immeasurable difference for your future. If your car is not running properly, you take it to a mechanic. You run to the medicine cabinet when you have a headache. Why should your attitude to stress be any different? Make a change. If that doesn't work, get help. Do it. Now.

BY THE WAY...

Just two little morsels of information I came across while researching for this section:

1 The origin of the word 'worry' is from the Old English *wyrgan*, which means to strangle or choke — this was originally a word of West Germanic origin. You wouldn't tolerate *anyone* choking off your windpipe all day every day, would you? (See page 390, Breathing.)
2 Researchers in UCLA have identified a distinct difference in the way in which men and women respond to modern stressors. Men still primarily manifest the **Fight or Flight** response while women seem to have evolved, and are more inclined to rely on, a response that has now been entitled **Tend and Befriend**. This healthier response may even be a factor in why women in the developed world typically live five to seven years longer than men.

'Laughter is the best medicine. Unless you happen to be diabetic, in which case, insulin is probably a better option.'
ANONYMOUS

Chapter 5

BREATHING

I have mentioned the matter of breathing correctly a number of times in this book; allow me to clarify what I mean. Healthy babies arrive on this planet breathing perfectly. And then they forget how. Somewhere around the age of seven, children stop breathing as nature intended. They begin to lose their flexibility, in many cases they start to lose their beautiful posture, and their breath turns foul (like an adult's). In a nutshell, they become short little grown-ups.

Breathing is *way* more than just the medical dictionary definition of a '*gaseous exchange between an organism and its environment*'. For the job-hunter, breathing properly can be the difference between success and failure in an interview. I am a qualified instructor of Chinese Martial Arts and, in the days when I used to

attend interviews, I was frequently asked if I had ever had occasion to use my martial arts skill. My answer was always, '*I'm using it now*' (which many interviewers seemed to find quite disconcerting). But it was true. I was sitting with good posture, breathing deeply and evenly, my whole body was warm and dry, my voice was strong and clear and my mind was buzzing away, noticing everything, well-fed with oxygen.

Have you ever slept in a stuffy room with all the windows and doors closed? You woke up feeling just how bad exactly? You know how nice it is to come out into the fresh air after a long session indoors (a lecture, a smoky bar, a meeting) with a lot of people? What is it that appeals so much about the ionised air in a forest or by the seaside? *Loooove* that oxygen.

DIAPHRAGMATIC BREATHING

If you or a family member have ever been through surgery, you will know how flapped Doctors and Physiotherapists get about post-operative breathing exercises. Here's why. Anaesthetics are known to have marked effects on respiratory drive and function, primarily a reduction in the efficiency of the lungs in expelling carbon dioxide (the bad stuff) due to diaphragm and chest wall relaxation, which decreases the volume of the lungs.

This decrease in lung volume is a major factor in a condition called *atelectasis* (failure of part of the lung to expand on inhalation) which can persist for more than a day in about half of all surgical patients. This is a big problem for a number of reasons, the two most important being:

1 A rapid, shallow breathing pattern, combined with the residual effects of anaesthesia and post-operative pain-killers, inhibits coughing, impairs the clearance of mucus and significantly contributes to the risk of post-operative pneumonia.
2 Oxygen (the good stuff) is a vital component of the healing process, so the medical community are always keen to restore a strong breathing pattern in surgical patients.

Accordingly, after surgery, physiotherapists show up in droves and cheerfully force you to breathe deeply, blowing into tubes and other gizmos, causing all kinds of pain and discomfort – this is why they are universally referred to as '*physio-terrorists*' by patients. This kind of concentrated, high-volume breathing is *very* sore if you have just been cut open and stitched up, but should present no problems for you, fair reader, as you sit there relaxed in your chair. So if you are comfortable, let us begin...

THE FUNDAMENTALS OF CORRECT BREATHING

- Sit on a hard-backed chair in a well-ventilated room. Get your backside well to the rear and sit up straight, so that the seat back catches your lower spine. Close your eyes.

- Imagine that a crane is lifting you up out of the chair by the top of your head. Wiggle your backside and your spine and neck until you can feel that you are sitting up really straight; put your hands in your lap.

- Now breathe out fully through your mouth – far beyond what you would normally do – think of it as 'discharging' the old air. Concentrate, and *squeeze* out all the old, stale carbon dioxide. Breathe in again sharply, preferably through your nose if you can. Hold that breath for a few seconds and then discharge the old air again, squeezing until you are empty.

- Place your left palm on your solar plexus (the little hollow in the centre of your chest just at the bottom of your ribs) and your right palm 3–4 centimetres below your navel. And breathe in again, less sharply this time. See which parts of you expand and contract as you breathe. Repeat the cycle five or six times, holding the breath for a few seconds each time.

- Open your eyes. See how you feel.

- Now try this – slump forward a little in the chair. You don't have to double over but incline your body forward quite a bit. Take in as deep a breath as you can and hold it for a moment. Now sit up straight again and see if you can fit any more air in by sucking in sharply. With bad posture, you limit your lung capacity by up to a third. Start to get comfortable with, and conscious of, sitting up straight and allowing air to flow smoothly into your body.

- Adopt your upright position with your hands on your mid-section as before and try this: as you breathe in, allow your abdomen to swell. See if you can gently and consciously prevent your ribs, collarbones and shoulders from rising as you inhale – rather, channel the air *downwards* by expanding your belly.

- If you are paying attention, your left palm will become aware of your diaphragm tightening on each in-breath. Your diaphragm contracts downwards on normal inhalation, which makes the thoracic (chest) cavity larger. When you practise focused diaphragmatic breathing like this, you facilitate this expansion and minimise the tension in your upper body.

- Feel your belly – it expands and becomes quite firm and round on each in-breath and relaxes on each exhalation. Now start helping it by pulling gently inwards with your right hand each time you breathe out. Find the muscles involved. *Feel* the muscles involved. Once you become aware of them, you should be able to take conscious control of them and get them working each time you draw in and expel breath.

A *caveat* here – don't overdo this kind of breathing at first. Most people will feel quite light-headed after only a small number of repetitions the first time they try this. Stop every few breaths and check how you feel. Walk around. Have a glass of water. If you overdo it, your head will be *swimming* with oxygen and that is not a pleasant feeling. In early practice, you may also become aware of the palms of your hands and the soles of your feet becoming somewhat clammy. This is quite normal and will pass with time.

STANDING EXERCISE

Once you are comfortable doing this in the sitting position, it's time to move on to the standing exercise.

- Stand with your feet parallel, about 15–20 centimetres apart. This narrow stance ensures that your legs are straight and 'fall' from your hips to the ground. Just as you learnt to sit up straight, you need to get comfortable with standing with an upright posture.

- Establish your foundation first – rock gently forwards on to the balls of your feet and then bring your heels back in contact with the floor. Do this a couple of times until you become aware of just how good it feels to have both of your feet in solid contact with the ground. Rock back on to your heels and then bring your toes down a few times as well. Now, with your feet flat on the floor, lift your toes up off the ground and then bring them *sloooowly* back down and 'grip' the floor with them. Imagine your feet as suckers holding you firmly to the floor. (Some people find it easier to envisage their toes as claws, biting into the ground.)

- Use the technique of imagining the crane gently lifting you by the top of your head to align your neck, spine and buttocks, and then bring your palms to your mid-section as before.

- Do a couple of 'discharging' breaths. Then practise your breathing cycle – this time with a definite pattern. Do a fairly short cycle at first: inhale for a count of four, hold for a count of five and exhale for a count of six. (I refer to this as a 'plus one' breathing cycle.) You can extend this over time to a count of six, eight or ten for the in-breath with the same 'plus one' for the hold and exhalation.

- To rid yourself of residual tension in your shoulders, neck and upper chest, bring your shoulders up so that they are level with the tops of your ears. Really *squeeze* to get them up there. Then visualise heavy weights suspended from your elbows as you hold your breath and very gradually allow your shoulders to be drawn downwards by the weight on an out-breath. Get used to keeping the tips of your shoulders and the tops of your ears as far apart as possible. You might need to repeat this a couple of times to get used to it; but once again, the growing awareness of your body and the feeling of being able to consciously control it is just *glorious*. (Most of us are completely unaware of the tension that we hold in our bodies – particularly if we are habitually sedentary in our work. This make-it-*really*-tense-and-then-relax approach is an excellent method for finding your physical stress points and gradually eliminating them. Relaxation Response therapy is built around this concept of tense-and-relax and I highly recommend that you try to find a class near you and give it a go.)

- Try taking your increasing awareness inside yourself now. Feel the coldness of the air as it enters your nostrils. Do this a few times. Then 'follow' the air – see how far down inside yourself you can still consciously sense it. Feel the expansion of your abdomen.

- Place your hands over your kidneys (just below the bottom of your ribs either side of your spine) and see if you can become aware of a sensation of 'filling' in this region on each in-breath.

- People report all sorts of warm, pleasant and tingling sensations throughout their bodies as they become more practised with this sort of correct breathing. While you are getting familiar and experienced with this routine, do just a handful of these breath cycles and then take a break.

- As you walk around, become aware of your feet on the floor – notice how your heel comes into contact with the ground, then the rest of the foot, then how you push off with your big toe as you move forwards. Just breathe naturally and relaxedly as you walk around.

IN TIMES OF CRISIS...

Once you become comfortable with diaphragmatic breathing, it can be a tremendous refuge and source of strength when things get stressful in your life. Develop your routine and build it into your Weekly Planner (see page 413). You might prefer to do it in the morning or in the evening – experiment to discover the optimal time for you. The middle of the day, when your body is at its most sluggish, is not a good time to practise.

Make sure that you practise in a well-ventilated, quiet area. The room should be comfortable – neither too hot nor too cold – and you should ensure that your practice will not be interrupted.

Five minutes of this calming unit before an important meeting, interview or presentation can make an enormous difference. Your muscles are relaxed and well-fuelled with oxygen. Your brain feels light and clear. Your posture is more commanding. Your mind is calm and so are you.

You cannot breathe diaphragmatically if your jaw is tight or your throat is constricted by tension, or if your stomach is knotted with worry or your shoulders and neck are aching – you just *can't* breathe fully and properly when there is tension in your body. Hence the difficulties after surgery, when your whole body is tight and sore.

When you are active, busy or keyed-up (but not in outright Fight or Flight) your brain is in a Beta cycle. Meditation and dreamless sleep, by contrast, are natural Alpha states – that is, the brain's electrical activity cycles less rapidly. Developing a breathing routine like the one above is the natural equivalent of taking a Beta-blocker – you will reduce your blood pressure, slow your heart rate and stop tremors in your hands and voice.

Some people get so het-up in advance of having to speak in public that they take tranquillisers for the psychological symptoms or Beta-blockers to help calm the physical symptoms of anxiety. (There was a professional snooker player in the 1980s who suffered from a hand tremor that he controlled with the use of Beta-blockers.) However, being a little jittery like this is normal and desirable (see page 326, Public Speaking at Interviews) so drugs are not to be recommended – they can impair your performance and quickly become a crutch, plus they can have a broad range of very nasty side effects to boot. Beta-blockers in particular can cause cold extremities, nausea, sleep disturbance, impotence, lassitude, breathing difficulties and dangerously low blood pressure.

Far better to allow nature to take its course. Accept the sense of tension in advance of stressful events as a normal and healthy part of your preparation. The butterflies in your stomach are telling you two things: (1) You *care* about this event. It matters to you. It may make a difference to your life. And (2) you have an edge – you are keyed up, tuned in and ready for the battle ahead. For long-term stress, however, you should *definitely* take action. Develop your relaxation and breathing routines, take charge of your stressors and, at the physiological level over time, both your circulatory and respiratory systems will be enhanced by deep breathing and your lymphatic system will be stimulated, helping to clear toxins from your body more efficiently.

Gee, I wonder if any of that could be handy in a job-hunt?

AFTERWORD

> *You can't tell a business how it can operate? Well, I say this: Oh, yes, we can! We can legally require companies to build safe products, to ensure safe workplaces, to pay employees a minimum wage, to contribute to their social security, and to follow a host of other rules that we, as a society, have deemed necessary for our well-being.*
>
> **MICHAEL MOORE IN *DOWNSIZE THIS!***

Seven enforced career changes...
If you retired tomorrow...
If you died tomorrow...
Your job can evaporate overnight...
What are you afraid of...
The Bogeyman is out there...
If you were told you had six months to live...

I have used a lot of negative imagery and what-ifs in this book, because the stuff we're talking about here is important. If you are sitting there, stressed out because you don't have a job; or because you *do* have a job that you hate; or because you are frustrated, unhappy and unfulfilled and feel utterly powerless to do anything about it; you need to WAKE UP!

All too often we don't question our values or attitudes, we don't re-frame our thinking, we don't take constructive action on a stressor, until we absolutely have to. So you're in a job you don't like. You've accumulated some debt. Your boss is on your case. The project isn't going well. A key player won't take your call. Your in-tray is jam-packed with three weeks of correspondence that you haven't had time to even look at. You are *crushed* with the strain of it all. What are you going to do next? Where can you even start? Where are the aspirin, 'cos here comes another one of those oh-so-familiar headaches.

The phone rings and you groan with frustration. It's your partner, calling from an ambulance. One of your children is being rushed to hospital with suspected meningitis. Now you're awake! You're firing on *all* cylinders. Your headache is gone. Is there *anything* from the list of stressors above that really matters now?

You will almost certainly not float through life without having to face and survive a bunch of these crises. Elderly relatives will die. Children will have accidents or horrendous illnesses. Friends and colleagues will stab you in the back. Businesses you are involved in will fail. You will lose jobs or make poor career choices. You will have debts. You will crash cars. Lumps will fall off your house. Etc. Etc. Etc. Etc. There's a whole lot of stuff in your life over which you have little or no control. My point is this: if you have control in a situation, *any* control, USE IT.

I make no apologies for all of this negative imagery; I have found that images of flowers and bunny rabbits don't tend to make people sit up and think in quite the same way. Nevertheless, I hope that reading this book wasn't too cathartic and painful an experience for you (we go through a *lot* of tissues at *Fortify Services*). At the very least, I hope you found it useful and entertaining. If not, I hope you found something in it that makes one per cent of a difference to your career or to your chances at interview next time round.

It doesn't all come down to what is written on your gravestone – who are we kidding? (Although Stephen Covey does have a very interesting eulogy exercise in his *Seven Habits of Highly Effective People*.) Very few of us really make a difference in the organisations we work for. Very few of us change the world substantially for the better (or worse), but how happy and fulfilled we are in our daily lives makes an *enormous* difference to those closest to us. And that has ripples...

I said at the outset that you needed to build your approach from the ground up and that your starting point needed to be an acceptance of the realities of the marketplace. If you feel that I have overstated the case and that it's not that tough out there, and if you are able to sail merrily and unhindered through the world, I am delighted for you. Happy trails and good luck.

On the other hand, if your experiences to date bear out some of what I have said and you have decided that it is time to take some of the control back into your hands – happy hunting!

GET SHORTLISTED.

CHANCE FAVOURS THE PREPARED MIND.

REMEMBER IT'S ONLY A JOB.

'My heroes are the ones who survived doing it wrong; who made mistakes, but recovered from them.'
BONO

APPENDICES

THE SPOUT MODEL

Competence:

	SITUATION	PROCESS	OUTCOME
	How did the situation arise? Anything I can learn for the future to prevent this from happening again?	Best-practice or seat-of-the-pants? How/where did I learn to use this approach? Did it all work or are there elements that I can improve upon the next time?	Marks out of 10 for me. Marks out of 10 for the organisation. Medium–long-term impact of this?
1			
2			
3			

4

5

6

7

8

9

THAT WAS THEN, THIS IS NOW

	10 YEARS AGO	5 YEARS AGO	NOW
Age			
Marital status			
Number of kids			
Accommodation			
Mode of transport			
Recent qualification			
Recent training			
Recent self-improvement			
Job title			
Organisation			
Boss's title			
Key responsibilities:			
1.			
2.			
3.			
4.			
Number of staff			

	10 YEARS AGO	5 YEARS AGO	NOW
Budget I control			
Key skills for the job:			
1.			
2.			
3.			
4.			
Measures of success:			
1.			
2.			
3.			
4.			
Key things I learnt:			
1.			
2.			
3.			
4.			
5.			
6.			
Accomplishments:			
1.			
2.			
3.			
4.			
5.			

ANNOYANCE CHECK-LIST

VERBAL	1ST SESSION	2ND SESSION	3RD SESSION
'You know'			
'Kind of'			
'Sort of'			
'Like'			
'Emmm'			
'Hmmmmm'			
'Let me see…'			
'Buuuuut'			
'Sooooooo'			
'Thaaaat'			
'Weeeeeell'			
'I think'			
'I believe'			
'I feel'			
'I suppose'			
'I would say'			
'Challenge'			
'In all honesty'			
'I'm not sure'			
Profanities			
Other?			

NONVERBAL	1ST SESSION	2ND SESSION	3RD SESSION
Pointing your finger			
Enumerating on your fingers			
Making quotes with your fingers			
Interrupting the interviewer			
Finishing interviewer's words			
Jumping in with an answer			
Speaking too quickly			
Speaking too loudly			
Needing to start your answer again			
What was the question?			
Losing your train of thought			
Nervous laughter			
Bobbing your head excitedly			
Lunging forward and back			
Perched on your seat			
Lounging in your seat			
Fiddling – hair, jewellery, etc.			
Bringing hands to face			
Other?			

WEEKLY PLANNER

TIME	MONDAY	TUESDAY	WEDNESDAY	THURSDAY	FRIDAY	SATURDAY	SUNDAY
06.00							
07.00							
08.00							
09.00							
10.00							
11.00							
12.00							
13.00							
14.00							
15.00							
16.00							
17.00							
18.00							
19.00							
20.00							
21.00							
22.00							
23.00							
00.00							

☐ – Work ☐ – Domestic ☐ – Crucial ☐ – Food for the Soul

FAQs

'I have been working for over 12 years now and I just can't get my CV shorter than three pages. What should I do?'
Part 2: Chapter 3, CVs – The Basic Information (see page 66)

'How do you write a profile of yourself? I have heard that putting one of these at the top of my CV will really help my chances of getting to interview, but where do I start? What do I include or leave out?'
Part 2: Chapter 7, Me... At a Glance (see page 110)

'Why do they ask those weird questions at interview? What are they really trying to find out about me?'
Part 3: Chapter 3, What's Really Going On... (see page 148)

'I'm well qualified. I have great experience. I'm a hard worker and I'm good at what I do. I'm even a nice person! WHY WON'T ANYONE HIRE ME?'
Part 3: Chapter 4, Early Preparation (see page 152)

'I hate talking about myself and I always find it difficult when they ask me about my strengths. How do I tell them my good points without seeming to blow my own trumpet too much?'
Part 3: Chapter 5, Getting Ready to Talk About Yourself (see page 155)

'I heard somewhere that you should only wear light-coloured tights to an interview. Why?'
Part 3: Chapter 11, Dress Code Dos and Don'ts (see page 187)

'I hate the "Tell us a bit about yourself" question at the beginning of the interview. Where do I start? How long should I talk for? How much detail should I include?'
Part 4: Chapter 1, Introducing Yourself Well (see page 209)

'What the hell am I supposed to say when they ask me what my weaknesses are?'
Part 4: Chapter 2, Talking About Weaknesses (see page 215)

'They always ask if I have any questions at the end of the interview, but I'm afraid to get too pushy, so I usually just say, "No". Is it okay to actually ask them questions?'
Part 4: Chapter 3, Asking Them Questions (see page 219)

'What do I do with my hands?'
Part 4: Chapter 7, Body Talk (see page 289)

'Should I use humour or tell jokes in an interview?'
Part 4: Chapter 7, Body Talk (see page 291)

'Is there any advantage in going for a mock interview session?'
Part 4: Chapter 7, Body Talk (see page 293)

FURTHER READING

Here are some of the writers and thinkers that I enjoy on an ongoing basis.

CAREER AND PERSONAL DEVELOPMENT

Richard Nelson Bolles – his *What Colour is Your Parachute?* is an absolute must-read for anyone considering a career change. His humour, compassion and experience shine out of every word.

Martin John Yate – *Parachute* has some very useful ideas on using the internet as a job-hunting tool; Yate has written an excellent book called *Online Job Hunting* which gets into the micro-specifics of that process. If the net is going to be an important route for you, this is well worth the cover price.

David Allen – the productivity guru. *Getting Things Done* has changed the lives of many of my stressed-out, swamped clients. Practical, focused and totally effective. If it doesn't make a difference for you, then you must be some sort of Superior Being.

Carmel McConnell – *Change Activist* looks at how to not pillage the planet in the pursuit of your career. A lot less Greenpeace-y than it sounds, this book is bouncy and immediately valuable. There is a good balance of exercises and thought-provoking material to didactic content, and the interviews are interesting too. A lovely book – engaging, useful and passionate – I have recommended this one to many friends and clients.

Steven Covey, Charles Handy and **Edward de Bono** – anything you can read by these guys is worth the time. Alternative viewpoints, common sense writ large and some big leaps in thinking. Many readers remark that the material in their works is not so much new as something you've always thought, but have never been able to articulate…

BUSINESS THINKING

Tom Peters and **Peter Drucker** – the big boys. Always worth it. Catch Tom live if you can.

Jonas Ridderstrale and Kjell Nordström – their *Funky Business* and *Karaoke Capitalism* are engaging and illustrative of the ephemeral nature of corporate life today. If you still don't believe that there is no such thing as a job for life these days, read these excellent books.

Scott Adams – his Dilbert strip is mandatory reading for those of us who can't take executive posturing too seriously, but his *Dilbert Principle, Dilbert Future* and *God's Debris* are seriously thought-provoking, and I don't know about you, but when I hear someone that cynical say, '*Have you considered this?*' I listen.

Ken Blanchard and Spenser Johnson – the must-read *One Minute Manager*. Simple, simple stuff, that every manager should know and apply, but few do. Opinion among my client base is polarised on Johnson's *Who Moved My Cheese?* If you like it, you'll *love* it.

Barbara and Alan Pease – their books on the differences between men and women are funny, immediately applicable and the situations they describe are instantly recognisable as true. **John Gray** is the other big noise in this space with his *Mars and Venus* books. Not management thinking *per se*, but you try getting ahead in this world without understanding how the other 50 per cent of the planet thinks…

Various – executive autobiographies can sometimes be worth reading, particularly if they relate to an industry or company that you are interested in working for.

THE BIGGER PICTURE

Noam Chomsky – amazing thinker, extraordinary writer, espousing change-your-whole-world-view ideas. Not for the faint-hearted – this is not light reading by any stretch of the imagination, but the inarguable simplicity of his thinking is more than worth the effort.

Bill Hicks – Hicks described himself as 'Noam Chomsky with dick jokes.' American 'comedian' who died in 1994 from pancreatic cancer. I put comedian in inverted commas because he used comedy as his vehicle, recognising that he would be locked up if he espoused these ideas while standing on a soapbox outside the White House. If you are sensitive to invective and extremely pejorative terminology, Hicks is probably not for you. For my money, **George Carlin** is the only soapbox comedian left on the circuit today who is worth listening to in the same way.

Ken Wilber – another fabulous mind. His *A Theory Of Everything* describes societal and personal evolution in terms we can all recognise happening around us.

Michael Moore – *Stupid White Men* and *Dude, Where's My Country?* left all thinking readers depressed and foaming with rage. His earlier *Downsize This!* is well worth a read, too. There has been a lot of angry reaction to his fast-and-loose approach, but his central themes still make for very interesting reading/viewing.

Naomi Klein – *No Logo* was a runaway success and *Fences and Windows* looks set to do the same. If you don't work for a big corporate, you may be alarmed at some of what you read here.

Henry Rollins – better known as the lead singer in the Angry-White-Guys-With-Guitars bands Black Flag and The Henry Rollins Band, Henry also tours with what he calls 'spoken word' shows. Depending on the night, he can talk about the big stuff that is happening in the world today or material that is very personal indeed. A case-study for how to spell-bind an audience and a plain-speaking man who leaves me high on language every time I hear him.

Richard Bach – *Jonathan Livingston Seagull* and *Illusions* do in allegory what Covey *et al.* do by instruction. Fabulous, questioning writing. Couldn't recommend him more.

INDEX

The world is like a ride in an amusement park. And when you choose to go on it, you think it's real because that's how powerful our minds are. The ride goes up and down and round and round, it has thrills and chills, it's very brightly coloured and it's very loud and it's fun... for a while. Some people have been on the ride for a long time and they begin to question, 'Is this real, or is it just a ride?' And other people have remembered; and they come back to us, and they say, 'Hey! Don't worry, don't be afraid, ever. Because... this is just a ride.'

BILL HICKS